Also by MAURICE SAMUEL

Non-fiction

THE PROFESSOR AND THE FOSSIL (1956)

CERTAIN PEOPLE OF THE BOOK (1955)

LEVEL SUNLIGHT (1953)

THE GENTLEMAN AND THE JEW (1950)

PRINCE OF THE GHETTO (1948)

HARVEST IN THE DESERT (1944, 1945)

THE WORLD OF SHOLOM ALEICHEM (1943)

Fiction

THE SECOND CRUCIFIXION (1960)

THE DEVIL THAT FAILED (1952)

WEB OF LUCIFER (1947)

These are BORZOI BOOKS,
published in New York by ALFRED A. KNOPF

Little Did I Know

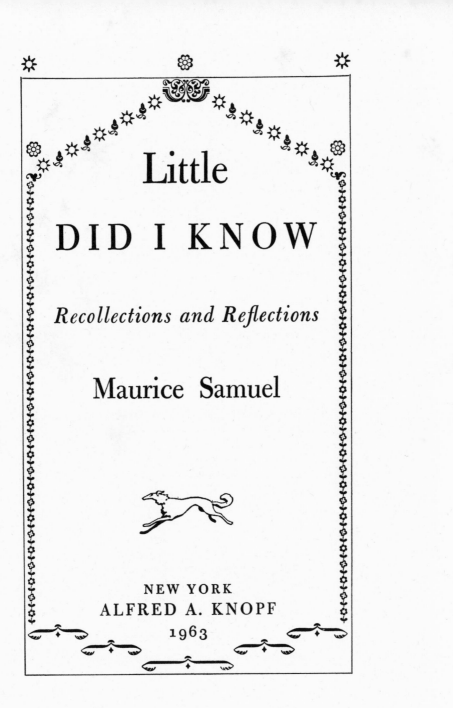

Little
DID I KNOW

Recollections and Reflections

Maurice Samuel

NEW YORK
ALFRED A. KNOPF
1963

L. C. catalog card number: 63–17832

THIS IS A BORZOI BOOK,
PUBLISHED BY ALFRED A. KNOFF, INC.

FIRST EDITION

A portion of Chapter XVIII appeared under the title "The Maggid" in *Midstream*.

ACKNOWLEDGMENTS

MOST of the following pages were written, in their original form, during the summer of 1961. I have added and changed much since then, but always in the spirit of the first draft, so that the additions and changes are a prolongation and clarification of a mood. This is the only artifice I have employed; everything here recorded is as faithful to fact as copious notes and a self-serving memory can make it.

A small part of the material was published long ago; another part, more recently. In a few places I have dipped into my own books. For permission to re-use larger or smaller fragments of my articles I wish to thank the following periodicals: *Commentary, The Congress Bi-Weekly, Harper's Magazine, The Jewish Frontier, Midstream,* and *The New Palestine.* For permission to quote I am also indebted to Harper and Brothers, New York (*Trial and Error,* the Autobiography of Chaim Weizmann); Atheneum, New York (*Chaim Weizmann, A Biography*); Ryerson Press, Toronto (*The Rocking Chair and Other Poems,* by A. M. Klein); Reynal & Company, New York (*Felix Frankfurter Reminisces*). The material quoted from *The World's Work* was later used by the late Ambassador Morgenthau in his autobiographical *All in a Lifetime.*

✤ vii ✤

Contents

✤

Part *1* Descent to the Beginning

I.	*My Virgilian Uncle*	3
II.	*Time Present, Place Here*	27
III.	*The Twig Is Bent*	32
IV.	*Recall*	51
V.	*The Clan*	71
VI.	*Insulation*	91
VII.	*The Fathers of the Clan*	101
VIII.	*Patchwork*	119
IX.	*Our Shtetl Roots*	133
X.	*Time Present, Place Here*	142

Part *2* Cities and Men

XI.	*The Eruption*	159
XII.	*Chaim Weizmann*	179
XIII.	*The Scientist*	202
XIV.	*Founding Fathers*	210
XV.	*Of an Old Tragedy and a Bitter Farce*	226
XVI.	*Hieroselyma Est Perdita*	254
XVII.	*"Writer and Lecturer"*	266
XVIII.	*The Maggid*	286
	Epilogue of High Moments	310

PART 1

❀

Descent to the Beginning

CHAPTER I

My Virgilian Uncle

❀

Among the people who rise out of my past to claim first mention in this book, my uncle Berel is the most persistent. This would have surprised him. He played only a brief role in my life, and had no idea that it was of any importance. He must have supposed—if he ever thought about it at all—that when he was dead and gone I would call him to mind affectionately now and again, but less and less frequently, less and less clearly, as the years passed; and that by the time I reached his age he would be among the ghostliest of my memories. I, for my part, surely did not look so far ahead; but now I am much older than he was at the time of our intimacy, and I find myself thinking about him more and more frequently, and seeing him more and more clearly. It is, in fact, impossible to disallow his claim.

So there he is, Uncle Berel, my mother's brother, Berel Acker, the tailor, who does very little tailoring, making most of his living, such as it is, from repairing, cleaning, and pressing. I usually see him in profile, at his work table before the window facing north on grimy East Fifteenth Street, between First and Second Avenues, while I sit at his right, and we carry on long conversations which on his side are punctuated by what are known as Bronx cheers. He is in the late forties; he has a squat figure, a round, brown, wrinkled face with Tartar cheekbones and overhanging mustaches. He chews an extinguished cigar stump, and his little brown eyes twinkle when he turns to make a point. The Bronx cheers are not derisive; they are modest, mechanical, and professional; he produces them by taking a sip of water from the glass on his left and, with a circular flourish of his bowed white head, spraying from between pursed lips the skirt or pants he is pressing by hand. He ought to have a pressing machine, but for various reasons he has never managed to save up the price; and among these reasons is an admitted disquiet of soul in the presence of a New World innovation which would sever another bond between him and the good old days in Rumania, where he was born and grew up.

There is a constant tug of war between Uncle Berel and me. He wants to talk about things he thinks I know, and I want to hear him on things I know he knows. He would like me to clarify for him once and for all how they measure the circumference of the earth and the earth's distance from the sun; or how a microscope magnifies; or how one can reconcile the obvious uncertainty of man's life with the obvious solvency of insurance companies. I keep steering him toward the details of his occupation and his memories of Rumania.

Uncle Berel is a mixture of shrewd realism and uncontrollable sentimentality. He is a meditative man from two consecutive and contradictory causes. His wife (I barely saw her in America, she died soon after my arrival) was homicidally talkative and threw him back on himself; now he is a not disconsolate widower and much alone. He is a sharp observer and a close reasoner; but he also has fantasy. He hangs his customers on the rack in provocative combina-

4

tions: Mr. Michelson the grocer next to Mrs. Tuchverder-
ber the matchmaker, a priest's soutane next to a rabbinic
kaftan. He would make a good novelist, though he did not
get more than a *cheder* (elementary Hebrew school) education, has never made a formal improvement on it, and
speaks only Yiddish and Rumanian. When I suggest in all
seriousness that he could produce, if not a novel, then a
new and homely *Sartor Resartus,* and explain that it is a
sort of philosophy of clothes, he says: "Beh! A philosophy
of *shmattes,* rags, maybe, if I were a writer like you." For I
am already a writer, a fact attested by an impressive collection of rejection slips.

"Very good, Uncle Berel! A philosophy of old clothes.
There have been so many Jewish old clo' men; it's a tradition."

"Maybe you're having a little joke with me," he answers.
"And yet what I do here is no small matter. Here comes an
old suit, a beggar, a scarecrow, fit for the garbage can. I
take nothing in my hand, as you might say, just a spit of
water and a hot iron. I neither add to the cloth nor sub-
tract from it, I make a flipflop with the iron and hopla!
there's your suit, a regular gentleman"—but he says
"gentledendle," to indicate disesteem—"not to be recognized. A resurrection for the sleeper in the dust, as the
siddur (prayerbook) says. And the things I learn about
customers, even if I've never met them and somebody
brings their clothes to me, the things I learn—oh, ho!
Black coffee beans in the pants pockets—he chews them to
cover his breath, because he drinks and he's afraid of his
wife; cigarette butts in the vest pockets—a miserly soul;
chewed toothpicks—nervousness, bad manners, and close-
set teeth. And the stains! A world of stains, from the lapels
to the pants cuffs; and what they sometimes tell you isn't
fit to be spoken of. Has your writer friend—"

5

"Carlyle—"

"Has he anything to say about that?"

"Not that I remember."

He removes the cigar stump, sips water, and swoops down over the table like a benevolent hawk, reminding me of Dante's "Ha! Ha! Thou stoopest!" Emptied, he tries to switch the conversation; if not Carlyle, then something about actuarial tables; but my Yiddish is defective, I am relearning it after years of alienation; and I was never very good at mathematics. I push him back to his old clothes. It turns out that in his own way he feels actuarially and has formulated for himself a version of Emerson's Law of Compensation.

He feels himself to be a sort of economic barometer, or, rather, a recorder of barometric readings. Mr. Michelson's grocery store is the barometer, and the mercury Uncle Berel watches is represented by Mr. Michelson's suits. When the operators, cutters, hat-makers, pressers, and salesgirls on the block are out of work or on part-time, their diet is low in *lox* and high in potatoes; then Mr. Michelson's takings are poor and his suits lose heart and acquire lustre in longer absences. When times are good and *lox* is again in the ascendant, Mr. Michelson's suits pick up *joie de vivre* and come in as often as every other Thursday. But there is more to it than that.

"I tell you," says Uncle Berel, "it is a marvelous world. I stand here and reckon it out. When people are out of work they don't have their clothes mended and pressed very often, and therefore I too earn less, which is only right. Good! But you might think I am in danger of starving to death. Not at all! For if people have no jobs they can't buy new clothes; so the suits and skirts grow older and older, and it has been cleverly arranged that the older they get the more often they need mending and pressing. The mind of man can't look through the deepness of it all."

6

On certain subjects Uncle Berel and I are so hopelessly divided that we have dropped them by tacit consent. I am a newly converted—self-converted—Zionist. I believe that some day, all going reasonably well, we shall have a Jewish homeland in Palestine. It depends largely on us. Uncle Berel is immovably skeptical. The division, to mix a metaphor, is an impasse. "Yes, we will." "No, we won't." "Why won't we?" "Beh! For one thing, they won't let us." Who are "they"? Uncle Berel makes an impatient gesture with the flatiron, giving it a little rapid clockwise and counter-clockwise flip before he plumps it down; that is all he can do, for though his emotions are strong the flatiron is heavy. "Everybody!" But his skepticism is not hostile. When the issue was first raised between us he admitted that he too had once dreamed dreams, but they had faded away, or rather had been extinguished suddenly.

"Once upon a time, years and years ago, when Theodore Herzl"—he pronounced it "Todder"—"was alive, I thought for a moment, yes, maybe it will happen. There is a man who is received by kings and sultans. That must have meant something. They knew him for what he was. A Prince. It was a sudden light, and it went out. That's the kind of luck we have. Now it's *farfallen*, done for, not *bashert*, not destined. Today—tremendous nations locked in a life-and-death struggle"—it was the winter of 1914–1915—"where do we *Yiddalach* come in? I respect you, you've been to college, but on this matter, if you'll pardon me . . . Who's going to lead us now?"

I too revered the name of Herzl, though I knew little, at that time, about the personality—royal indeed—fusion of sophisticated Viennese journalist, Messianic prophet, and master organizer—who within a decade of his death had become folklore. But I gave Uncle Berel names, which he shrugged off. "Do you call that a Herzl?" The greatest among the Zionist leaders who were then arising I did not

7

mention, though I had met him in person. My ignorance of the Zionist movement was extensive. I had no idea of the role Chaim Weizmann had played and was playing in it. How, then, was I to guess that a still greater role awaited him, or, even more remote from probability, that he would admit me to his friendship and exercise a far-ranging influence on my life?

Another subject I soon learned to avoid with Uncle Berel was socialism. Here I cannot speak of a division; Uncle Berel simply wasn't interested. My fierce insistence on the equality of all men elicited from him not a repudiative squiggle of the flatiron but a meditative "Mm—nn—yeh!," neither approving nor disapproving, followed by a long silence. At that point, I believe, Uncle Berel's respect for my college education was weaker than usual. I left it at that.

I think of Uncle Berel as Virgilian because he was for a period my guide through various limbos of folk and family memories. I responded to them as a fascinated outsider, for though they were mine I was detached from them; nearly half a century had to pass before those of the memories which I shared with him (I migrated in 1900 from Rumania, where he was a frequent visitor at our home, at the age of five) became something more than disconnected little pictures in a gallery, and fused into a deep-toned, mysterious, and magic interior totality. When I was nineteen my childhood seemed to me to have been somebody else's, and it is only recently that I feel it to be more visibly and palpably mine than it was then or during the intervening years. There was, to be sure, much talk at home, in Manchester, about Rumania; Uncle Berel, however, did not merely talk about it; he conducted me into it.

8

He had a ritual. Every Saturday night, whether his barometer stood at Fair or Foul, he went to a "service" at a certain little Rumanian Jewish restaurant on the lower East Side. (I have forgotten its name, and it surely closed its doors long ago.) It was nothing like Moskowitz's famous rendezvous, then on Houston Street. The premises were a basement four steps below the dirty street level; there was no instrumental music; the prices were modest. Uncle Berel's fellow-celebrants were all Rumanian Jews, elderly tailors, shoemakers, candy-store keepers, machinists, pressers, who knew each other from of old by first name and the name of the town or village of origin: Leibu of Macheen* and Itzik of Pitchiniagu and Getzel of Barlad and Moishe of Glodorlui and Chaim of Podoturk and Mendel of Fokoshan. Ostensibly—and, as far as their consciousness went, genuinely—they assembled to eat *karnatzlech, beigalech, mammaligge,* and *kachkeval,* to drink what they called and apparently believed to be Rumanian wine, and to play *sixty-six* and *tablenette.* They spoke Yiddish peppered with Rumanian phrases, and the conversation reverted in rhythms to old times. They remembered the Chismijui of Bukarest, and the Red Bridge of Yasse, and the *shool* (synagogue) of Vaslui. (But they said *sheel* for *shool,* whereas I, relearning my Yiddish among *Litvaks*—Lithuanian Jews—here in America, said, and still say *shool;* I also say *man* (husband) instead of the Rumanian Yiddish *mon,* and *veib* (wife) instead of *vaab:* I sometimes even slip into *die* before *veib,* that is, I use the feminine article instead of the neuter, Litvak Yiddish having no neuter article and *veib* being perversely neuter in Rumanian Yiddish, as in German.) From time to time Uncle Berel took me with him, and I enjoyed it intensely,

* Throughout these pages, as an act of piety, I reproduce Rumanian names and words phonetically, Macheen for Macin, etc. I have identified the places on the map but cannot bring myself to distort them back into accuracy; so also with certain nouns.

9

as observer rather than as participant. To my uncommitted and unenchanted palate *karnatzlech* were simply cigar-shaped rolls of chopped meat, overspiced and underdone; *beigalech* (not to be confused with *beigel*, which has been described as a doughnut dipped in cement) were merely meat patties, *mammaligge* a cornmush cake, *kachkeval* a rank cheese, none of them particularly appetizing. To Uncle Berel and his cronies these foods were sanctities; it was not an ordinary eating and drinking; they ate and drank time, they smacked their lips over the pathos of distance and irretrievability; their tastebuds had transcended their neural functions, serving as ministrants to the sweet melancholy of divided and uprooted souls.

I have long wanted to write about these and other spiritual-associational values of food. It is not language alone, or even chiefly, that distinguishes man from the animals. A goat crops the grass but a man ingests the landscape and the heavens above it, and even a solitary meal can be an *agapë*.

One would have thought that these emotions were associated for Uncle Berel and his cronies with the exile's vain-longing for the land of his birth, with remembered joys of a time and place, both lost forever. In Uncle Berel's case it was certainly nothing of the sort. He hated Rumania and never had a good word for it. He had grown up in a period of mounting Rumanian anti-Semitism. When he was a young man, thousands of Rumanian Jews were being driven from the country by poverty and repression. (Oh, idyllic, halcyon days, when Jews were driven from a country instead of being incinerated in it—if only Uncle Berel could have known how considerate the Rumanians were!) Many of those who could not buy railroad tickets, or even hire a horse and cart, had formed into large groups which wandered westward on foot, begging their way, singing

songs which have now become a little segment of the folklore. Uncle Berel had started out with one such group and
had turned back, but whether it was his feet or his voice
that gave out I do not know. He became a tailor, made
enough money to buy passage for himself and his family
as far as England, and later was helped on to America.
Why did he, like the other frequenters of that restaurant,
seem to hark back to a time of good eating and drinking,
a time of high living and contentment? It was a psycho-
optical illusion. These were the foods they had loved and
never had enough of; what they harked back to was simply
their youth.

Uncle Berel put up a fight against the illusion. "What
black year is it," he asked, wrathfully, "that makes me want
to shed tears of love for Rumania when I hear a Rumanian
song? *Vulech gonef!* (Wallachian rogue!) who didn't let a
human being live! *Vulech gonef!* With his 'Hey, *Zhidan!*'
(sheeny!) and his 'Don't stand here!' and 'Keep out of
there!'" And once he flabbergasted me by an extraordinary outburst quite out of keeping with his native good
humor. There was a fat woman singer in our little restaurant. She sang Yiddish and Rumanian songs, without ac-
companiment; the former I understood, and some of them,
like *A Brievalle der Mammen* (Send Your Mother a Letter)
and *Eli, Eli* (My God, My God, Why Has Thou Forsaken
Me?) were dreadful; others, from Goldfaden and the folk-
repertoire, were often beautiful. The Rumanian songs I
did not understand, and why on that evening that particular song did what it did to Uncle Berel I shall never know.
I was watching him and saw his eyes becoming moist; suddenly he stood up, drew a fifty-cent piece from his pocket,
and hurled it across the room through the open door onto
the steps, whence it bounced back with a shrill ringing.
"Na dir, kurveh!—take it, whore!" howled Uncle Berel.

The woman continued to sing as she made for the coin, and Uncle Berel sat down, quivering.

He resented Rumania's shameless gate-crashing into his loving reveries of the past; it was a parasitic and defiling intrusion. But once he was launched on a sentimental binge Rumania always nicked in for an utterly unmerited place. He saw it, and was helpless to prevent it. It was as though a refugee from a German death camp, sole survivor of a large family, were to hear a performer in a cabaret singing an innocent German folk song, and weep because it reminded him of his childhood. Uncle Berel also chided himself, with the same clear-sighted helplessness, for his disinclination toward a pressing machine. He was a believer in Americanism and progress, but his heart was stuck in the past; and what sharpened his resentment was his view of Rumania as the very embodiment of willful backwardness and moral beastliness.

"A stinking land!" he said. "Not the land itself, which is lovely enough—such a year on all of us!—but the people. No, not the people, the *cham,* the *tzaran* (peasant), the stupid mass, but the *preetzim* (the aristocracy and the rich), the government, which keep them ignorant and brutish. Not for nothing did your mother carry on to make your father leave the country, so that your brothers and you wouldn't have to be Rumanian soldiers. Ask your father what *that* meant."

I knew something about "that," but there was an odd difference-in-agreement between my father's way of telling it and Uncle Berel's. My father had served in a Rumanian cavalry regiment called (as he pronounced it) the *Rawooshoren.* There were at home, in Manchester, two photographs of him in uniform, and in the larger, tinted one he was heroically mounted, resplendent in uniform, sabre and all. He had risen to the rank of sergeant, a

12

considerable achievement for a penniless Jew. As a child I had not been able to reconcile the dashing hero on horseback with the rather grim and frustrated shoemaker who was my father. The stories he told of his service were hair-raising and if only half true more than justified my mother's terrors and Uncle Berel's animadversions. The savagery of the non-coms toward the privates was equalled by the contempt of the officers for both. An unbridled sadism passed for discipline, and the quartermaster's service was corrupt through all its levels, so that the uniforms were ragged and the food, poor enough by regulation, was tampered with. I grew up with the notion that the Rumanian army was a hell. I suppose it couldn't have been as bad as all that—and yet a strange incident interpolates itself at this point.

I was in Paris, on leave, in the spring of 1919, a sergeant in the A.E.F., waiting for my demobilization. Coming late one night out of the Rat Mort on the boulevard Clichy, I was accosted under a lamp by two Rumanian officers. Their lips were rouged, their eyes ringed with mascara. I had the impression that they wore corsets. They said something to me in Rumanian, and I recognized an obscene word I had heard from older people in our Manchester group. I started back with such terror and loathing that they in turn started back from me and made off, laughing vilely. I wanted them to know that I had understood them, and I wanted also to insult them. So I shouted after them: "Hey, *Zhidan!*" It was the only offensive Rumanian word I could think of. There may have been a second purpose, to this effect: "And you're the people who despise Jews and call them *Zhidan*." It is of course absurd to base one's judgment on a few reports and individual episodes—but I am recording my experiences and nothing more.

With all his acknowledgment of the ghastly conditions in the Rumanian army, my father remembered his soldier days with pride. And when England declared war on Germany in 1914, and I as a pacifist refused to join up, my father was contemptuous of me. I also refused to remain in England while others were enlisting (conscription did not come till two years later). In November 1914 I left for America; my mother rejoiced; Uncle Berel, for his part, approved wholeheartedly.

"You couldn't have done a more sensible thing. I only wish the Jews could all get out of Europe, instead of having to shoot at each other, *mir nisht, dir nisht,* because *goyim* like to fight. They've always been at it, and they always will be. *Ich hob sei alle in d'rerd*—they can all go to hell."

By the spring of 1917 my views had changed and my pacifism was tottering. I had become anti-German, and though not an American citizen, I could see where I would stand if America entered the war. I had to prepare Uncle Berel; so there were sharp exchanges, and it almost came to a quarrel.

"What do you mean, Germany is the aggressor?" asked Uncle Berel. "What kind of language is that from *you?* England has a lot of colonies, Germany has hardly any, and she wants her share. You're a socialist and a Zionist, aren't you? You believe all men and all nations should be equal."

"There shouldn't be any colonies, Uncle Berel."

"Right. But there *are* colonies. What difference does it make to you who has them?" He would break into the peculiar Yiddish singsong of logical discourse which has passed from the Talmudists to the folk. "I-if there were no colonies at all, and i-if Germany were going out to get some, I would say that Germany had to be stopped." He added, hastily: "Maybe," fearing he had yielded a strong

14

interior position on which he might have to fall back later. "As it is, you want to defend an old thief from a young thief."

"Let it be so, Uncle Berel. I say an old thief is better than a young thief. He's tired, and his conscience bothers him, and he wants to make amends and be respectable. When he dies and there's no one to inherit he leaves his money to charity. He even practices charity before dying. A young thief has a fresh appetite; you can't let him start the whole dirty business all over again."

"I don't see your old thief in such a state of exhaustion," said Uncle Berel, sarcastically. "According to the papers, he's giving as good as he's getting."

That was how the main arguments went, Uncle Berel repeating *"Ich hob sei alle in d'rerd"* and I insisting that "they" were not all alike. I had forebodings about Germany, though perhaps not clearly on Jewish grounds. We skirmished on the question of "atrocities," which Uncle Berel laughed off as propaganda. Behind the spoken arguments were emotions we could not refer to; Uncle Berel was as fond of me as I of him; he trembled for me, and he felt some responsibility toward my mother. I knew I was going to disappoint and grieve both of them.

Then America entered the war and I had to make my decision. I did not want to return to England, nor could I bring myself to enlist in the regular army; I was afraid of making myself ridiculous among professional soldiers. When the draft law was passed I took out my first papers so as to come under its operation, and to my immense relief my number was in the first batch—eight hundred and something. I received my training at Camp Upton, Long Island, and there Uncle Berel, dispirited but affectionate, would visit me, bearing always a gift of salami and black bread. I could not convince him that we were not only well fed but perhaps overfed; and he never became reconciled to my decision.

One Sunday morning I took him round the system of trenches we had dug—a replica of a section of the Western front—and were learning to storm and defend. Uncle Berel looked long and earnestly, then turned to me. "These holes in the ground—you're supposed to let yourself be killed rather than give them up?" "Yes, Uncle Berel, that might be the order." "*Vey, vey,*" he mourned, "can human lunacy go further? Fool! If the other man wants them so badly that he's prepared to kill for them, let him have them! Go away and dig yourself another lot of holes."

He took a horrified, almost morbid interest in the details of my military activity. He conceded that the American army was nothing like the Rumanian, but the whole thing was mad anyhow. One circumstance made a peculiarly painful impression on him. My regiment, the 307th Infantry, had a large contingent of New York East-Siders, some of them recent arrivals in the country with very little knowledge of English. I was in Company F, and my captain, a likable lawyer named Davis, asked me whether I would not take over two squads of the newcomers and teach them the rudiments of close-order drill in Yiddish. It was a request rather than a command, and in an evil hour I accepted. My Yiddish had improved considerably in the last three years; I was reading the classics with enjoyment and already entertaining thoughts of translating Sholom Aleichem, Yal Peretz, and Mendelle into English. (I had made the personal acquaintance of Sholom Aleichem shortly before his death in 1916.) Uncle Berel had been indescribably delighted by my increasing proficiency in the language, but he was profoundly shocked by the use to which I was now putting it. He was also

16

puzzled: where did I get the military terminology? He had never heard of such a thing in Yiddish, Jews had never fought in that language.

I told him that I gave the commands in English and explained their execution in Yiddish, with illustration. *"Ven ich zog* 'Te-en-*shun!'* you must stand up straight, *ot azoi*, like this, feet together at an angle, *ot azoi*, shoulders drawn back," and so forth. I confessed to Uncle Berel that I found the assignment not at all to my taste. The men didn't take me seriously, because of my Yiddish. They were willing enough to be soldiers, but they looked on me as an impostor. They argued with me, and one man, Strauss, a thickset Russian Jew, was particularly objectionable. "Look, Samuel, I've been standing and walking on my feet for over twenty years, and I haven't fallen down since I was a baby. I can stand like this, and I stand like this"—he took up various postures—"and I'm still standing. Give me a gun and I'll shoot all the Germans you want, but for God's sake *fardreh mir nisht a kop*—don't drive me out of my wits with that rubbishy left right, left right! Just tell me where to go and you'll see, I'll get there."

"Strauss," I said, "I'm teaching you what I have to teach you. Go tell the captain."

"And another thing," answered Strauss. "You want to say 'Attention'? Say it. Don't shout 'Te-en-shun!' and get red in the face. You want to say 'Forward march'? Don't yell 'Faw-waw-*harch!*' Say it plainly, reasonably, like a human being."

"Isn't he right?" asked Uncle Berel, and went back to his lament. *"Vey, vey,* you take a beautiful language like Yiddish, a dear homey language, and with it you not only want to teach men to kill, you also want to turn them into idiots. For the sake of a hole in the ground. *Feh!"*

17

I look back nearly half a century and wonder how far Uncle Berel would have carried his principles. Would he have agreed with Epictetus, who says: "If a man steals your lamp it is your fault for having a lamp"? I also wonder how in his brief Zionist interlude Uncle Berel the pacifist foresaw the emergence of the Jewish homeland. I dare say it was somewhat as follows: a large number of Jews would realize, under the magic of Herzl's persuasion, that the time had come for them to rebuild their country; some would go there, others would help them; the nations of the world, under the same spell, would applaud; the Arabs would receive the Jews with open arms: a Messianic picture.

Was my own view, in my socialist-Zionist-pacifist days, any less naïve? With all that we have witnessed since, the answer seems to be emphatically no. Yet there was a time before, during and after the First World War—the "war to end wars," the early days of the League of Nations— during which men far more sophisticated than Uncle Berel or I foresaw reasonably happy solutions of many general and particular problems. There were leading Jews, *and leading Arabs*, who believed, or at least officially declared that they believed, in fruitful Jewish–Arab co-operation. I digress at this point in order to defend myself—in my own eyes, too—against the charge of utter *shlimihlishness,* and I quote an extraordinary letter remembered by few. It was written by the Emir (later king of Iraq) Faisal, the head of the Arab delegation to the Paris Peace Conference of 1919, and addressed to Professor (later Justice) Felix Frankfurter, who was then active in the Zionist movement and co-operating with Chaim Weizmann, the head of the Zionist delegation:

Dear Mr. Frankfurter:
    I wish to take this opportunity of my first contact

with American Zionists, to tell you what I have often been able to say to Dr. Weizmann in Arabia and Europe.

We feel that the Arabs and Jews are cousins in race, suffering similar oppressions at the hands of powers stronger than themselves, and by a happy coincidence have been able to take the first step toward the attainment of their national ideals together.

We Arabs, especially the educated among us, look with the deepest sympathy on the Zionist movement. Our deputation here in Paris is fully acquainted with the proposals submitted by the Zionist Organization to the Peace Conference, and we regard them as moderate and proper. We will do our best, in so far as we are concerned, to help them through; we will wish the Jews a most hearty welcome home. . . .

We are working together for a reformed and revived Near East, and our two movements complete one another. . . .

People less informed and less responsible than our leaders, ignoring the need for cooperation of the Arabs and Zionists, have been trying to exploit the local differences that must necessarily arise in Palestine in the early stages of our movements. . . . I wish to give you my firm conviction that these differences are not on questions of principle, but on matters of detail, such as must invariably occur in every contact with neighboring peoples, and as are easily dissipated by mutual good will. Indeed, nearly all of them will disappear with fuller knowledge.

Philosophers will tell you that what has not happened could not have happened—a wonderful expression of the self-assurance of hindsight. But many things looked possible in 1919 to men of good will, and if their hopes were disappointed it does not prove that the pessimists were wiser.

In the course of the decades the things I learned about Rumania from and through Uncle Berel, and those I heard of at home in Manchester, and those I recall myself, have become submerged in the uniformity of that strange, clear, submarine light that now rests on all my childhood memories. Transpositions may have taken place; things told may, by repetition, have acquired the intensity of things lived; things lived may have fused with things told; all are equally "factual."

The Jews of Rumania used to have a reputation as *Lebejungen,* high-livers, short on learning, much given to the world and the flesh, if not the devil. They, and to some extent Ukrainian Jews, also from a fat land, were contrasted with the lean and hungry intellectual *Litvak* (Lithuanian Jews). It may be an individual accident—my birth into a low economic stratum, the family destiny, my mother's temperament—but my personal memories do not bear this reputation out. Rumania is touched with sadness for me. In Uncle Berel's restaurant I once heard from the entertainer a song that had been a favorite with my mother, about the miseries of the Jewish conscript. I recall it very clearly:

> How many bitter tears my parents shed
> Before they saw me grown to man's estate;
> Now far from home I must lay down my head,
> The road is closed and bolted is the gate.
>
> So sing this song with me, my brothers dear,
> Your youth is gone, the happy time is done.

Now you have reached your first and twentieth year,
The next three years you are King Carol's son.

Doleful enough words, and a doleful melody went with them; but even when she sang a song of cheer (I mean, as far as the words went) there was a disconsolate catch in my mother's voice that would have infused a cosmic dejection into *A-hunting We Will Go!* Uncle Berel told me that as a girl my mother had been a jolly and lively creature, which was as difficult for me to reconcile with my image of her as it had been to identify the dashing cavalryman in the resplendent uniform with the careworn, overworked, embittered mender of old shoes who was my father. It appalled me also to learn that once upon a time my mother had been able to read and write, and had corresponded with my father in their courtship days. I knew her always as an analphabet, though wonderfully intelligent. Years of sickness and the struggle for a livelihood, especially after we migrated from Rumania, first to France and then to England, had beaten her down and atrophied, by disuse, such literacy as she had once possessed.

My mother had a sweet voice and knew many songs. In her girlhood in Yasse, and then during a stay in Bucharest, she had been a frequenter of the plays and operas of Abraham Goldfaden, the founder of the modern Yiddish theater. Besides those arias of his which have become Yiddish folklore (he was a kind of higher-level Stephen Foster to East European Jewry), like *Rozhenkes un Mandlen* (Raisins and Almonds), *A Pastuch Is Amol Geven* (A Shepherd Once There Was), and the like, she had memorized passages which have not caught on in the same way, and which I have not heard again except at long intervals, when there has been a Goldfaden revival. (Just a few years ago, on the West Coast, a Hadassah group which I addressed put on an excellent performance of Goldfaden's *Shulamis*, and ladies on either side of me, seeing me wipe my eyes furtively, said: "This must mean a great deal more to you than it can to us." It did.) Whatever my mother sang was flooded with melancholy. The cheerful Pilgrim's Chorus from *Shulamis* became a funeral march, so that, when I heard it rendered with the swing and high spirit Goldfaden had undoubtedly intended for it, I was shocked as by an act of irreverence. As to what my mother did with the intentionally doleful passages, I can only say that by comparison the heartbreaking recitative of Jeremiah's Book of Lamentations on the eve of the Black Fast sounded like an epithalamium.

Uncle Berel told me that my mother began to change when she had to settle in the village of Macheen, where my father had set up a shoe-repair shop. She was a city girl, accustomed to the movement and gaiety of sizable places like Yasse and Bucharest and Braila. I remember with a vividness which places the experience beyond suspicion of dream or the recounted incident how my mother used to sit on the stoop of our house in Macheen and bewail her fate. Dead from the front of the house the dirt road ran off toward the Primeria (town hall), with Todoracu the barber on the right and *Sooreh die blecherkie* (Sarah the tinsmithess, i.e., the tinsmith's wife) on the left, and farther along, also on the left, the synagogue and the *mikveh* (ritual bathhouse). Our street, which was the dead end of the Primeria street, stretched one way to the Turkish quarter and the crossroads lantern which was the pride of Macheen, the other way to the glittering Teena (Danube), which made a bend and came round to the back of our house. Across more than six decades I hear my mother keening as she stares away, holding my head in her lap: "*Gevald, vus bin ich farkrochen in der veest*—God

22

help me, how did I land in this wilderness? Fields and
fields and fields, peasants and peasants and peasants. And
the nights! Death itself!" It is from that childhood experience, I sometimes think, that I have brought over my
aversion to the deep countryside. I cannot bear its special
silence. I am overcome by a shudder of fear when I have
to walk alone at night along a deserted country road. It is
not the fear of assault, or of some mishap, and certainly
not of ghosts; it is an unnamable horror which sends me
at top speed toward the light of a house and human company.

The memory of those locations—town hall, crossroads,
synagogue, Turkish quarter, lantern—I checked with
Uncle Berel long ago, and more recently with my older
brother, Mendel, who was in Macheen until the age of
eleven. But the sound of my mother's voice and the words
she uttered I shall never be able to check with anyone.
The impression she left on me is in one sense a private
affair, but in another sense the very opposite; for it is of
the *Golus*, the Jewish Exile. Those words: *"Vus bin ich
farkrochen in der veest!"* That voice, that sense of the lost
and the exiled!

There comes over, from my mother, from my childhood,
I should even say from my infancy, and also from my youth
and from Uncle Berel, a feeling of the dominant spirit
of *Golus* desolation, and behind it, faintly, I hear the
wailing of the muezzin on the minaret which was visible
from our yard. Uncle Berel's "Beh! They won't let us"
seems in my recollection to echo a general hopelessness and
listlessness with regard to the Jewish condition among the
Jews of my early years. "They won't let us" and "Who are
we to undertake such an extraordinary enterprise?" As my
mother had lost the ability to read and write, so the Jews I
grew up among seemed to have lost, also through trans-

mitted disuse, their faith in themselves as the creators and managers of a Jewish homeland. For a moment Herzl had broken through the paralysis; then, with his death, ancient habit had reasserted itself and—as I was to learn in the Zionist movement—it would take decades of agitation and frightful cataclysms to rouse the will and establish the self-confidence of the Jewish people. I call to mind the legend of Tarquin the Proud and the nine Sibylline Books. The Erythrean Sibyl offered them to the Roman at a creatain price; he refused; thereupon she burned three of them and offered the remainder at the same price. He refused again, and again she burned three books and offered the remainder at the same price. In the end Tarquin bought the three for the money which would have got him nine. So with the Jews; they dallied until they had to build their homeland after the two most vital Jewries—those of Poland and Russia—had been either destroyed or cut off from the rest of the world.

We Zionists talk in our propaganda of the electric shock which passed through world Jewry when England issued the Balfour Declaration in 1917, supporting the plan for a Jewish homeland in Palestine. Yes, the reaction was vivid. I also remember out of my childhood how Herzl's brief and blazing career produced a similar effect in our humble, uninstructed corner of the Jewish world, and how his sudden extinction plunged us into mourning (the cliché is in this case a literal description). However, I also remember that the wonder and worship that blossomed round Herzl had had no practical results in my environment—they seemed to be waiting for him to do everything himself, like a Messiah—nor were the results impressive anywhere outside the little band of passionate devotees. The masses did not move at Herzl's call, and they did not move even after the Balfour Declaration. And yet, speaking for the world I grew up in, and the world round Uncle Berel, it was not a fundamental indifference. It was in part distrust of the world at large ("They won't let us"), in part distrust of self ("Who are we, etc?") and in part that Messianic attitude in a secular form. For Herzl had been a genuinely Messianic apparition, secular in externals, folkloristically sacred in essence, and thwarted by death.

Uncle Berel was "electrified" and confused by the Balfour Declaration. I was at the time of its issuance already a soldier. I had by then worked for, among others, the Zionist Organization of America, the Jewish Education Bureau of New York, a raincoat manufacturer in Cleveland (that lasted two days: I left unobtrusively after having sewn some dozens of sleeve tabs into the armpit ends of the sleeves), and in the pit of the Goodyear Rubber plant in Akron (that lasted some months). I had done some hoboing in the Middle West, and had written two novels the manuscripts of which I was fortunate enough to lose, thereby saving myself a small fortune in stamps alone, and I had published several short stories in Mencken and Nathan's *Smart Set*. On one of my leaves I went with Uncle Berel to his restaurant. He wavered that evening between gratitude for the Balfour Declaration, suspicion of duplicity, distrust of destiny, and above all doubts as to the capacities of the Jewish people.

"A *ness*, a miracle," he said. "Excellent, *anshtendig*, decent," and so on, diminuendo. "Let's suppose that England means it and the other allies agree. Is it *bashert*, destined, and can our *Yiddalach* do it? *Es leigt sich nit off'n sechel*—it somehow doesn't make sense."

Somewhere along the line, in centuries of exile, humiliation, and everlasting displacement, the Jews seem to have formed an attachment to their misery. The sense of earthly futility, too, was to them part of Jewishness. There was not only acquiescence in their status, there was also a lachrymose enjoyment of it. On the evening to which I refer, the entertainer sang a Rumanian refrain I had heard from my mother. All I remember of the words is:

> *O saracu Plevna nostra,*
> *Ah, aman aman, ah, aman aman . . .*

The first line means: "Alas, alas for our Plevna," and I take it to refer to the famous battle or battles of Plevna in the Turko-Russian war of 1877, in which Rumania had had a part ("Old, unhappy, far-off things and battles long ago"), and what the second line means I do not know. But I remember that in the song occurred the names of Osman Pasha and Skoboliev, and when she uttered them my mother made a gesture of horror. The song is also associated in my mind with one of the earliest, perhaps *the* earliest visual recollection out of my childhood—a squad of soldiers in dusty, gray-white uniforms marching past our house toward the Turkish quarter. In my mother's singing there was a great compassion for the soldiers, and a touch of despair at the bloody antics of the *goyim* in which Jews were compelled to join *mir nisht dir nisht,* as Uncle Berel used to say. And both Uncle Berel and my mother had a deep-rooted if unformulated conviction that the world, with its privileges and triumphs, was not for the Jews until something like a Messianic transformation had taken place.

CHAPTER II

Time Present, Place Here

❀

I

I AM WRITING this book in the land Uncle Berel said "they" would never let us have. I keep thinking: "How wonderful if I could get him a visitor's visa from wherever he is—assuming he could get a passport—and show him round: 'Look! It has happened after all!' " I have had this thought about others, about relatives and friends, my parents, my *rebbe* (Hebrew teacher), those who have long been keeping Uncle Berel company, but about him in particular, because he was so obstinately persuaded that it could not happen, and because he would be so pleased to be proved wrong.

But it is also because I am living in the Weizmann Institute of Science, where they are answering questions he used to ask, and many others he could not have thought of. I am playing Uncle Berel, as it were, to the scientists here. "Tell me something about the mechanism of heredity. What is the situation today in atomic science? By what means do they plot the structure of a molecule? How do you prepare a program for the electronic computer?" I have been trying, over the last few years, to make good— to whatever extent it is possible, so late, with so little equipment—a painful defect in my education. It is a

wonderful adventure, the most exciting I have ever undertaken; and it brings me very close to Uncle Berel.

One thing in particular I would like to tell Uncle Berel.
"Do you remember asking me: 'Who's going to lead us
now? Where will we find another Herzl?' And do you
remember that I never mentioned the name of Chaim
Weizmann? Well, he was the man, as great in his own
way as Herzl. From boyhood into old age he labored for
this land. His share in it is incomparably the greatest of
his generation. And if it were not for him I would certainly not be here. I don't mean in Israel, but at the
Weizmann Institute." And I can imagine Uncle Berel
murmuring: "It is a marvelous world . . . the mind of
man can't look through the deepness of it all."

When I first saw Rehovoth nearly forty years ago there
was of course no Weizmann Institute; there was hardly a
Rehovoth. The area was part habitation, part orchard and
orange grove, but, like the rest of the country, mostly
wilderness. Its largest population was of jackals—their
diminishing tenth and eleventh generations can still be
heard lamenting in the nights—and the road from the tiny
village to the nearest town, Tel Aviv, was sand, into which
the wheels of the diligence sank several inches. It took four
or five hours each way; now the taxi makes it in twenty
minutes (thirty with a sensible driver) on the metalled
road. Rehovoth, with its twenty thousand inhabitants, is
bigger than Tel Aviv was then, and a twenty-fifth part of
what Tel Aviv is now. Furious traffic pours back and forth,
local buses and trucks, buses and trucks to and from the
northern cities and Beersheba, private cars, motorcycles,
tourist buses. Behind its gates the Institute is, to all seem-
ing, a world apart.

It is a lovely place, eighty acres of multicolored garden
and lawn and grove, with green predominant, but rich in

scarlet and mauve and purple, Monterey and Kashmir cypresses, pine, flame tree, bougainvillea, and poinciana regia. I am under a constant tugging toward the outdoors, even in the heat of the day, but I parcel out the hours with a stern hand. In the morning I write, in the afternoon receive my teachers; toward twilight I leave the Faculty Club House and stroll from building to building: Nuclear Physics, Experimental Biology, Electronic Computer, Heavy Water Tower, Plant Genetics, library. My favorite walk is along the shining tree-lined road which ends in a spacious marble-paved plaza; from here a narrow, sandy track leads between lantana, oleander, honeysuckle, geranium, and rose bushes to the grave of Chaim Weizmann. A plain, horizontal marble slab bears his name in Hebrew, nothing more, no mention of honors or other worldly circumstance, not even dates of birth and death. To the right, on the little hill, is the stately house in which I so often sat with him in his latter years, and from which we could look down on the spot he had chosen for his burial place.

II

It is the complete division, for me, between two non-communicating worlds that has triggered off so powerfully the impulse to write about my inner life. I am a collection of memories and emotions, loves and hates, sweet silent thoughts, delights pertaining to persons and books, deep attachments—to my people, to America, to Israel, to England—recurrent longings to be "better" than I am, glimpses of a Power for which I accept the name of God; and all this has no bearing on, no connection with what I am trying to build up as the concept (I will not say "picture") of scientific "reality." I find the two worlds incommensurable. Is it because I am a tyro in science? Is it because science is still in its infancy? Men whose intelligence I respect, whose scientific competence is attested in high places, tell me that in time a connection will be established between thoughts and emotions on the one hand and the measurable behavior of atoms and electrical charges on the other; at least a connection of rigid correspondence. For the moment all I understand, and that only in part of course, is the reasoning behind the Crick-Watson model of DNA, the tables of the atomic shells, the logic of the Stern-Gerlach experiment, the procedures of X-ray crystallography, some of the reports on electroencephalography. There is aesthetic as well as intellectual fascination here, but this emotion is irrelevant except as the driving force toward study. Or, if it is relevant, we must think in a new way about the manner of its operation.

I pondered this problem as I stood late one night before WEIZAC, our Weizmann Institute electronic computer, which is kept working twenty-four hours a day throughout the year. He (I use this pronoun because there is no neuter gender in Hebrew, and I prefer "he" to "she" because I cannot associate complete absence of emotion with the feminine) is pretty old, having been put together seven or eight years ago. He was quite a man, or rather, quite the thing, in his prime, that is, on the day he was completed—computers differ from living things like men and other animals in being at their best when born and falling into obsolescence more rapidly. Not that old WEIZAC has deteriorated; kept in good order he performs as well as ever. He is simply outclassed by the new computers, one of which is being constructed next door to him with his self-less assistance.* The new computers will also be outclassed

* As I correct proofs in America, I learn that old WEIZAC is done for. He computed himself out of existence on the question of whether he was worth keeping. I shall miss him.

in a few years. We may soon have a computer (or have we one already?) that can not only keep itself in order but improve itself to keep pace with the progress of man's needs. WEIZAC is unable to process the material I have just referred to, my loves and hates and moral qualms, even if the mathematicians were able to program them. But tomorrow, or the day after . . .

I stand before WEIZAC and his lights blink at me. Control instructs Input: "Feed information to Memory"; instructs Output: "Print information from Memory"; instructs Memory: "Transfer information to Processor" and: "Send information to Control"; instructs Processor: "Process information received from Memory and transfer back to Memory." In a matter of a few seconds a million million "Yes-No, Yes-No" operations produce the answer to the programmed question. It would have taken mathematicians weeks or months to work it out. And yet WEIZAC is a primitive; there is even, in that blinking of his, a suggestion of the animistic, and more than a suggestion in the terminology of his parts.

What will his sucessors be like?

I go out from his presence into the star-studded night and stroll in the silent garden. I feel that I represent millions and millions of my kind: I shall have to get used to certain things; but when I have done that, what will I be like?

CHAPTER III

The Twig Is Bent

❀

STATISTICALLY I am dead several time over. If Uncle Berel had been an actuary, he would have known that anyone born in 1895 in such advanced countries as England and America had an even chance of being alive at fifty; it was less than an even chance for one who was born and continued to live in Rumania. My mother bore nine children, three of whom died in infancy; two little brothers, Aaron and Naphthali, I never knew; I remember as in a vivid dream a sister called Bessie, and I remember the pall that fell on the house with her death. As regards the family, then, I had two chances in three of surviving my infancy, but that is only the beginning of the list of hazards.

I was born together with a twin sister, Hannah, who died in 1955. When we came into the world, my mother had three infants and two youngsters to look after, and the double addition was too much for her. I was put out to a Turkish wet nurse who nearly settled the problem when I was a few months old. In letters my father wrote me shortly before his death in 1924, he told me how I peaked and pined and was discovered, on an unexpected visit, in such filth and misery that I was snatched back home. In respect to that episode alone, I overcame a ten-to-one hazard.

Now suppose my mother had not nagged my father to leave Rumania and I had stayed on there for the rest of my undetermined life; what would have been my chances of surviving the Hitler time, to say nothing of intervening dangers? Or suppose we had settled permanently in Paris, where we stayed for nearly a year before proceeding to Manchester, and suppose I had been a French conscript in the First World War; or suppose I had served in the British army instead of the American; or, serving in the American army, suppose I had been sent to the front instead of getting no nearer to it than the advanced zone, whence I was recalled to serve in GII. There were also many private narrow escapes in my life, though these are perhaps part of the general statistical table; once I nearly stepped into an elevator shaft on the twentieth floor when the elevator was not there, and once a farmer in Ohio shot at me when I was stealing peaches from his orchard. It was night, and he missed, but I heard the bullet like a mosquito near my ear, and I ran like mad. However I look at it, I am astonished at being here.

On the other hand, if I have defied statistics till now, statistics will turn their tables on me in the end. I shall assuredly die before my time. We all do, with an uncollected statistical life expectancy.

A more subtle statistical puzzle lies in the fact that I grew up into me and not somebody else. The probabilities pointed at a kind of me that depresses the me I became. For, granting me a normal span of life, what would have been my opportunities had my family stayed on, as the majority of Jews did, in Rumania? "Fancy," I often say to myself, "not having the treasures of the English langauge and literature to ransack! Fancy not to have known at first hand the greatness of England and America. All that I have read, all that I have seen,

> cities of men
> And manners, climates, councils, governments,

(a little exaggeration here), the spiritual and intellectual excitements which have not yet ceased to visit me, would have remained unrealized.

I became a socialist and atheist around the age of thirteen, whether before or after my *bar mitzvah* (confirmation) I cannot remember. Probably after, because, being a contumacious youngster, I would no doubt have refused to go through with the ceremony if I had considered it "intellectually dishonest."

But the evil seed sprouted before the ceremony; during my last months at *cheder* I was, with my pointed questioning and challenging of sacred things, the affliction of my *rebbe,* a large, fat, and decent man with a vast black beard, a hypochondriac wife, and no pedagogic skill whatsoever. That Manchaster *cheder* on Waterloo Road might as a matter of fact just as well been in Rumania for all the relationship it bore to the surrounding world: the front room of my *rebbe's* house, thirty to forty boys between the ages of six and thirteen jammed into it, various groups chanting their lessons separately, a marvelously organized bedlam. And yet I am still troubled by my wicked behavior toward my *rebbe,* and if it sounds queer that one should brood occasionally on boyhood sins more than half a century old, we have St. Augustine's warrant for it; he in maturity remembered with passionate weeping how at the age of seven he had stolen some pears, not because, like me in Ohio, he had been hungry, but just for

34

the hell of it. How much of "just for the hell of it" lingers in us till the end!

My *rebbe* was a man of learning and in some respects not more than two or three centuries behind the times. He taught me Hebrew so badly that I quickly and willingly forgot whatever I had picked up in seven years of *cheder* attendance. He was, however, a gifted storyteller, and when he went into the *Midrashim* (the ancient, extra-Biblical homiletic and folkloristic literature), he held us fascinated. He was equally effective when he expounded the *Pirke Abot* (The "Ethics of the Fathers," a section of the Talmud). But the *Midrashim* and *Pirke Abot* came only once a week, the Saturday afternoon treat. He also expounded then the beauties of the ancient Jewish moral and civil codes; he dwelt on the laws of *Peot*, the leaving of the corners of the harvest field to be gleaned by the widow, the orphan, and the stranger, and of the fruit that lay on the ground after a windfall. From the *Pirke Abot* I learned at the age of eight or nine that I would avoid sin and egotism if I remembered what my origin was—a putrid drop; also that he who puts on flesh is only providing food for worms. I must say that my *rebbe* did not seem to me to be troubled by this last bit of information. He was overweight and very fond of cookies and tea between regular meals. During the week he tried to drum *Chumash* (the Pentateuch) and Rashi (the great medieval commentator) into us by the brute force of repetition.

When I became a socialist, the laws of *Peot* outraged me. Why should some men be so well off that the poor could subsist on their leavings, and why should the Law countenance this situation and even enable the rich man to collect heavenly merits by its means? I understood only much later that there was being implanted in me a deep regard for the moral element in ancient Jewish pre-

35

scription and legislation, and I regret that I was not able to tell my *rebbe* of my change of view.

My conversion to socialism and atheism was the unexpected end result of an event that occurred when I was twelve and a half years old. I won a scholarship to the Manchester Secondary School. I think I was the first in our clan and in our whole Rumanian Jewish colony, then fairly new in Manchester, to perform the feat. It was a very good scholarship; free tuition for five years and an "Exhibition" of five pounds for the first year. My parents were awestruck by the generosity of England; they contrasted my good fortune with the melancholy experience of my two older brothers, who had topped their classes in the village school of Macheen and had been harassed and insulted for their Jewish pushfulness. As for me, I celebrated the event by a revolution in my reading habits and in my thinking.

Until then I had devoured weekly ten or a dozen boys' magazines: *The Boys of St. Jims, The Boy's Friend, The Boy's Leader, The Union Jack, The Gem, The Marvel,* and the like. Since these magazines used to cost an English penny (two cents) each, and my weekly pocket money, delivered every Saturday afternoon, was a ha'penny (halfpenny), I had to enter an organization of twenty boys or more, nearly all from homes as poor as mine, and all equally addicted to this type of literature. Two of us bought one magazine and twenty of us would have ten magazines to pass around. Occasionally double-numbers were issued in gorgeously colored covers, price twopence, and if ordinary numbers were musts, double-numbers were double-musts. We usually managed somehow, and gorged on the thirty-two-page issues. When the news arrived that I had won the scholarship, I was filled with a sudden horror of my wasted life. I made a solemn vow to put away folly and frivolity and to prepare myself for greatness.

36

Whether or not I immediately began to ply my *rebbe*
with outright socialistic and atheistic questions I do not,
as I have said, remember; if I did not, I sailed very close
to the wind, an exceedingly ill wind, for this I do remember: my *rebbe* foretold that I would come to a spectacularly
bad end, and that in my downgoing I would involve large
numbers of Jews, if not the entire Jewish people, and
probably a contingent of gentiles as well. In our Manchester–Rumanian semi-ghetto, socialism and atheism
were blindly but not quite unjustly yoked together, and
with them, not quite so justly, a disrespect for the
decencies and for the welfare of Jewry.

It was a predominantly unhappy time for me, though
shot through with ecstatic interludes. I was frustrated in
my search for knowledge. The new reading material I
hankered for was expensive, and the juvenile section of
the public library did not carry it. There was in those days
a publishing enterprise called The Sixpenny Rationalist
Reprints—Herbert Spencer, Ernst Haeckel, Joseph Mc-
Cabe among others. But who had sixpence? The bloated
rich. There was also a secondhand bookstall in an alley
near Shudehill, where tattered copies of the Reprints could
be had for twopence. Twopence was my weekly allowance
after I had won the scholarship, and though I earned or
cadged a few pennies now and again, I never had enough.
In this new world I had entered there were no companions
with whom to pool resources. I used to borrow the Reprints at a penny a time; I also used to borrow surreptitiously. I have long been convinced that the cadaverous
young man who ran the bookshop knew all about my
unpaid borrowings, and it has occurred to me that such
business practices accounted for his cadaverous appearance.

I resented my poverty and was in some ways ashamed
of it. I could not make friends with more prosperous fellow

high-school students. The front room of our house was used by my father as his shoe-repair shop, while everybody else's front room was a parlor. There wasn't a room for talking in.

My deepest source of unhappiness was spiritual. I wrestled in the usual adolescent fashion with ontological problems which gave a nihilistic background to my social and moral thinking. I also dabbled in, rather than studied, astronomy. I managed to get hold of an ancient telescope with a one and a half inch aperture, and constructed a clumsy hand-worked equatorial which moved so jerkily that it was worse than nothing, except for the pride it gave me in my workmanship; but I never went beyond the mathematics of the three Keplerian laws. It was all loosely observational, a sidereal Cook's tour, watching for Halley's comet and sketching the mountains of the moon and looking for nebulae and asteroids. I had unforgettable moments, and I never see the Pleiades without recalling the cry of terror and bliss that escaped me when I first turned my ramshackle little telescope on them. But as I probed the heavens I saw our planet, our solar system, and our galaxy shrink into insignificance. The clockwork of the stars and planets was reflected back for me into human affairs, exposing will and purpose as illusions. Life was meaningless and all our striving a vain gesticulation: slogans, movements, dreams of human improvement, martyrdoms—nothing but a predetermined jigging of matter. The greatest thinkers of the ages were in no better case than the most benighted clods, and to the wisest I conceded at best only a superior sophistication in self-delusion.

Among the first paperbacks I bought—I shall return to the occasion—were certain works by one Robert Blatchford, a widely admired socialist and science popularizer, and those that left the profoundest impression on me were his *Merrie England, Britain for the British,* and *Not Guilty, a Defense of the Bottom Dog.* Blatchford's name was always linked with two others, Victor Grayson and H. M. Hyndman. They were the terrible trio of revolutionary England fifty-odd years ago. Grayson was a young socialist member of Parliament, Hyndman was the elderly intellectual leader of the British Labor Party, which had just begun to make a respectable showing in the House of Commons. To me they were the Trinity, and their fates were various. Grayson disappeared from England and not much later died obscurely in a little town in Australia. Blatchford, who at one time edited the socialist daily, *The Clarion,* became a reactionary and a spiritualist after the First World War. Only Hyndman, the most substantial of the three, carried on consistently until his death in 1921. By then much had happened to me. I had settled in America and established my friendship with Uncle Berel; I had done my two years in the American army, I had been a secretary on the Morgenthau Commission which investigated the Polish pogroms of 1919. I had been demobilized in Paris, where I had opened a public stenography office for Americans, I had served as interpreter on the Allied Reparations Commissions in Berlin and Vienna, I had mastered Yiddish and was learning Hebrew, I had married, and I had returned to America with my first publishable novel.

But to go back. Blatchford's effect on me in my adolescence was shattering. He was a Sinaitic voice and everything he said was law. I remember, fifty years after I last read him, phrases of his which were like hammer blows. On the irreconcilability of interest between worker and employer he quoted a Hindu proverb: "I am bread, thou art the eater, how can peace be between us?" On the unsuspected dormant strength of the working classes he said:

39

"They are like the lions in the zoo; every keeper knows
that they can, with a sudden effort, break the bars of the
cages; but the lions don't know it." On the problem of
the lowest kind of labor in a socialist state and who would
do it, he said: "We can make it attractive by shortening
the hours. But at least we won't see fat aldermen guzzling
oxtail soup at dinner while factory girls starve." I am not
sure of the exact phrasing, but I am sure of the key words.
I went about repeating them somberly to myself. "Fat aldermen guzzling oxtail soup!" What a revolting picture! And
the juxtaposition with starving factory girls! I took it that
oxtail soup was the most luxurious and expensive kind of
soup in existence; not necessarily tasty, but gratifying to
the sense of power and exclusiveness, like peacocks' noses
at Roman banquets. That aldermen were fat, and that they
guzzled, was self-understood; I was filled with indignation
and disgust. Equally self-understood, because Blatchford
said so—also because it was such an appealing thought—
was the lion's tragic unawareness of its own powers; and I
tagged on to Blatchford's scientific discovery some lines
from Shelley:

> Rise like lions after slumber,
> In unvanquishable number;
> Ye are many, they are few.

At thirteen I became a stump speaker for the Socialist
Party, stupefying the neighborhood and vindicating my
rebbe. I also went out, as a prodigy, to neighboring towns:
Oldham, Wigan, Altringham, Irlam o' the Heights (pronounced Irlamathites, like a sect, or a Biblical tribe). At
street corners near and far I thundered in a treble against
Winston Churchill when, having been promoted to a
cabinet post in Asquith's government, he contested a by-
election in Manchester. I defeated him. But it was his Tory

opponent, Joynson-Hicks, who got in, and not the socialist I had supported, a certain Daniel whose second name I have forgotten. The Churchill supporters sang, to the tune of *Tramp, Tramp, Tramp, the Boys Are Marching:*

> Vote, vote, vote for Winston Churchill
> He is sure to win the day.
> Don't be fooled by Joynson-Hicks
> And his dirty Tory tricks . . .

I sang with the socialists:

> Dare to be a Daniel,
> Dare to stand alone . . .

(which we pretty nearly did) and:

> The people's flag is deepest red,
> It's shrouded oft our martyred dead;
> And ere their limbs grew stiff and cold
> Their heart's blood dyed its every fold.

What the victorious Tories sang I do not remember.

At one point in my earlier socialist career I was a fiery supporter of Lloyd George, the Liberal, because he advocated the nationalization of land. The Liberals had a quite extraordinary song which even today would smack of extreme leftism if not of barricades. Like many English political songs, it was borrowed, as to melody, from America—this time *Marching Through Georgia:*

The land, the land, 'twas God who made the land!
The land, the land, the ground on which we stand!
Why should we be beggars with the ballot in our hand?
God made the land for the people.

My high-school and university years were filled with political and intellectual excitement, and with extremes

41

of mood that were almost manic-depressive. I got to know the Lancashire weavers and their clog-and-shawl-wearing wives, and I conceived an enduring affection for certain little places and groups—warm, eager, hopeful talk, kindly faces and bad teeth, fish and chips after the meetings, or sometimes only chips carried out of the chip shop on a piece of newspaper. But I was not at ease in my early socialist phase. I suffered from recurrent longings for a Jewish way of life. I was troubled less by my atheistic than by my socialist philosophy. "Jewish atheist," while obviously unorthodox, was somehow not impossible; "Jewish socialist," with its implication of cosmopolitanism and rejected Jewishness, was. I lived in a marvelous muddle, which I shall describe further on.

In my post-high-school socialist phase I was acutely uncomfortable for other reasons. At the university, to which I won a three-year scholarship at sixty pounds a year (a large sum in those days), my socialist comrades exasperated me by their dogmatism, by their intellectual bullying (I was all persuasiveness, of course), and above all by their addiction to the phrase: "For the simple reason that . . ." The simple reason was never satisfactory; besides, "simple" was a reflection on my intelligence; worst of all, they were always implying that a good socialist never asked fundamental questions.

Among my comrades in those days was a volcanic, diminutive redhead, Ellen Wilkinson, who ultimately became a cabinet minister in the Labor government. Another was a tall, lean young man with a death's-head face, J. T. Walton-Newbold. He told us that he was going to die soon of consumption, and he looked it. He broke that promise and many others. He, too, entered Parliament and later went from socialism to Communism, from Communism to Fascism. Wilkinson and Walton-Newbold were ready to stake their lives on the prophecy that no great war would ever be fought in an industrialized area; the proof was the last imperialist war, the Russo-Japanese, which had been fought out in the empty spaces of the Far East. War, they said, there would be, but not where productive property would be endangered; the *Pax Capitalisma,* an echo of the *Pax Romana,* forbade it.

I, on the other hand, was ready to stake my life, or at any rate talk others to death, on the thesis that there would not be any kind of war any more. Let a war be declared, I said, and the workers, the toiling masses, would rise in their might—workers never rose in anything else for me— and pull the imperialist conspirators from their place of power to establish universal and everlasting brotherhood and peace.

My sharpest disagreements with my fellow-socialists were provoked by their rigid historical and economic determinism. I agreed that socialism was the only conceivable moral order, but how could that which was automatically inevitable also be moral? I continued to chant loyally: "The nationalization of the instruments of production, distribution, and exchange," but in spite of despondent lapses into a wider mechanistic philosophy—during which I hadn't the slightest interest in mankind's future or my own—I found the "inevitability" of socialism not only incompatible with a theory of morals, but personally offensive as well. If the world was moving to perfection under an iron law and at its own pace, it needed no help from me; I was making a fool of myself arguing with people to bring about what they could neither accelerate nor delay. "Inevitability" took the heart out of me.

This frustration did not face me in Zionism. Herzl had, to be sure, declared the Jewish state to be a historic inevitability, but Zionists were not as a rule given to historic

43

determinism. We believed that a Jewish state ought to be created in Palestine; to work for it was right and proper whether or not we succeeded. We differed in our estimates of our chances, but we were content with a belief in the feasibility of our program. Those that went beyond—and there were many—appealed to faith, not to historic determinism.

In New York I discovered for the first time that there was such a thing as a socialist-Zionist movement. There may have been a branch of it in Manchester, but I do not remember coming across it. The Zionists I knew were anti-socialist, the Jewish socialists anti-Zionist. But more pleasing was the discovery that one could be a socialist within the general Zionist movement, which was strongly tinged with liberalism. One could, through the Zionist congresses and funds, support socialist-oriented enterprises in Palestine, and thus work for socialism at large by creating a socialist Jewish state. I did not join the socialist-Zionist party. I had had enough of "inevitability."

In our few exchanges on Zionism and socialism I prophesied to Uncle Berel that a Jewish homeland would, when it came into being, play its part in making a better world, and in my new-found passion for the Bible I quoted: "For from Zion shall go forth the Law and the word of God from Jerusalem." I kept my fingers crossed, as it were, for the second half of this famous verse, for after all I was an atheist. I interpreted "Law" in my own way, the law of economic equality.

Well, here I am in the Jewish homeland, which was something of a mirage fifty years ago. It is a remarkable phenomenon—certainly, despite many defects, a progressive force in world affairs; but it is not socialistic or ever

44

likely to be of its own free will. Nor do I want it to be, for I no longer believe that "the nationalization of the instruments of production, distribution, and exchange" is the best managerial formula for a country's affairs—or even a good one. I don't believe it to be workable, at least not until human beings are at such an advanced moral stage that system is irrelevant. What is more, I don't believe that "the toiling masses" want all-round economic equality; they want a decent life, a sufficiency with security, and freedom spiced with the play of reasonable differentiations; and if they can get all this without economic equality, they will gladly concur.

In this they are morally right, with a profound intuitive and practical rightness. I see the problem now in a totally different light. It is a destructive baseness which impels men to say: "This is what I want for myself, and I won't let others have more."

Long after I had seen Uncle Berel for the last time I came across a passage from Karl Marx which helped me to crystallize permanently my rejection of economic egalitarianism.

A house may be large or small, but as long as the surrounding houses are equally small, it satisfies all social requirements of a dwelling-place. But let a palace arise by the side of this small house, and it shrinks from a house to a hut. The smallness of the house now indicates that its occupant is allowed to have either very few claims or none at all; *and however high it may shoot up with the progress of civilization,* if the neighboring palace shoots up in the same or greater proportion, the occupant of the small house will always find himself *more uncomfortable, more discontented* . . . [My italics. M.S.]

45

What a ghastly indictment of human nature, what a despairing prospect for the human species! I know it is not easy to define "sufficiency," but I am sure that if a man has to survey his neighbor's portion before he can decide whether his own is adequate, the very concept of "sufficiency" disappears; the principle of measurement has ceased to be appetitional satisfaction and has become envy. But envy is unappeasable; it is watchful, touchy, self-promoting; it discovers differences where there are none, so that if objective economic equality could be enforced, the feeling of it would not follow. Thus the demand for an unattainable feeling of equality becomes the enemy of an attainable satisfaction; it is the sacrifice of humanity on the altar of a nobly immoral principle.

Together with the chanted "nationalization of" etc., other slogans of the early days have taken on a hollow sound. "Workers of the world, unite! You have nothing to lose but your chains . . ." When the slogan was coined, a hundred years ago, it was a barely permissible propaganda exaggeration; by the early part of the twentieth century it was a disastrous falsehood. The German and Italian workers had something to lose, and they lost it to Hitler and Mussolini. The workers of Russia had less to lose, except in prospect, and it will be some time before they realize what they lost unnecessarily in order to improve their condition.

But I have more than that to say about the socialist movement. If its theoretical base now looks to me like nonsense, I am still filled with admiration for its practical achievements and with gratitude for the part it has played in my life. The modern Western world would today be a charnel house if the socialist movement had not intervened. Its courage and idealism, if accompanied by wrong reasoning, sprang from the right moral instinct. Imperfect our modern Western world certainly is, but one can only think with horror of what it would have been without the great socialist movement. The classic capitalists were mostly horrible, conscienceless men. Their historic function was to make the breakthrough, to squeeze out of the workers the indispensable accumulation of investment capital. Driven by obsessive greed and lust for power, they performed their function with furious—and unnecessary— brutality. The pace could and should have been slower; the withholding of surplus profit need not have been so extortionate. When the breakthrough came, the capitalists had no intention of calling a halt; they wanted the accumulation to go on forever, to their own undoing and that of society. Their kind is still with us, an unteachable, irreclaimable minority; they are the blind troglodytes who fought the New Deal at every step and, ragingly impotent to nullify it, will continue to fight its extension. (To use an Irishism: there are some people who will not thank you for saving their lives until they are dead.) But if they are a minority today, that is due to the socialist movement and its wide peripheral influence; and if the socialist movement is everywhere in decline, it is because the creative changes it has forced through have outdated it.

What a scurvy trick history has played on the Communists, and no wonder they loathe the socialist movement with a convulsive loathing. It was their original hope to step in where the capitalists had done all the dirty work and take over as angelic liberators. But, being able to seize power only in pre-capitalist countries, they are forced to do their own dirty work, and they are doing it no better than the early capitalist commissars. No, they are not doing it as well; they are forcing the pace even more brutally, and they have repressed the inventiveness and resourcefulness of individual competitive greed.

I remember with even greater admiration the socialist-Zionists who, under infinitely difficult conditions, prevented the nascent Jewish homeland from developing into an early-capitalist exploitative state based on cheap labor. Israel would not have its place among the world democracies had it not been for the primitive *kvutzot,* the later *kibbutzim* (it is well to note that this word is now international), and the workers' co-operatives. In Israel, too, the socialist movement has completed its mission. The labor leaders of Israel still call themselves socialists, but it is an honorific title; they have no program for universal nationalization. The *kibbutzim* themselves are becoming village corporations with equality for all members, a decent form of life which somehow, to the distress of the "socialist" leaders, is not spreading. And in America the socialist-Zionist movement which is committed to the support of "socialist" Israel is entirely middle class.

What remains in me of my one-time socialism? Only the moral element and a certain, informed alertness to capitalist hypocrisies and dodges. My social philosophy is an amalgam of what my *rebbe* and the Prophets (it is a long time since I have winced at "the word of God") taught me and what I have read, from my youth onward, in leftist books, including Karl Marx and Engels. I am what Communists call a "reformist" and a "rotten liberal." My views on the techniques of social amelioration come from a layman's acquaintance with economics, history, psychology, etc. My instincts are with the worker as against the employer simply because the employer is as a rule better off. But I no longer believe, as I used to, that the worker is always right vis-à-vis the employer; and I am grateful that workers have now improved their condition to the point where they can sometimes be in the wrong.

I also brought out of the poverty of my childhood and

youth, and out of later economic hardship, a distaste for rich people, though, like the anti-Semite with regard to Jews, I make exceptions. Some of my best friends . . . Also a distaste for expensively elegant women and women who like to have men spend money on them, either from greediness or as a lift to their vanity. I could never afford their company, which I would not accept as charity. I have no pleasure in posh hotels and restaurants. Most of all I dislike "easy spenders"—who are seldom easy givers; they show a contempt for money out of excessive deference to it; they stand treat to those who have no need of it because they want to be appreciated "on a higher plane." And that contempt of theirs for money is in more ways than one a contempt for human beings—for the careworn who must watch their pennies, for the fools who are impressed by easy spending. Easy spending and easy giving are psychologically as well as arithmetically in conflict; an easy spender wants to be surrounded by good humor and good fellowship, the sight of misery upsets him without moving him.

I often wish I could have talked all these things over with my *rebbe*, Kalman Moskovitch. It is not unlikely that if I had argued with him from the moral postulates he taught rather than as a "scientific" socialist, we would have found much in common; but the only time I saw him after I left Manchester was not propitious for leisurely discussion.

It was in 1929, in Palestine, as it was then called, two days after the bloody anti-Jewish riots of that year. On August 25 I set out with Colonel Frederick Kisch, the Palestine Chairman of the Jewish Agency, on a tour of the cities and settlements. I had put on my old American uni-

form, hoping to impress, if not intimidate, any Arabs we
might encounter on the road, and we carried revolvers. We
went north from Jerusalem, visited Beth Alpha and Heph-
zibah, the two little *kibbutzim* at the foot of Mount Gilboa
that had stood off an Arab invasion of the Valley of Jezreel.
Then we proceeded to Safad in Galilee, where a number of
old people had been murdered.

I knew that my *rebbe* had settled some years before in
that ancient and sacred city of the Cabbalists, and when I
asked Colonel Kisch whether we might not spend ten minutes looking for him, so that I might send a message to
Manchester, he readily agreed.

We found him in one of the narrow, crooked, sloping
alleys on whose gray, crumbling walls centuries of Jewish
learning, piety, poverty, and Messianic conjuration are almost visibly encrusted. When he came to the door I recognized him at once, though his beard was now completely
snow-white. He stared at me, puzzled, until I said, in my
recently acquired Sephardic Hebrew—a pronunciation he
would associate with Christian priests: "*Rebbe, eincha
makir oti*—don't you recognize me?" Then his eyes
brimmed over, he uttered a loud cry, and answered in
Yiddish (for like all religious Jews in those days he reserved
Hebrew only for prayer and study): "Moishe! *Redst takke
loshen koidesh, ober fort vi a goy*—you do indeed speak
Hebrew, but it's still like a gentile!"

CHAPTER IV

Recall

❀

STEP BY STEP over the years Manchester has receded, not from my affections but from my sense of reality, and all that was in it has undergone a change into another incarnation. Visit by visit I have seen faces age, and one by one disappear: parents, uncles, cousins, a friend here, another there. New faces have come up in swarms, nephews, nieces, grandnephews, grandnieces, and I have long since lost count. Yes, yes, I too have become a grandfather, but I did it openly, while they did it behind my back; I did it naturally and imperceptibly, while they did it in stealthy leaps and bounds. I appear on the scene at intervals, belonging less and less, more and more a historical oddity, the vague one who went away to America a long, long time ago. I am an indeterminate identity to the young, a subject of occasional unurgent questions: "Was Great Uncle Joe his brother or his cousin?" (My brother Joe, nine years my junior, died in his wonderful manhood in 1949. I date my old age from his death.) I am reintroduced or introduced for the first time to little strangers and half-strangers whose fleeting curiosity is a forecast of the oblivion awaiting my name; they move me to confused reflections, for this one has my father's chin, that one my mother's eyes, and a third my ears—floating fragments of the dead and near-dead handed down by the genes in a sure but anonymous and fragmentated immortality. I feel my limbs, my organs, and my physical peculiarities being shuffled out into the future, a pack of cards mixed with other packs.

They hardly know me and they know not at all that Manchester world in which I grew up. They are neither immigrants nor the children of immigrants, but second-generation English. Their parents are well-to-do—we would have called the poorest of them rich. Education? They can't imagine not going to high school and perhaps university, scholarships or no scholarships. Rumania means less to them than Italy to third-generation American-Italians. The Lower Strangeways of my childhood and youth is almost equally alien territory to them, a shattered and battered slum through which they pass rapidly on visits between the upper- and middle-class areas they live in—Didsbury, Higher and Lower Broughton, Prestwich. It was in decline, with little room to decline in, even before the Second World War; now, half obliterated by bombings and meanly restored here and there, it speaks to me in a voice made intelligible only by love, like an old and indigent friend who has lost his teeth and wears a cheap, ill-fitting artificial set. The one glory of Old Strangeways, the Assize Court, vast, black, magnificent, a sooty Moses perched in precarious majesty on its tower, holding two sooty Tablets of the Law—that terrifying many-turreted palace which judges entered from horse-drawn carriages announced by scarlet-coated trumpeters—is, or was on my last visit, a roofless shell, though the ugly jail behind it is still in business. Delphiniums grew for several years on the vacant lots now covered again by repulsive little structures. Lower down on Strangeways the side and back streets remain, with some changes: Norfolk, mostly gaps (one is where our house stood, at number 5), Suffolk, Bedford, Trafalgar (sudden and incongruous bravura!), Choir, Enid, Perkins, Melbourne, Broughton Lane. What have my grand-nephews and grandnieces to do with that blighted wilderness, and what can they imagine of the forebears who inhabited it half a century ago? Only I, a *revenant*, poke around periodically, finding fewer and fewer living traces. Rosenberg's butcher shop is still there—what a handsome man he was, with his Napoleon III beard, more like a noble killer of men on the grand scale than a retail purveyor of animal carcasses—but of course he is long dead, and when I intruded to ask about his son Ruby, with whom I went to school, I found that he too was dead. Gordon's fruit and vegetable shop is still there, and the Brunswick pub, but where is old white-whiskered Maude, the shoemaker's supply man? And Saunder's and Wagstaffe's toffee shop, kept by two twittering old maiden ladies given to amateur recitations, is gone, too. Pincu's barbershop went long before, in my time, when he ran away from his wife and family to America, shortly before the one-eyed book-and-prayer-shawl dealer stole a bride's dowry (twenty gold pounds!) and disappeared without a trace.

We came from a country still largely medieval. Well-to-do Rumanians in the larger towns were no doubt nearer to the nineteenth century, but my parents knew nothing of coal fires and gaslights, which they approached in Manchester with amazement and uneasiness, coaxed into their use by blasé and much-amused relatives who had preceded them by several months. In Rumania we had burned *penkes* (faggots) in an iron stove in the middle of the room, not clumps of black stone in a hollow in the wall behind a grating. A kerosene lamp was a natural thing, an inflammable metal tube sticking out of the wall smelled of witch-craft. We clung to the lamp even after we had become familiar with gas, and I used to be sent out after a penny-worth of "lamp oil" at a time. The greasy feel of the bottle, which I clutched to my bosom for fear of dropping it, is still in my fingers, its smell is still in my nostrils. But you could do things with the lamp that you couldn't do with the gas bracket; you could stand it on the table on which father could lay the Yiddish newspaper or magazine or book supplied by the one-eyed dealer, and we could cluster round and listen, entranced, in an intimate circle.

We clung to other primitive usages brought out of Rumania; in the preparation of coffee, for instance. My father was a great coffee drinker, and he took it *à la turque,* highly concentrated and highly sweetened. Coffee was not a brown powder that came in cans; it was green beans that came in bags. We roasted and ground it ourselves. The roaster was a hollow metal cylinder a foot in length and a hand's-breadth across. It revolved on an axis that pro-truded at one end in a sharp point and at the other in a long handle. You stuck the point into a chink at the back of the fireplace, and you turned the handle with the right hand while you held the axis in the hollow of your left. The coffee beans rattled above the glowing coals, a deli-cious odor was wafted from the roaster. Every so often you pulled it away, opened the sliding door with a rag, and peeped in. When the beans had acquired the right shade of black-brown you poured them into a basin to cool. When you were done with the roasting you poured the beans a cupful at a time into the grinder, another cylinder, smaller, narrower, heavier, of yellow brass. You held that between your knees, gripping it with the left hand and turning the wooden handle with the right. What a busi-ness! It must have taken a couple of hours to prepare half a pound of coffee, and I don't know how many thousands of man-hours, as they call it, were expended in the Samuel household before we surrendered to prepared coffee. Except for the coffee *à la turque,* we drank it heavily mixed with chicory. I used to think it a necessary ingredient, and missed it when I left home. I only realized later that the chicory was an adulterant put in for reasons of economy.

The roaster and grinder we brought with us from Rumania, like the family candlesticks. We also brought along a wooden bowl to chop meat in and a small chopper. Meat grinders were already in general use, and Rosenberg the butcher may have had one. If he did, my mother turned from it as Uncle Berel turned from the pressing machine. It wasn't right not to do the work yourself, or to delegate it to an outlandish machine that hadn't the human touch, and this applied particularly to the chopped liver for the festive Sabbath meal on Friday evenings. Mother chopped on other days too, I suppose, but the sound of a pious chopping in a wooden bowl haunts my memory of Friday afternoons, a ghostly tattoo which speaks sometimes of a lost world and sometimes of superfluous labors added to the unavoidable drudgery which went into the care of a household of eight.

These objects and customs brought from Rumania were accompanied by others which were not without their parallels among our gentile neighbors in enlightened Manchester. My mother suffered cruelly from gallstones and jaundice. The idea of an operation terrified her; she took all kinds of medicaments, some, including Karlsbad water —of which she drank innumerable bottles—prescribed by doctors, others, unknown to the pharmacopoeia, prescribed by charwomen, one of whom, I remember, was represented by her colleague as an authority on "the janders." Years later I realized that her specialty was jaundice. Twice my

55

father managed to send my mother to Karlsbad, on the suggestion of the doctors that if she drank the waters straight from the well, instead of from bottles, she would be cured. This was in later, more affluent years, when my father had a shoeshop; still, it entailed a great financial effort; between that and doctors' and druggists' bills he struggled along and might have managed but for two weaknesses, one for extending credit indiscriminately, the other for cosigning loans. My mother had a whole collection of Rumanian folk remedies, among which were a paste made from bird droppings and a stocking soaked in urine and laid across the throat; what these were specifics for I do not remember.

My father was a victim of lumbago. He, too, consulted doctors and quacks impartially. In Rumania he once underwent a grisly cure; on the advice of a peasant acquaintance he had himself enclosed naked in the freshly split carcass of a cow. He always wore a tight band of red cloth round his waist, and since it was always slipping, he would rewind it two or three times a day, performing a slow and stately circular dance in his long underwear. He must have been told that a supporting belt would give him more relief, but he would not forego his cummerbund.

Our home cooking, like that of the other homes in our group, was as Rumanian-Jewish as it could be made in the new surroundings. *Mammaligge* we had when corn meal was available; *kachkeval*, the real rank kind, was a rare event. The other dishes so beloved of Uncle Berel were somewhat more frequent, but still for festive occasions only. We had meat twice a week; *gefillte* fish, chopped liver and chicken, were mandatory for the Sabbath eve, and the meal was always topped off by a dessert of carrots boiled with honey and raisins. Chicken goes together in my mind with Friday-night candles and, by later association, with

Zionist banquets and a dessert of long speeches. *Hollishkes* —chopped meat and rice wrapped in cabbage leaves and boiled sour-sweet—were my mother's specialty. It is a Rumanian-Hungarian dish. Our *rossel* was a variant of the universal meat-and-vegetable dish, nearer to an Irish stew than to a goulash. A great standby was *flocke-eeta* (as we pronounced it: a Rumanian Jewish scientist at the Weizmann Institute has kindly supplied me with the correct spelling, *facaluiete,* which makes no impression on me); it consisted of boiled mashed kidney beans covered with a dark sauce and burnt onions. It tasted "loovly," as they say in Lancashire, and had the consistency of plaster of Paris just before it sets; one could count on it to lie on the stomach pleasantly until the next day. For the rest, we had cheese, olives, onions, and lots of bread. When melon was obtainable, melon and bread was a meal; rye bread with garlic rubbed into the crust, or white bread with halva, was also considered a meal. If you had enough bread you only needed the *tzimbroit,* the with-bread.

Uncle Berel imposed himself on my childhood memories by his renewal of them when I came to America, and his thoughtful Tartar face is superimposed on *mammaligge* and *karnatzlech* and *beigalech* and *katchkeval.* The Rumania my parents spoke of so frequently fuses with Uncle Berel and his cronies in the restaurant of New York's East Side. Buhush, Glodorlui, Fokoshan, Podoturk, Barlad, Yasse, Braila, the towns and villages which colonized my Manchester world were never forgotten by us, either. There were some who had long spasms of homesickness till the end; my father was one of them, and he would dream of resettling among the scenes of his brilliant military career. There was much in England he never became reconciled to, and English cigarettes were high on the list. He was a passionate smoker, though smoking was forbid-

den him, and he choked on Woodbines, which were five
for a penny. In exceptionally good weeks he treated himself
to half an ounce of Rumanian tobacco and a booklet of
Rumanian cigarete paper; I can't imagine where he got
them. The cigarette paper was called Dorobantul, manu-
factured by the Fratelli Braunstein of Braila, and on the
cover was the magnificent colored picture of a hussar. What
with his nostalgia for the good old times and his fixation on
Rumanian tobacco, my father actually returned to Rumania at the age of fifty-eight, alone; within six months he
was back in Manchester. It was no longer the same place,
and if it had been, he was no longer the same man; perhaps
even the tobacco didn't taste as it once had, at the source.
My mother, however, had all of Uncle Berel's loathing of
Rumania: she did not even sentimentalize about it.

My father was a disciplinarian with a passion for cleanliness and order. His favorite word—he uttered it sternly,
an army command—was *Curitzenye* (cleanliness)! In our
first Manchester home, in Norfolk Street, there was no bath
when we moved in, and my mother used to bathe the children Saturday nights in a tub before the fire (only recently
did the question occur to me: where and when did my
parents bathe?). As soon as he could scrape up the money,
my father had a bath and boiler installed. Almost as badly
as Rumanian tobacco he missed the steam baths which the
Jewish community had maintained in Macheen, together
with a ritual bath for the women, near the synagogue. I
remember the steam bath well, with its wooden tiers and
clouds of steam, with men ascending the tiers Adam-naked,
smiting each other with willow withes and shouting glee-
fully in unnatural voices while the peasant attendant
dashed bucket after bucket of water on the red-hot stones
below, so that the steam came hissing up in wild burst after
burst. It recurs to me as a vaguely symbolic scene, half

apocalyptic, half quaint, half William Blake, half Marc Chagall. I stayed at ground level, which was hot enough for me, envious of and terrified by the berserk hardihood of the grown-ups.

I got along badly with my father, and reconciliation came only after I had left home. The long letters he wrote me in 1923–24 were not only his life history but his apologia, as were mine to him. I had by then learned to admire the elemental strength of his character, and his autobiography confirmed my admiration with many vivid details.

He had run away from his native village of Glodorlui and a harsh stepmother at the age of eight or nine. (Leaving the village at dawn, he had paused at the top of a hill, lowered his trousers, squatted, and cried: "Glodorlui, kiss my ass!") He had wandered and starved among strangers, falling in with mendicants and criminals such as Mendelle Mocher Sforim, the grandfather of modern Yiddish literature, describes in his *Fishke the Cripple*, the scum of the Jewish world. (I did not know in my boyhood and youth that there was a Jewish criminal class; occasional malefactors, yes, like Pincu the barber and the absconding bookseller, but not a class.) He somehow got himself apprenticed to a shoemaker, who instead of teaching him the craft turned him into a household slavey. He found another employer, who taught him but swindled him out of his pay. He found a third and a fourth—he seems to have been as set on becoming a shoemaker as I have been on becoming a writer. In one letter he described how, being in rags, he stole a pair of trousers and ran off, was pursued, caught, stripped, and left half naked in a snow-covered field. In spite of the kindness he found now and again, it is almost beyond me that he did not turn into an irreclaimable criminal. It all happened nearly a hundred years ago (and in another land; besides, the man is dead), but my stomach turns over when I think of the little boy who was to become my father begging a piece of bread at strange doors, sleeping in the open or on bare floors, and guarding through it all the original gift of his integrity. I have called him dour, and he was; yet he had his expansive moods, when he loved to read aloud to the family. I was unjust to him; all of us were; it is some consolation that we reached an understanding before the end.

He came of an enormous family, the partial records of which I have put together from what he told me and from later encounters with brothers and cousins of his in France, America, and Israel. His father, a widower with several children, married a widow by the name of Kossover, also with several children, and several more were born of the marriage. In French they call it *enfants de trois lits,* in Yiddish "mine, yours, and ours." I have a list of thirteen. The original family name was Weissbuch, but an older brother of father's, Tuli (Julius), having evaded conscription and being on the run, came to Macheen for a while and changed his name to Samuel. My father, to help him out, followed suit, with the result that my oldest brother, who had been "christened" Samuel, went through life like an echo. My father's paternal grandfather, the terminal of my researches, was called Naphthali, and by transposition of the Hebrew letters, Pantoul. He was a bee-keeper, and in his old age went to die in Palestine, settling in one of four sacred cities, whether Jerusalem, Tiberias, Hebron, or Safad (my *rebbe's* retreat), I have not been able to find out. There are legends that, rejuvenated by the Holy Land, he married again and begat numerously, like Abraham of old after the death of Sarah; but what he left behind in Rumania, namely, my father's father and my father's uncles and aunts, seems to have equaled, whether by one or more marriages, my own grandfather's tripartite household.

Among my father's Rumanian-Jewish contemporaries in Manchester many did not get beyond a rudimentary command of English. My father rejected the language almost *in toto,* and what he acknowledged he subjected to dictatorial transformations. For Trafalgar Street he said *Interfolger,* for Mazeppa *Moozet'n,* for Enid *Heener.* He used to send me to Maude's shoemaker supply shop for *neintzigshteel shmoolerletz:* nails, nine sixteenths, small heads. Here and there I perceive a clue to the principle behind the transformation. *Heener* is Yiddish for hens, *neintzig* means ninety, *shmool,* narrow, and *letz* a clown, or a kobold; but *Interfolger* and *Moozet'n* and *shteel* hang in the air. He heard us children sing "London Bridge Is Falling Down" and reissued it as *Unterdebikl svorendak.* It was useless to correct him, for that was what he seemed to hear no matter how pedantically we chopped the words into syllables for him. *Boodegaren* was his version of Board of Guardians (a free-loan institution) till the end of his days; he may have been assimilating it to *Bulgaren*—Bulgarians.

Sometimes he fell back on plain Yiddish. A shilling was a *berdel,* a little beard, because of the likeness of Edward VII on many of the coins; a gold sovereign was a *ferdel,* a little horse, because of St. George mounted and slaying the dragon. Thus a guinea (a pound plus a shilling, no longer coined or in circulation, but still widely used in pricing) became, attractively enough, *a ferdel mit a berdel,* a horselet with a beardlet; but a sixpenny piece (half a shilling, colloquially a "tanner") remained substantially English though modified by a Yiddish diminitive suffix into a *sixpensel.* The charming and exotic florin (the two-shilling piece), which few Englishmen connect with Dante's birthplace, my father ignored; for the plural of shilling he reverted to his private English: *shillakkes:* beardlets would

61

have been too suggestive of a congregation. Into certain transformations he put a touch of derision and parody: *shillakkes* was one of them. More understandably, he pointed up the absurdity of "key," phonetically the Rumanian Yiddish for cow, and since our house key hung on a string behind the front door, and my father could not bring himself to imply that one could open a door with an ordinary cow, it was always *die kih mit'n shtrik*, the cow with the string. There was, however, no mockery in *fallink* (short flat *a*, accentuated) for farthing, the smallest English coin, worth one half of a ha'penny, now discontinued.

During our first year in Manchester my father's earnings were small and, though supplemented by my brother Mendel's (who never went to an English school and nevertheless developed a taste for the best in English literature), kept us on a bare subsistence level. In the second year my oldest brother, Sam, came on from Rumania, where he had been left for lack of fare, and with three workers in the house it was a little easier. But Mendel and Sam were, respectively, eleven and fourteen years old when they arrived in Manchester, and the total income cannot have been, at first, more than two pounds ten shillings a week. There were seven of us to feed and clothe, and when my brother Joe was born in 1904, eight. In their later teens my older brothers made good money as clothing machinists, and my father saved up for a shoeshop. My twin sister Hannah, my younger sister, Dora, and Joe the baby, were not helpful until much later.

Two pounds ten a week, even for a family of eight, was somewhat above slum average in England at the turn of the century. But we had special calls on our income: the *cheder, kosher* food, which cost more, the Passover celebration, with its own expensive dietary demands, the synagogue seats for the High Holy Days. There was a quasi-religious injunction to buy the children new clothes for Passover and the New Year; we were better dressed than our gentile schoolmates. We gave more to charity (this I learned later); here and there a wandering beggar, now and again a collection for Russian pogrom victims; there were Rabbi Meir the Wonderworker's collection boxes for saintly scholars in the Holy Land, and the blue-white boxes of the Jewish National Fund for the redemption of the Holy Soil. It was unthinkable not to contribute something toward the dowry of an orphan bride; and then there were immigrant relatives—sixpences, shillings, and even half-pounds.

My mother was more generous than my father, but my father gave beyond our means without really wanting to. I have referred to his habit of cosigning loans right and left; he never learned from experience, and it was not unusual for him to be paying off for six or seven defaulters at a time; the sums were considerable, anywhere from three to five pounds. My *rebbe* undertook, at my mother's tearful prompting, to speak to my father, and he pointed to the text of the Book of Proverbs: "My son, if thou be surety for thy friend, if thou hast stricken thy hand with a stranger, thou art snared with the words of thy mouth . . . thou shalt smart for it." But my father was never cured of this ancient and not wholly dishonorable weakness.

A heavy charge on our resources was snobbery. The dread of being thought poorer than we were made us poorer still, though this is not a specifically Jewish affliction. Outside of misers, mendicants, saints, and other exceptional cases, everyone wants to be thought better off than he is. It was our Jewish misfortune that we had more indices of status than our gentile neighbors; our advantage over them was our abstemiousness. No one in our circle was a frequenter of pubs, and we drank, sparingly enough, only on festive occasions. We played cards, not for money; also Lotto (imported from Rumania), which has recently become an international vogue, if not an epidemic, under the name of Bingo.

Let me add that if our charity was not free from exhibitionism, its foundation was nevertheless compassion. Charity is enjoined equally on Jews and Christians, but Jews for various reasons have developed the virtue to a higher degree. The Jewish Biblical text runs: "If thine enemy be hungry, give him bread to eat; if he be thirsty, give him water to drink" (Proverbs). The operative strength of the tradition among Jews is brought out by a curious Yiddish curse: "May you some day be in want and come to me for help and find me destitute"—i.e., "I know I'll obey the law and yield to pity if I only can; I'd rather be starving myself."

My mother must originally have had an iron constitution to live on, as she did, to the age of seventy-two, surviving my father by eight years; but her latter years were much lightened by improvement in family circumstances. She was of a deeply pious nature, and though she could not always prevent us from drinking milk after a meat dish (forbidden by the dietary law), she never permitted unkosher food to enter the house. However, she did not go so far as to keep two sets of dishes for meat and milk meals. She taught all her children the morning prayer which must be recited as soon as one opens one's eyes, the *Moidie Annie,* as she pronounced it, praising God for returning our souls to us after the night's sleep. She did not know what the Hebrew words meant, neither of course did I. I long wondered who "Moidie Annie" and "Beany Shmussy" were, and discovered in due course that the first was, in Sephardic Hebrew, *modeh ani,* "I acknowledge," and the second *bi nishmati,* "in me my soul." This was followed

64

by a Yiddish prayer, in which we undertook to do any good thing that good and pious people asked of us.

I need hardly say that my mother never failed to bless the candles on the Sabbath eve, first spreading a fresh white cover on the table. That gesture of the circling hands with which she gathered in the light and carried it to her eyes, and the accompanying prayer uttered in a mysterious whisper, come back to me powerfully. So does the Passover, which was observed with most of the minutiae: the symbolic cleaning out of the last traces of leaven with brush, shovel, and taper, the renewal of the household—a thorough spring cleaning—the complicated, charming, and exciting ritual of the *seder* (a religious family Feast of Liberation filled with symbol and song—and good things to eat) on the first two evenings, the replacement of bread by matzoth for the prescribed period of eight days. Most powerful of all has been the effect of the Rosh Hashanah and the Yom Kippur, the New Year and the Day of Atonement. I chafed at having to stay at my father's side in the synagogue for hours at a stretch, but when the ram's horn was blown I trembled with awe and wonder. Not that the sound itself was necessarily imposing—the *shofar*-blower was often less than adept—but something passed through the little synagogue, a hint of mystery and of immeasurable stretches of time. A sound of weeping went up from the women's gallery, where my mother sat, and when she came home red-eyed and kissed us children, and I mumbled shyly to her in the traditional formula—or as near as I could get to it in my faulty Yiddish: "May your prayers have brought you a good year"—my heart was wrung. I do not doubt that later experience has thrown back on those seasons and festivals an emotional response which was weaker in my childhood, but a response was there and imbedded itself in me. It is a common observation that the rituals of self-identification which Jews abandon last are those of the New Year and the Day of Atonement, and the saying of the *Kaddish,* or Sanctification, on the anniversary of a father's or a mother's death.

My mother, whose dream it was that I would some day become what she called *Kreiserrabbiner* (she meant *Kreis-rabbiner,* chief rabbi of a district, but confused *Kreis* with *Kaiser*), was more religiously inclined than any of her relatives or acquaintances, though I do not remember a single non-religious family in our circle. Neither were there any outstanding pietists, except for my mother's father—an unexpected development, I was told, of his extreme old age. My father had lapsed into average piety from a higher standard in Rumania, where I remember him donning the phylacteries and prayer shawl at home. At sundown on Friday he laid aside his last and his tools, and covered his workbench in the front room with a cloth, which he did not remove until Sunday morning. Throughout the Sabbath he used to refrain from smoking, according to the law, and I used to wonder how he did it. I drew on memories of my father for the portrayal of the Ebionite rabbi-shoemaker in my novel *The Second Crucifixion.* Their characters were very different, but certain behavior patterns were the same; so, I am sure, were some of the techniques of their craft.

My mother was a woman of strong natural intelligence, and I loved to sit and chat with her, letting her do most of the talking. She understood people, and had sensitive views on right and wrong, on the becoming and the unbecoming. She had a meditative, even philosophical strain. I remember how, late one Friday night, when she thought she was alone in the room, she apostrophized the dying candles, and likened their spluttering to the protest of human beings summoned by death. *"Vus tzankt ihr azoi, lechtlech,*

66

why do you bicker so, little candles? Will it help you at all?
Had you been made longer, you would burn longer,
but some candles are born short and some are born long,
and God made some lives long, some short." So Sholom
Aleichem's Tevye the Dairyman might have spoken; and
I was again reminded of my mother when I read Marcus
Aurelius many year later: "Why do you protest that your
life is not longer than it is? You might as well protest that
you are not taller than you are."

She was fond of the folk phrase: "Long as the Jewish
exile"; "My troubles are long, long as the Jewish exile."
One of her favorite songs came from a Goldfaden opera:

> While the ears of wheat are tender,
> Young and light and short and slender,
> While the ears of wheat are tender,
>   They are safe always;
> The wind cannot take hold to shake them,
> Nor the raging storm to break them,
> The wind cannot take hold to shake them,
>   In their youthful days.
> But with time grown heavy-weighted,
> To destruction they are fated.

The song is a parable of man, and also of the Jewish
people; it is a warning against luxury and pride and pos-
session, though it seems to contain a certain fatalism: can
the grain help ripening? Another of Goldfaden's arias, also
a favorite with my mother, was less involved, and preached
the same lesson.

> A shepherd lived in days of old,
>   Of Abram's holy seed;
> And prospering in field and fold,
>   He learned the sin of greed.

So turning from his shepherd's trade
He sought the mart where gold is made
 And lost his home and land;
Then beggared, racked by hunger's pains,
He sold himself to toil in chains
 Beneath the oppressor's hand.

(The translation is free, and lacks the folk simplicity of the original.)

The theme of merited exile runs through the Jewish folklore of two thousand years: Biblical in origin, filling the Yiddish phase of Jewish life, echoing a remote, happy, forfeited past.

In Manchester, as in Macheen, my mother had little opportunity to indulge her girlhood love of the theater. A Yiddish strolling company came at long intervals to play in the Derby Street Jewish Workingmen's Hall, but the cheapest seats were sixpence, in the rear. She found a kind of substitute in my father's readings, at which I too was an enthralled listener.

The closing circle of memory connects again with experiences long forgotten and reveals how much more they did for me than I was aware of for a time. The reading sessions were held irregularly, being dependent on the arrival of new material at the bookseller's—periodicals and books, mostly from America. There were novels by Shomer, an immensely popular hack, but also stories by the living classics, Sholom Aleichem, Yal Peretz, and Mendelle Mocher Sforim. My father would hold forth and we would listen, moveless, enchanted, to whatever had come to his hand, infantile trash or first-rate literature. For the ritual had its own beloved appeal. It was escape and sublimation; our surroundings faded away together with our personal worries; we were in other lands, other ages, tasting the luxury of sympathies which entailed no obligations.

The ecstasy with which I listened was heightened by the terror of finding myself suddenly thrust out of the circle. The sessions lasted late into the night, and if my presence was detected after ten o'clock I would be packed off instantly—there was no nonsense with my father—and then I felt as though I were being thrust not only out of the circle but out of life and into my grave. Oh, how bitter it was to know that the fascinating story was continuing to weave itself under the lamplight while I, for my alleged youthfulness—and suppose there was a certain speciousness in the allegation, was this the time to bring it up?—remained in dark ignorance, and would never, never know how it all came out. I could of course ask my mother the next day, but that would have been useless; her version never jibed with mine. They were in fact different stories, the one she followed and the one I built up for myself as I listened to my father's voice. The very titles of the books had a special content for me.

One of them, by Shomer, was *Groisfierst Constantin,* and the sound of it was as majestic as it was unintelligible. I knew that *grois* meant big, but *fierst* was a blank, and I did not know that Constantin was a man's name. I imagined a giant of some kind engaged in mysterious movements and holding impenetrable conversations with beings as mysterious as himself. I would try, while falling sadly asleep, to continue the story for myself, but, outside the circle of the lamplight and beyond the reach of my father's voice, my inventiveness went dead.

A long time afterwards it dawned on me that *Groisfierst Constantin* meant only Grand Duke Constantine, and the magic went out of the title.

Another novel of Shomer's which my father read out to us was called *Der Reicher Betler,* The Rich Beggarman. I knew what each word meant separately, but the combination was a challenge to my imagination. The fantastic individual it denoted presented himself to me in two forms. In the first he was actually a mendicant, going from door to door with his burlap sack, unaware that he was rich; as I saw it, his true condition was being concealed from him by a magician. I thought of him also as an echo of King Solomon, who became a wandering beggar when his likeness and his throne were both usurped by the demon Asmodeus, his inveterate enemy. In the second form (which, I later discovered, was the right guess), he was a rich man who, after an absence of many years, returned to his native village pretending abject poverty in order to test his relatives and friends. The second form was my favorite, because I could more easily project myself into the role; at some future date I would, after a similar absence from home, take revenge on my father by showering him with unexpected riches, heaping coals of fire on his head, never even mentioning his heartlessness in ordering me to bed in the middle of a reading.

Many words and episodes connected with those readings made permanent places for themselves in dormant memory cells, and their emergence into consciousness depended on chance, above all the chance that I would turn back to Jewish things. And perhaps this was not chance at all, but a ripening in darkness and an inevitable pushing through to the light, and chance only in the sense that we remain alive by chance.

CHAPTER V

The Clan

❀

MY FATHER was the only member of his family to settle in Manchester. The others who left Rumania—they were counted in the dozens over the years, some under the original name of Weissbuch, others under the adopted name of Samuel—scattered in all directions. I met two Weissbuch uncles in Paris, one a fur dealer, the other a conductor on the International *Wagons-Lits;* and what an odd thing it was to have my own uncle punch my ticket when I made the trip from Paris to Warsaw in 1919. I met a cousin of my father, a Weissbuch, in Rochester, New York. He was a kindly well-to-do pawnbroker who had much to tell me about the past generations. There are Weissbuchs and Samuels in Florida and California, in Canada and Australia. Of many I have only the report. They are all descendants of old Pantoul, that great replenisher of the earth.

One large group stayed on in Rumania, and those that survived the Nazi occupation were ultimately caught in the Communist trap. A few managed to get out and found their way to Israel. I had not known them in person, nor had we ever communicated, and the circumstances under which we finally came together had all the improbability of a Hollywood fantasy. If the legends of old Pantoul's

continuing fertility in the Holy Land have any foundation
in fact, I may very well have made contact there with third
and fourth cousins at various removes, but I have never
identified one of them.

My mother's family came to Manchester in full force,
part of it moving on, as I have told, to America. I have a
group photograph taken in 1902, in the squalid backyard
of 5 Norfolk Street, on the occasion of my aunt Chaya's
wedding, which was celebrated in our upstairs front room.
Uncle Berel is in it, a billycock set jauntily on his head, a
cigarette dangling from his lips. I am there with my twin
sister Hannah and my younger sister Dora, in the front
row, seated on the ground, and into my face only a Words-
worth could have read trailing clouds of glory; I see instead
a suggestion of the Mongoloid. All the older people are of
course dead, so are most of the younger ones, and a good
sprinkling of the infants.

The venerable white-bearded figure near the center is
my grandfather, who lived on another twenty-odd years
into the nineties, some even saying a hundred. Neither he
nor anyone else could speak with certainty, for there was
no official record. Nor could there be, in his case, an appeal
to the personal memories which served for my parents'
generation in the absence of birth certificates. "Let me
see," one would say. "I was brought to bed with Itzig when
Malkah married. I remember it, so may God grant us all
long and prosperous years, like yesterday, because I
couldn't go to the wedding. And Leizer was born exactly
eleven months after that; and if you want an absolutely
infallible sign, Sarah the tinsmith's wife, may she rest in
peace and busy herself in our behalf"—it used to trouble
me that the dead were supposed to rest in peace and nevertheless run about among the influential residents of Paradise interceding for the living—"came to me right after the

wedding and said—" To which the protocol reply would
be: "God be with you, Fanny, you've surely taken leave of
your senses. You're confusing Malkah's marriage with
Mirel's, and for an absolutely infallible sign, you danced
at Malkah's wedding, and Sarah the tinsmith's wife, may
the mention of her name bring us long life, was there and
said to me: 'Look at her, she's in the high months, may no
harm befall her, and she dances like a young girl.' And I
even told you at the time, and you answered: 'Let those
that begrudge me my happiness dance not at weddings but
with the fever.' Well, am I right?" Which would bring
forth laughter and amazement: "*I* danced at Malkah's
wedding? May evil spirits dance on the heads of the enemies of our people." So it would go on amicably, to the
enjoyment and edification of both sides, for this was part
of the culture, the clan's oral chronicles, the "begats," what
Thomas Mann in *Joseph and His Brothers* calls "fine
talk," until the matter was settled, or rather dropped, each
side brooding and looking for other confirmatory associations to be cited when the subject came up again. But the
limit of disagreement would usually be a year or two,
whereas in my grandfather's case there was nothing to go
on but rumors diverging by decades. To me he was of such
inhuman antiquity that ten years either way made no difference.

He lived, after grandmother's death, with Auntie Chaya,
and was treated with touching respect by his son-in-law
Leibu, or Leon. I would see him shuffling about the house,
or down the street, and would try to avoid him because he
never failed to ask me whether I had "*davvened*" (said my
prayers) that morning. It was a rhetorical question; nobody
in our circle, himself excepted, used to say the long morning prayers, and he knew it. I used to think that he only
wanted to embarrass me. Actually it was a form of greeting.

Sometimes I saw him in Uncle Leon's warehouse on Upper Strangeways. He would wander among the crates picking up discarded pieces of string and tying them together until, after a few months, he had a ball six inches or so across. As he went about this occupation, he would hum a synagogue melody, as if to sanctify his labors. Now and again he would stand still, contemplating a piece of string, trying, I supposed, to make up his mind whether it was worth saving. Uncle Leon would accept the completed ball gravely, saying: "Father-in-law, you really shouldn't put yourself out." And grandfather would answer: "You never can tell when a thing will come in useful." He spoke then as if from infinite depths of practical wisdom.

He tried a few times to interest me—and no doubt others of his grandchildren—in his pious exercises, especially after Uncle Leon had made him a wonderful present of a book which he had obtained from the one-eyed bookseller. It was a very fat book set in a great variety of types, here and there twenty lines of heavy, quarter-inch letters running across the page, and underneath them two or three columns in eighth- and tenth-inch type, here and there boxed inserts so tinily printed that I wondered how grandfather could read them even with the thick-lensed steel-rimmed spectacles which he balanced delicately on the hump of his bulbous nose. The large type was Hebrew, the smaller Yiddish; and grandfather would read a passage in Hebrew, then a passage in Yiddish from below. He did not understand Hebrew, and never knew whether the Yiddish was a translation of what he had just read in Hebrew; it might be a translation of an adjacent passage, or a commentator's interpolation, but he was moved by the sound of the Hebrew not less than by the meaning of the Yiddish. He read everything in the same doleful chant, following the text with a bony, hairy finger, and interrupting himself now and again with: "Gold! Precious as gold!"

74

A few years ago I came across the book in America, and the title of it flashed back into my memory. It was the *Korban Minchah* (The Afternoon Temple Sacrifice), a devotional compilation of the daily and some of the festival prayers, *The Ethics of the Fathers, The Book of Esther, The Song of Songs,* and a variety of selections from the *Midrashim* and the later *Musar* (morality) writers, a true folk book with many ingenious as well as homely parables, with stories of saintly figures, admonitions against worldliness, warnings of hell fire, promises of heavenly bliss. The Yiddish is of a century ago in style and spelling, and it carried me back to grandfather's childhood, and set me thinking of the generations that had fashioned the language to their purpose.

He once gave me, without knowing it, the fright of my life. I was passing by the privy in Aunt Chaya's yard (inside toilets came later in the family ascent, toilets in the bathroom still later) when I heard his voice from inside, raised in the familiar devotional lament: "Do you call this shi—ing? This isn't shi—ing at all! Merciful God, Lord of the Universe, take me away from this sinful world." It sounded so horrible that my knees almost gave way under me. Understanding only the Yiddish words but not the condition they referred to, I thought that the old pietist had become insanely blasphemous.

He was the old man of the tribe, with something terrible about him. He was like a lump of eternity. His memory went back to the days before there was a Rumanian kingdom, before there was a Carol on the throne, and at family gatherings he would smile into his beard when the others referred to themselves as "we older people." He was not wholly of their world, for he had been born in the Austrian city of Kolomea, and had come to Rumania as a young man. He had therefore undergone two uprootings in his life, and the second one, which took place when he was in

75

his sixties, found him exhausted of all adaptability. It could be said of him that he really didn't know where he was.

My grandmother is in the photograph, too. She died in 1904, a date for which I have an absolutely infallible sign. When I went over with my father to the house on Mazeppa Street, where she lay, he insisted on taking along the Yiddish newspaper, *The Express,* and when I pleaded with him to leave it behind—I could not have explained my distress—he said, sternly: "What do you mean? It says here that the Japanese are smiting the Russians hip and thigh; everybody will be glad to hear it." For a moment I thought that he was including grandmother; either he had forgotten that she was dead or else he was under the impression that the dead could hear. But when we came into the room he shoved the newspaper into his pocket and he made no mention of the Japanese victories.

I wept for my grandmother. She was a loving soul in a small, shrunken body. At times she would produce a ha'-penny for me, and if I had already made my weekly contribution to the circulating library of our *cheder,* I would hasten to Saunder's and Wagstaffe's toffee shop and linger at the window in long, delicious, and salivating indecision. I used to think I was her favorite grandchild, but she had more than a dozen little grandchildren and each one had the same impression; such is the natural effect of a great capacity for love. None of us ever got ha'pennies from grandfather, and only once did he give expression to what might pass as an affectionate interest in me. That was on the Sabbath after my thirteenth birthday, my *bar mitzvah,* when for the first time, and in token of my entry into manhood and moral responsibility, I was called up in the synagogue to the reading of the weekly portion of the Prophets. I came through without a flaw, chanting, with all the traditional trills and roulades, the opening of the story of Samson. Flushed with pride I went back to my place between my father and grandfather, and grandfather leaned over and implanted a loud public kiss on my forehead. It rang through the synagogue and made a tremendous impression on me; it was as if a cannon had been fired in my honor.

Grandmother's was the second family death I witnessed, the first having been that of my shadowy little sister Bessie in Rumania. At the age of five or six I had gone through the common childhood preoccupation with death, my own and that of others, and was reminded poignantly of it when my first granddaughter, at the same age, snuggled close to me and whispered: "You're not so old, Grandpa Moish; you won't die yet for a long time." But at nine I had forgotten my early terrors, and the transformation of my grandmother into an image which was laid in a box and carried out of the house amid hand-wringing and loud sobbing was a totally new, totally unexpected, and ghastly event, bewildering and shattering in its effect.

How could such a frightful thing happen? What was the matter with the grown-ups, the bosses of the world, that they should let themselves be pushed around in this incomprehensible fashion, not lifting a finger, but rather joining with abandon in the monstrous procedure? There was so much frightening play-acting, too: the bucket of water at the outside door into which you had to dip your fingers entering and leaving, the mirrors and pictures turned to the wall, the entering and leaving without salutation, the sitting in stockinged feet on low stools, the tearing of the lapel of your coat. I wept for my grandmother and felt I was part of a conspiracy; I wished I could thrust into her hand all the ha'pennies she had ever given me; she might need them where she was being taken.

77

Other ha'pennies came from Auntie Chaya, and sometimes farthings. In my childhood the farthing had status. You could get for it an indestructible piece of toffee, or a "kali-sucker," a paper bag with a hollow straw stuck into a quantity of sickly-sweet white powder. You could also get at the chemist's shop a stupefying scientific device, a small sheet of rice paper perfectly blank but for an asterisk in the top left-hand corner and a printed motto on top: THE MOST MARVELIOUS INVENTION OF THE AGE. You folded the sheet at the edges, stood it up like a miniature table, and applied a glowing match tip to the asterisk. Then wondrous things came to pass. Thin trails of red fire started out from the asterisk, ran complicated courses which never crossed, and having become extinguished left behind a burned-out profile of Queen Victoria, or King Edward VII, or Buffalo Bill. We used to debate whether the asterisk was committed in advance to a particular portrait, and it is a matter for regret that I cannot recall which side I took, though I do recall the gist and tone of the arguments. To some it seemed unlikely that such ingenuity should be dissociated from free will and intelligence; against that was the patent fact that there were only three designs. The metaphysicists among us opined that even this limited choice constituted free will; the materialists answered, with precocious scientific acrimony: "You don't know what the bleddy hell you're talking about; it depends where you touch the star."

Auntie Chaya was fat, motherly, and jolly. Her children were too young to be my playmates, but I liked her house and used to hang about it, though only in part for the ha'pennies and farthings and tidbits. Before Uncle Leon rented his warehouse on Upper Strangeways, he kept part of his stock at home, and I was fascinated by the endless variety: brooms, chamber pots, toilet paper, hasps and staples, hand mirrors, writing paper, mufflers (scarves), loofahs, toothbrushes, shoelaces, shoepolish, pots and pans, locks and keys, spectacle frames, dustcloths, caps, slippers, cups, saucers, gas mantles, all in a bewildering jumble. The multitudinousness of objects gave me the impression that Uncle Leon was enormously rich. I longed to grow up and be like him, the possessor of countless *things*, and it surprised me that Auntie Chaya seemed to take no interest in the marvels of the two stockrooms.

She was an avid listener at my father's readings, and the only one who ever interceded for me at the dread moment of dismissal, though to no effect. I would try to sit next to her on the sofa, out of my father's line of sight, and shielded by her bulk, which I assumed she had accumulated for my special protection. The warmth of my childhood memory of her must have had something of the physical in it, she was such a cosy, reassuring bulwark. If only she hadn't started so violently at some tragic turn in the story, or laughed with such head-to-foot heartiness at the comic passages, breaking like a seismic disturbance into the web I was spinning for myself!

Uncle Leon was lean, prematurely bald, nervous, talkative, and clever, given to sarcastic clowning and spasms of intellectual curiosity different from Uncle Berel's in that they were more penetrating but also more self-conscious and exhibitionistic. The first of our clan and the only one of his generation to become well-to-do, he was generous even in comparative poverty. He "went on markets," that is, he had stalls, miniature Woolworths, which he opened in a number of surrounding towns on market nights. There he sold the contents of his stockrooms. It was cruel work, as hard on the mind as on the body. It called for the memory of a Macaulay and the stamina of a Peary. After a busy evening which lasted until after eleven, one was too exhausted to write down the needed replacements; besides, there was the repacking and recrating to do. One simply had to remember, whether in Oldham, or Wigan, or Altringham, or Macclesfield, what to ship in for the next time.

Two circumstances added to the burdens of this occupation: a certain amount of thievishness among the customers, and the uncertainty of the Lancashire weather. There would be four or five salesmen inside the stall, which was in the form of a hollow square. When one of them spotted marauding hands near another salesman's pitch, he would shout in Yiddish: "Mick, *tzvei-tzen*—two-ten," meaning, "Two eyes to watch ten fingers." But there was no guarding against the weather. A sudden squall would empty the market place, and once the crowd had dispersed it never reassembled; and if the squall developed into a good old Lancashire storm the repacking would have to be done while gusts of wind tore at stanchions and canvass, and sheets of rain passed and repassed over the exposed wares. From such profitless evenings Uncle Leon would return home, sopping wet and bedraggled, close to collapse. No wonder he used to complain that he went not on markets, but on *makkes*, calamities and curses.

In my high-school days I used to turn an occasional shilling by going along to help. The towns I have mentioned were also those I used to visit as a socialist agitator, so that I appeared in them in two capacities; from soapboxes I exposed the evils of the profit system and from behind my uncle's stalls gave practical demonstrations of it.

Some time before I entered college Uncle Leon sold the stalls and became a wholesale supplier to the poor devils who bought them. He engaged me one Sunday every month for stock-taking and what he called bookkeeping. Before my first day of employment I hurriedly consulted a friend

who was attending commercial school and reported back
to Uncle Leon that I would need a journal, a ledger, and
sundry other records. I had improvised, with much labor
and to my own admiration, a system for entering debits and
credits and drawing up balance sheets, and I began to
explain it. Uncle Leon listened for a minute or two with
a faraway and slightly compassionate expression, then
drawled in that peculiarly sarcastic way of his that used
to get under my skin: What debits? What crebits? What
do you think I am? A Lewis's shop, a Baxendale?" He was
referring to prominent Manchester firms. "Here!" He
handed me a penny notebook. "Write down what I say.
Wachtell owes me four pounds eight shillings for the last
two months. I can get loofahs cheaper from Feitelson's.
Jacobson says I'm a swindler because the rent is going up
on the Altringham stall I sold him and I promised him it
wouldn't. He's a liar; I didn't make any promises and the
rent isn't going up. He's trying to squeeze me for better
prices, but it'll help him as much as leeches help a corpse.
There's no money in my chamber pots; I've got too many
and they take up room. Wherever I turn I stumble over
chamber pots. I'll offer them for three shillings less on the
dozen. Why aren't you writing?"

"What shall I write?" I asked. "That wherever you turn
you stumble over chamber pots? And where do you want me
to write it?"

"There! Right there!" pointing to the notebook.

"On the same page as Feitelson and the loofahs and
Jacobson is a liar?"

"Certainly. Do you want a separate book for each of
them?"

The preparations with which I had thought to impress
him were going for nought, and with them the value I had
set on my services.

"What kind of system is this?" I asked.

"Who needs a system? I have everything in my head."

"Then what are you writing it down for?"

He meditated a while, and said softly, in Yiddish: "In case I close an eye," meaning in case he died.

There was only one proper answer to such a remark, namely: "Bite your tongue off." Exasperated, I forgot tradition and my manners and said: "But nobody will understand this rubbish."

"So they won't understand. What difference will that make to me when I'm nine ells underground?"

He didn't want a bookkeeping system. He needed, for the conduct of his business, only the bills and receipts he kept skewered in his roll-top desk; for the rest he relied on his memory. He never had me read back to him what was written in the notebook; nor did he ever look at the long stock lists we compiled; he dictated only by way of rehearsal. His memory, while still phenomenal, was not quite as good as in the market days, but just to watch me write was all the help he needed.

I would bill him regularly ten shillings for the day's work and settle as regularly for half a crown (two and a half shillings). I argued that I was being paid at something like fourpence an hour, which was wage slavery. He was not to be budged. He was as hard in business as he was generous outside of it, and if I had asked him for ten shillings as a gift, or even a whole pound, he would have given it to me. He once explained: "If you're kind in business you won't be in it for long and then you'll have nothing to be kind with. Besides, the man who's kind in business is ashamed of it and is called a fool, whereas if he's kind out of business he lets everybody know he's a *feiner mentsch*— a gentleman." This last was an unjustified sneer at himself, for he was an unostentatious giver. He supported my grandparents, he was always helping relatives—a half-crazy sister in Paris, a brother in Smyrna, and a cantankerous old mother, Charney, who was with us for a while—she is in the group photograph, a massive, square-jawed matriarch. There was a rumor that she had once kept a whorehouse in Constantinople.

Later Uncle Leon left the hardware trade and turned to moneylending, operating on the same principles—ruthlessness in business, generosity outside of it. He was the only one of the older generation who was not horrified by my socialist activities. He had a social philosophy which was nearer to anarchism than socialism. Human beings, he thought, were fundamentally good; their natural impulse was to live together in harmony without the interference of laws and governments; but something had gone wrong somewhere, and instead of harmony there was universal discord and hatred. *"Vi vilde chayes*—like wild beasts!"* When he talked like that you would have taken him for a sentimentalist and a softy; actually, he was shrewd and realistic, with a sharp insight into human weaknesses and no little capacity for exploiting them in business.

I was sometimes present when he was making a sale, and I would be spellbound by the performance. There was something of the actor and much of the Levantine in him. His tongue ran on so, and he put up such a show of eagerness and confusion that the buyer lost his bearings. His favorite phrase was: "I'll tell you what I'll do with you!" —uttered in the tone of a man who was sick and tired of bargaining and was resolved to get out of a nasty situation at a ruinous loss. "I'll throw in a gross of toothbrushes at half price and the black year take it—to hell with it! And if you're not satisfied I'll give you two months' credit *and* the cash discount." Then he would smite himself on the

forehead with his open palm: *"Sha!* Wait! As Queen
Esther said, if I'm done for, I'm done for. I'll tell you
what I'll do with you! I've just received a shipment of
combs, beauties, here, take a look. I ordered them for—
well, never mind who, why should you have it on your
conscience? Put them on your stall and they'll go like hot
cakes, one-two-three! Aha? You pretend you don't like
them but there's a glint in your eye. Good! Put them on
one side, and take a look at this job lot of shaving mugs, I
got them cheap and you can have them for nothing! For
nothing! And I'll tell you what else I'll do with you—"

He offered concessions, combinations, reductions, bonuses, with machine-gun rapidity, and the remarkable
thing was that he never overreached himself; more re-
markably still, he never really put anything over on a
buyer. "I wouldn't do that. I'd lose the man. But I know
the business a thousand times better than he does. Only
I want him to think that *he's* swindled *me.* He goes away
laughing to himself and considers himself a genius. And
take my word for it—everything I give him he'll sell at
a decent profit. So everybody's happy."

Since he was a moralist outside business hours, I made
the point that he was corrupting his customers, encouraging them in the belief that they were successful swindlers.
"Ot hosste dir gehot!" he answered. "There you go! Am
I Moses our Teacher? Am I saving souls or am I selling
hardware? Isn't it enough that *I'm* honest? And if you
want to go into the little letters"—he was referring to the
marginal commentaries in the Talmud, about which every
Jew knows without having looked into a volume of the
Talmud—"if you want to go into the little letters, isn't
all business a swindle? You yourself, Mr. Socialist, say
so; and the bigger the business, the bigger the swindle."

As Uncle Berel would have made a good novelist, so, I

84

think Uncle Leon would have made a good Talmudist. He was more than a rapid reasoner; he saw into the essence of human situations and often expressed himself with aphoristic neatness. He once said: "If a friend does you a favor and reminds you of it, he cancels it. For he was making an investment, not doing you a kindness." Then again: "Favors aren't business transactions. If a man does you a favor and you can't return it, return it to someone else who never did you a favor. Kindnesses should circulate, not go back and forth between two persons." On one occasion a member of our clan spent much more than he could afford on an only daughter's wedding. Uncle Leon was highly critical, and when someone pleaded: "Look, after all a thing like that happens once in a lifetime," he answered: "*Narrishkeit*—fool-talk. Every Monday and Thursday a once-in-a-lifetime thing is happening—a wedding, a funeral, a *bar-mitzvah,* a circumcision, a reunion with a long-lost relative, this, that, the other. From once-in-a-lifetimes you're left with nothing to live on."

Uncle Leon had an older sister, Mallie, who was married to my mother's brother, Moritz. Among my older relatives I knew Auntie Mallie best because one of her sons, Mick, was for a long time my best pal. She was slightly subnormal and I disliked her for a reason which did not become clear to me until long after she was dead: she had the cunning of the mentally retarded against which the normal person is defenseless. Her stupidity was too quick-witted for us. One couldn't get through to her, for she was impenetrably armored against self-perception, and the notion that she had done wrong was as remote from her mode of thought as quantum mechanics.

If one of her children asked for something she didn't want to give, she never refused it outright; instead, she would say, soothingly: "Hush now, hush, you really don't

want that." In our life a refusal was a straightforward
thing, routine; you knew you couldn't always get what
you wanted; you protested, and made your peace with the
refusal. But this bland disfranchisement, this shooing
you out of the right to want, was maddening. You didn't
know where to take hold of it. You could cry, and keep on
repeating: "Yes, I *do* want it," but before long you found
yourself wanting not the particular thing but your right
to want it—which she would not concede—while the thing
itself had lost all interest for you, so that Auntie Mallie
was right after all! It was an indefinable, unidentifiable,
and intolerable species of torture which Auntie Mallie
had invented and patented. It was also a double injustice,
for it robbed you of the residuary equity of an honest
refusal; after all, a certain number of refusals built up a
claim of sorts, entitled you finally to some consideration.
This was the humane and natural law between children
and grown-ups, but Auntie Mallie stood outside it. What
could you claim for having ten times not been given what
you hadn't wanted in the first place? It was as if you were
being accused of trying to pile up counterfeit credits.

Another trick of hers in the same spirit was to ask for
a favor as if collecting a debt. I say "trick" but I am sure
she wasn't aware of it as such. She would say: "It's a long
time since you went an errand for me, so won't you . . ."
A long time might not have passed since you had done
something for her. How could you remember? You didn't
keep a notebook of services rendered. You were quite
helpless; she spoke amiably, with such tacit conviction,
that even if you happened to remember a recent service
it would have been graceless—as well as futile—to bring
it up.

She had a wonderful way of putting people in the wrong
beforehand whenever she anticipated criticism. She would

say, placidly: "Now listen to what I'll tell you, and don't
lose your temper, don't start screaming at me." This device was familiar to everyone who knew her, yet it was
invariably successful. Either one was immediately stung
into replying, angrily: "I'm not going to lose my temper,
and I'm not going to scream at you," whereupon she
would sigh patiently: "See, I told you," or else one would
exercise great self-control and reply: "Yes, go on," thinking—in spite of all past experience—to frustrate her; but
no, she sensed the suppressed irritation as a dog is said
to sense the released adrenalin in a frightened person,
and she would insist, gently, skeptically: "But I know
you're going to scream at me," and of course one finally
did.

With all this she was by no means unkind, she only
wanted her kindnesses to have the character of free, spontaneous, and unmerited offerings without the taint of a
quid pro quo. If she gave you an apple or a pear or a piece
of cake she made you eat it in her presence, while she
nodded approvingly and purred: "Good, isn't it?" She
needed praise in large quantities and made a play for it
under the most unfavorable circumstances. If someone
complained that the soup was cold she would answer
proudly: "That doesn't happen often with me, does it?"
She turned every lapse into an opportunity, which nobody
else ever seized, for the celebration of her virtues; one
could feel her pressing for good words, and it made one
uncomfortable.

Children are more sensitive than grown-ups to such
maneuvers of the ego. They have only just and barely
come to terms with the over-all accepted system of ameni-
ties, conventions, and shams; they react quickly and re-
sentfully to unscheduled demands on their powers of
pretence. I disliked Auntie Mallie because, as we would

now say, she crowded me. I could not have explained the relationship, I could not have given an acceptable reason for disliking her; thus I seemed to dislike her without cause, which put me in the wrong and therefore made me dislike her the more.

Her husband, Uncle Moritz, my mother's brother, kept a haberdashery, and the family lived in rooms behind and above it. There were many children, and an infant or two would usually be rolling about, half-naked, on the shop floor, sometimes befouling it. The business did not suffer as a consequence; it may even have benefited. The customers, nearly all from the Salford slums, were not finicky; they may have felt that such dirt and disorder meant lower prices, and the place did in fact suggest the last stages of a bankruptcy sale. It is not impossible that Uncle Moritz counted on the effect.

To me he was a sly and secretive creature. Indoors he always wore slippers, even when serving in the shop, and he moved quietly through the hullabaloo of his surroundings. He sported, incongruously, a small and distinguished beard which curved away right and left from the cleft in his chin—on the photograph he puts one in mind of Charles Evan Hughes or C. P. Scott of *The Manchester Guardian*. I was intrigued by his beard and disconcerted by his noiseless appearances and disappearances, and by his occasional, brief spasms of speechless rage. I had the impression that he hated his wife, and I had some difficulty in reconciling this with their fruitfulness. I have since come round to the view that he loved Auntie Mallie but could not stand the disorder and dirt in the midst of which he lived, even though they may have been useful to his business. But if he did hate her she certainly would not have known it; she lived out her cheerful life more or less incommunicado. In company, and particularly when the talk turned to "high matters," Uncle Moritz livened up; the higher they were, the more remote from everyday reality, the livelier he became. He had a peculiar fixation on somebody he called "Alexander Mukden," whom he considered the greatest non-Jew who had ever lived, even greater than Napoleon. It was a long time before I realized that he meant Alexander the Great (Mukden—Makedon —Macedonia). I surmise that he yoked him with Napoleon because both had left some mark in Jewish history; Napoleon had convened a Sanhedrin and Alexander the Great had received with friendliness a deputation of High 'Priests.

Having much to do with gentiles, Uncle Moritz acquired a working knowledge of English; so, for the same reason, did Uncle Leon, who, being the youngest of his generation, in time became comparatively Anglicized, turned from the Yiddish to the English press, and even lived to see virtue in bookkeeping. They were exceptions; the large majority of the clan, dealing mostly among themselves, remained to the end strangers to the language and ways of their tolerant host country.

My uncles Berel and Srul (Israel), with their wives Malkah and Rosa, vanished early from my childhood. I found them in America in 1914, but Auntie Malkah died soon after my arrival; if she had lived I would probably never have got to know Uncle Berel as well as I did. Uncle Srul, too, kept a cleaning and pressing store. He was spectacularly handsome but so vain, and so dull, that after half an hour with him I would be sweating with desperation. Auntie Rosa was very fat, a famous cook, and a compulsive eater; the poor woman grew and grew until she weighed over four hundred pounds and one was embarrassed to look at her. But she outlived all her contemporaries and died in her middle eighties. The frequency of my visits to Uncle Berel was kept secret from her and Uncle Srul, and I do not remember ever seeing Uncle Srul at Uncle Berel's Rumanian restaurant.

Dozens and scores of the members of the vanished Rumanian Jewish ghetto of Manchester maintain a ghostly clamor for admission to this record: Fish the fishmonger and Fish the fruit dealer and a third Fish, the "hoarse chicken-slaughterer," a pietist who had all the qualifications of a cantor except a voice; Aaron the shoemaker, who at one time worked for my father and created a scandal by opening a shoe-repair shop of his own round the corner; Mendel the milkman, who woke me every morning by shouting up and down the street; Kupperman the fruitdealer, who was pitied because he had insured his mother-in-law—a bundle of skin and bones—and she clung to life with unnatural tenacity, to weep, in the end, at his funeral. Mingled with these are some outsiders, Litvak or Galician or English-born Jews who endured a minor exile in our midst: Mooslin the watchmaker, a cripple whose twisted walk I was adept at imitating; Matz the pharmacist, who had a long nose and funneled his talk through it; Jenkins the tailor and Goodman the photographer and Davis the carpenter and Solomon the fiddler, whose sons were also fiddlers . . . I must turn them back; I must be practical, like the director of an immigrant-aid society: "Don't push; if you all try to get in at once, none of you will get in. Later, later." They eye me skeptically: "Look at him, dressed in a little brief authority. Quotas, eh? And favorites. Relatives first, naturally. We know all about it."

CHAPTER VI

Insulation

❀

IN THE MASS I welcome them all into the record, relatives near and remote, friends of the family and acquaintances, as the representatives of the Jewish people throughout a hundred generations, not the scholars and saints and teachers, but *amcho* (Thy people), the plebs. They knew themselves to be untutored, and were humble about it. Their reverence for learning had not its like among the gentiles, even of the upper class; it had a fierce and enduring quality, and its frustration by poverty was their greatest spiritual affliction. I cannot remember a single instance of sneering at book knowledge, such as I later came across among some Jews, and of course non-Jews too. Granted, there was no one in our little community rich enough to flaunt his worldly success in the face of an indigent scholar—if there had been an indigent scholar in our clan. But your true *grobber ying* (coarse boor) is contemptuous of learning even when he is himself no shining example of the advantages of ignorance. To him ignorance is a positive quality in its own right. "I'm a plain, practical man, and I don't hold with that fancy college stuff." Quite foreign to the outlook of my people would have been the word "egghead," which, though not coined by the poor and illiterate, has great currency among them.

Their life philosophy found partial expression in their attitude toward the world about them. They loved England, and in many ways admired her immoderately. The wealth of England fired their imagination; the rest of the world could subsist on her leavings; the Roman Empire had been a beggarly thing by comparison. My uncle Moritz said: "If I had a hundredth part of the paper that is thrown out daily in this country, I would be richer than Rothschild." Then, starting back from his own temerity: "What am I saying? If I had the string for the bundles of paper!"

Next to England they ranked Germany, partly for her language, which they regarded as an aristocratic Yiddish, respected but also parodied by them. Anyone who aspired to the reputation of a worldly intellectual was disqualified if he could not speak a little German, or what passed for German with them.

More than England's wealth they admired English justice. They invoked for England the Rabbinic saying that the just among the gentiles have their place in Paradise. They connected England's greatness with her generosity toward the Jews, but not as cause and effect. They cited Cyrus of Persia, whom God had called "My anointed"; Cyrus became great, then he encouraged the Jews to rebuild their homeland after the First Destruction. However, they could also argue that God had made him great for that purpose; and it was an article of faith with them that the fate of Pharaoh and Haman (and the Roman Empire) awaited the rulers of Russia and Rumania.

But their high regard for England had its reservations. They compared their own way of life with that of their neighbors in the adjacent Salford slums and knew it to be immeasurably superior. There was no drunkenness in our community, no animalism, no wife-beating, no recourse to violence. These defects were despised as specifically *goyish*. My people did not suppose that all poor gentiles were like that; the Saunders and Wagstaffe ladies of the toffee shop, and Mr. Maude, the leather merchant, were obviously decent people, though they and we and our Salford neighbors were more or less on the same economic level. But the gentiles in our midst were few, and those that wandered into our area on Saturday nights were mostly drunks and hoodlums, men and women loud of voice and free with their fists. At other times the grotesquely poor came our way: indescribably ragged, unwashed men who in the summer sold paper flycatchers to the tune of "Catch 'em alive, O catch 'em alive"; others collected *our* leavings for farthings—rags, bones, and bottles—chanting in the entries (back alleys) a nasal "Har! Hoe!" ("Rags! Bones!"?); misshapen, gnomelike charwomen who earned twopence yellow-stoning the front-door steps, and who were sometimes seen taking their earnings into the Brunswick pub. Nobody had ever heard of a Jewish woman going into a pub—it would have been considered a monstrosity—or of Jews bawling and brawling in the street; and the sight of a Jew being led off by a policeman would have been considered a communal calamity. Nor would we ever have permitted a Jew to show himself in the God-forsaken condition of the rag-and-bone and flycatcher men, unless he was, like poor *meshuggener* (loony) Benjy, a harmless lunatic who could be neither committed nor controlled.

My people were not quite fair; they forgot that in Rumania and elsewhere there was a comparable Jewish class, if with other defects. Yet they were not wholly unfair. Rumania was a miserable country, England was the world's richest and noblest, and there was no excuse. They felt, moreover, that a community is to be judged not only by

93

how the majority behaves, but also by what it tolerates
in a minority. A community in which "only" five per cent
of the death rate is accounted for by murder would—if
such a community is thinkable—properly be called a den
of murderers.

They were unfair in another respect. They had no idea
how much good humor, as well as native goodness, how
much courage—I could almost use the word gallantry—
there was in some of those tatterdemalion, occasionally
boozy charwomen. Nor did they make allowance for conditions different from their own. None of my people knew
the taste of "black labor," the exhausting, brutalizing
slavery of navvies, stevedores, steel workers, porters. They
were artisans—tailors, shoemakers, carpenters—or shopkeepers. On the other hand, it was not physical exertion
which frightened them away from the heavier occupations;
it was the horrible prospect of becoming mindless beasts
of burden. How could they have hung on to what they
called *"dus bissel Yiddishkeit,"* their bit of Jewishness?

This was how they referred to it, apologetically, knowing how far they fell short of anything like the ideal. But
their "bit of *Yiddishkeit*" was related, for them, to something much more comprehensive than a moral code. It
was part of a time-defying identity which they associated
with the *atoo buchartooni* (as they pronounced it), the
notion of the Chosen People. Asked to define the notion,
they would fall back on dogma and self-flattery; yet their
self-flattery had nothing to do with their real merit, which
they did not wholly understand, while I, of course, did
not understand it at all.

There was a point of view from which they looked down
on mighty England as a whole. "Looked down" is perhaps a little too strong; "felt sorry" is nearer to it. If they
could not say enough about English justice, their admira-

94

tion was based to some extent on the paradoxical fact that the English had never received the Torah, *our* Torah, the everlasting word of God. It made England's moral achievement all the more remarkable, but it was useless to deny that this handicap was bound, ultimately, to be England's undoing, as it had been the undoing of so many empires before hers. A great pity, a very great pity—such a wonderful people! But there it was. Theoretically the English might save themselves by becoming Jews, but that was unlikely before the coming of the Messiah, and then it would be too late, for by then empires would be a thing of the past, and everybody would have accepted the Torah.

If you wanted to see the fatal deficiency at its clearest you had only to look at the English institution of sports, before which my people stood baffled and dismayed. Athletics for the young it understood; person to person physical competition it also understood, again for the young— the foolishness of immaturity; one condoned it, one never encouraged it. But that people of mature years should assemble voluntarily by the thousands and tens of thousands and work themselves into a wild excitement watching others hardly less mature (in our world one was mature in the early teens) kick a ball round a field was evidence of that deep-rooted pagan aberration from which we had been rescued by the Torah. It was not a defect of simple ignorance. The educated English classes, far from disassociating themselves from the institution, were its pillars, and accounted it one of the glories of their civilization, perhaps the fount of all its other glories. Doctors and professors (the reverence with which we uttered such titles!) attended, unashamed, unrebuked, cricket, football, and boxing matches, and took the outcome passionately to heart. So much my people gathered from the Yiddish paper and from us children. Well, say what you like, there were undoubtedly men of great learning among the English, and they had written learned books, but what comparison could there be between these and the Talmud, or the Rambam (Maimonides)? When I pointed out that in our little world no one, my *rebbe* excepted, had ever so much as looked at a page of the Talmud or of Maimonides, let alone read a paragraph of an English philosopher, the reply was: "Socialist! So you think the *goyim* have something as good as the Torah? If they have, why do they behave like that?"

That question and reproach must have been addressed to me after the scholarship had made a new man of me. How I handled the problem I can no longer say, but until then I did not have to handle it because it had no reality, it had no place in rational discourse. As a reader of *The Gem, The Magnet, Pluck,* etc., I identified myself with the pukka and japeful young heroes of the British public (i.e., private) schools as portrayed by writers who had obviously never attended one. One just didn't ask Tom Merry and Harry Wharton what sense there was in sports. Thus, until my thirteenth year, I knew no inner conflict between my Jewish and my non-Jewish worlds; they divided me into two peacefully coexistent but non-communicating halves.

I did, on occasion, tell my parents that Mr. Fisher, one of the Standard Four teachers, sometimes played football with us, and that Mr. Sharples, our headmaster, had been a noted footballer in his young manhood, and was still proud of his record in the field. It was no use. The moral authority of England was circumscribed; Jewish was Jewish, *goyish* was *goyish*. My mother, in so many ways more permissive than my father, shared the common view on sports. She said: *"Narralle,* silly, just imagine your *rebbe* playing football with the *cheder* boys; *vus far a poonim vot doos gehot*—what would it look like?" It would certainly have looked mad: that bearded and portly pietist in his black gaberdine (or, unimaginably, bare-kneed in shorts), crouching between goal posts or dribbling a football down the field and shouting some Yiddish equivalent for "Pass!" or "Offside!" Maddest of all was the thought of him leaping into the air like Mr. Fisher to intercept the ball with his head. It illustrated perfectly the incommunicability of the two worlds, and because of this incommunicability there was no ideological or inner clash, only a clash of external wills. But when I turned "intellectual" and affected—intermittently, at any rate—a vast contempt for sports, quoting with relish Kipling's "muddied oafs," my parents were still in the wrong. For, as I saw it, they spoke from prejudice, I from reflection. Marvelous and eternal insolence of youth! They were the "not yet," I was the "no longer."

Football and cricket were of course not our only pastimes. There were "the hills," or, as my parents called it, *"de heels,"* an unbuilt area stretching from behind the northern side of Bury New Road to Hightown, half a mile away. This bleak, undulating expanse of clay was the land of our adventure and our Tom Tiddler's ground. Here and there its repulsive infecundity was emphasized by scabby eruptions of green, and in the middle of it was Gilly's Pond, forty or fifty feet across, in which by a miracle of ecology tiny fishes we called jacksharps lived. You sat on the bank and made a wild sweep with an empty jam jar when one of them darted by below you. Occasionally you fell in, and anyhow you splashed yourself from head to foot, which came to the same thing. When not fishing, you went Alpine climbing, for which you needed a length of wash line, purloined for the duration, and two or three companions. Tied to one another, you clambered up gentle slopes pretending fiercely they were perpendicular; you dug your heels in grimly, shouted warnings of mortal glacier depths, and organized intrepid rescue parties for the heedless or reckless. When the fishing or climbing was over, you labored in vain to remove the evidence from your clothes and tried to sneak into the house by the back door, dreading more your mother's heartbroken: "You've been on *de heels* again!" than the cuffing you expected from your father; dreading most of all to be caught with the jam jar and to have your jack-sharp—there was seldom more than one—thrown out with the muddy water.

The lure of "the hills" was heightened by two attendant dangers, a brick works and occasional gangs of pugnacious Salford youngsters of our age. Of these the first was the more serious. There was a deep gully where the clay had been excavated, and a gondola-carrying cable stretched on a downward slope from one end of the gully to the other. On Sunday the works were deserted, and it was a tremendous lark to haul the gondola to the top of the slope and ride it to the bottom, jumping off just before it smacked into the wooden buffer. This was a group enterprise; it took six or seven of us to do the hauling, though only two of us could ride at a time. We quarreled for the privilege of the ride, less for the pleasure of it than for the fear of being thought cowards. I am astonished that, as far as I remember, no one was ever killed or crippled.

A policeman was assigned on Sundays to keep trespassers off, but he took his duties lightly and absented himself for hours at a stretch. We posted sentinels at strategic points, and they had two warning signals. When the policeman was first espied, they shouted: "N.L.T.C.!" for: "Now, lads, the copper!" When he had approached within a certain distance, it was: "N.L.T.C.C.!" for: "Now, lads, the copper coming!" We could just as well have shouted the whole words instead of the first letters, but that would have lacked flavor.

The gang tussles were nothing like the "rumbles" of our modern American cities. No weapons, not even sticks, were used. There would be much skirmishing and shouting and bragging, for ceremonial purposes—it makes me think now of classical Chinese armies and certain prudent Italian *condottieri*—and sometimes a free-for-all from which you emerged at worst with a bloody nose. We would have been happy in this evidence of our valor if it could always have escaped the attention of our parents; but a bloodstained shirt or coat was infinitely worse than soaked clothing or a jam jar with a jacksharp in it.

I can still catch, across half a century and more, the note of despair in the voices of our parents. It seemed so disproportionate to our misdemeanors. I did not understand that they were troubled by something other and far deeper than torn clothes and wasted time. Our pastimes were so heathenish; we were behaving like *shkotzim,* young *goyim;* we were going in the ways of the unbelievers.

How should old people feel when the young seem to be abandoning them in a hostile world? The sense of security grows slowly, and there were times when my people were back in the past. There was evidence of anti-Semitism in the Saturday-night rowdies; it came from youngsters as well as from tipsy adults. We soon learned the words "Sheeny-makalairy" and "Smoggy van Jew." "Sheeny" by itself was bad enough; "Sheeny-makalairy" and "Smoggy van Jew," accompanied by an offensive gesticulation—a wagging of the flat, upturned palms about the ears—were more venomous. Some of this may have been coarsely good-natured, but my people were not of a mind to make fine distinctions; ancestral and personal memories were too strong. We were gratefully aware that England was adamant in the protection of our persons, and generous beyond praise in the acknowledgment of our human rights. Yet there was this echo of the "Hep! Hep!" of the Middle Ages.

The etymologies of "Sheeny," "Makalairy," and "Smoggy" are much debated. "Hep" is clearly traceable to the first letters of *"Hieroselyma est perdita"*—Jerusalem is destroyed, or damned. My people, indifferent to etymology, had an ear for essentials, and they had heard "Hep! Hep!" more than once in Rumania.

Among my most uncomfortable memories is that of .the contempt in which for a time I held this sensitivity of my parents and relatives. I enjoined them, as well as I could, to rise above their anachronistic timidities. We were, I told them, in the twentieth century, not the nineteenth, or the eighteenth, let alone the thirteenth, or twelfth. Recent pogroms in Russia, brutal discrimination in Rumania? "Yes, yes, I know. Why do you keep harping on that? They are the last remnants of a tyranny which tomorrow's revolution will sweep away forever. The Dreyfus case? Well, didn't France, the mother of revolutions, come out clean in the end? It took a long time, you say, and the struggle was fierce? I know, but even while the Dreyfus case was on, we got shelter in France, didn't we? And nobody molested us there. You do trust England and America, but even there you smell infection. And what about Germany? Do you smell it there, too? The trouble with you is," I continued, anticipating in the strangest way the arguments I met later in novels by American Jews, "the trouble with you is that you think of the gentiles the way the lowest gentiles think of us; we have horns, they say, and drink Christian blood." The trouble with *me* was that I was so fond of saying "the trouble with you is."

CHAPTER VII

The Fathers of the Clan

❀

THE JEWISH schooling of my elders in the community had for the most part been better than mine. It had, like mine, been limited to an old-fashioned *cheder,* but in Rumania, and for many more hours daily, very often without the competition of a Rumanian school. (But my father left *cheder* at the age of eight, and did not go to a Rumanian school. Where he picked up his Jewish knowledge, and how he learned to read so well, is a mystery to me.) They had studied the Pentateuch with the standard medieval commentary of Rashi; they were more familiar than I with the Midrashic folklore of legend and parable, which covered all of Biblical history and part of post-Biblical history. In the Jewish world this was considered the equivalent of an elementary-school education. It was not only poverty that had kept them from going further; Rumanian Jewry had a merited reputation for spiritual backwardness. But it would be a great mistake to interpret the depth and substance of their culture in terms of an English elementary education.

What they knew had been woven by continuous later repetition into their workaday lives. The average English adult who had left school and gone to work at the age of thirteen or fourteen hardly remembered, except as names, Boadicea, Alfred the Great, Hereward the Wake, Richard the Lion-Hearted, Queen Elizabeth, the Armada, Crom-well. How often would you hear them mentioned, let alone curiously discussed, in the English workman's home, or at his convivial gatherings, or in the pub? Among my people, the patriarchs Abraham, Isaac, and Jacob and their wives were household familiars; so were Joseph and his brothers, who together with the patriarchs formed the pre-people-hood group and moved about in a primeval world of their own; so were Moses, Aaron, Miriam, Amalek, Balaam, Og, King of Bashan, Joshua, Samson, Samuel, David, Solomon, Elijah, Mordecai, Esther, Haman, Ahasuerus, and the post-Biblical figures of Hillel, Yohanaan ben Zakkai, Eleazar ben Azaryah, Akiba, Bar Kochba. We talked about them casually, as well as reverently—or, as the case might be, abusively. We gossiped about them, and since they were quite alive to us, and therefore contemporaries, their his-torical order was in one sense irrelevant.

Their personalities owed more to legend and commen-tary than to the terse Biblical text. The Bible told us what they had done and we decided what to make of it, placing the emphasis where we chose, often without war-rant in the record. Abraham our Father was of course the first Jew, the "discoverer" of God; we would not have dreamed of challenging the fact; nevertheless, it was impos-sible for us to think of Noah, who preceded him by ten generations, as a *goy*. He was, to be sure, uncircumcised, but he had been naturalized from of old by an unofficial referendum. We did not intend thereby to diminish the uniqueness of Abraham's spiritual achievement or the sharpness of the division that he represents in human his-tory; we just could not leave Noah out in the cold.

The heroic and revolutionary aspect of Abraham's career somehow did not come off in the folklore. We knew about his struggle with the mighty Nimrod; we knew about his defiance of the fiery furnace; we saluted his faithful and indomitable spirit; but we preferred to dwell on Abraham's intellectual struggles with his heathen father, Terah, in which there was more of the hilarious than the heroic. Poor old Terah! We couldn't make a real villain of him; he was, after all, Abraham's father; so we turned him into a ridiculous old duffer who could be out-argued by the simplest child. Indeed, our favorite stories of the God-discovery were of Abraham's childhood and his precocious exposure of the impotence of his father's idols. What a hash he made of them—literally, chopping them up merrily and pretending in all innocence that they had fallen out among themselves—as the ancient gods so often did—and set upon each other mercilessly. But of course old Terah, scratching his gray head, wasn't to be convinced. *Old* Terah: the adjective accompanies his every mention, partly derisive, partly compassionate; Terah is senility; a young Terah, a middle-aged Terah was unthinkable. There he was, there he is, the obstinate old babbler, everlasting symbol of uneducable heathendom; and there stands the boy Abraham, or Abram as he was called first, gleeful and godly, axe in hand among the litter of limbs and noses and torsos of *teraphim*.

We did not make much of Abraham the warrior, though he once fought a notable action, he and his three hundred and eighteen household retainers, against Chedorlaomer, king of Elam, and his allies; he smote them by night and chased them north two hundred miles or so, and rescued his nephew Lot, whom they had taken prisoner at Sodom. (*There* was another ridiculous character, Lot the envious, Lot the sot.) No, Abraham was to us predominantly the grandfather figure, mild and magnificent, white-bearded and benevolent. The stormy years are behind him—the excitement of the Covenant, the argument with God about the destruction of Sodom, the painful tangle with Hagar and Ishmael and Sarah, the sojourn in Egypt, the long-drawn-out waiting for the true heir, the dreadful trial of the sacrifice. He is rich and honored and wise, he has found grace in the eyes of God and of man. Yes, of course, there is that marriage of his after Sarah's death, to some woman called Keturah, and there are half a dozen sons with outlandish names. We don't talk about that; we talk about Abraham's fabulous hospitality, we linger over it lovingly, inventively, giving it priority, almost, over his discovery of God. If this seems to show a misappreciation of values, we must consider that very few of us can be God-discoverers, but all of us can practice hospitality, be the scale never so humble. Besides, hospitality means life itself to a nation of wanderers. So we liked to recall periodically how Abraham was always on the alert for wayfarers, and how his tent had four doors, north, south, east, and west, so that the wayfarer would not even have to trouble looking for the entrance.

I once heard a warm argument around the subject of Abraham's quadriportaled tent between my uncle Moritz and a rag merchant by the name of Lamport. I have said that the only man of learning in our community was my *rebbe*. Lamport, the rag merchant, who for two or three years rented a cellar in Uncle Moritz's house, was not a Rumanian but a Litvak who had attended a Yeshivah, or Talmudical college, and his sojourn among us was a bright and memorable episode. He was a squat, swarthy young man, thick-lipped, lively, and talkative, chockful of quotations from Talmud and Midrash, delighting in the display of erudition even when he was sorting rags. He was a believer, but no longer a practicing pietist. He had shaved off his beard, but he seemed to miss it, for in discourse on sacred matters he clutched at his chin occasionally, as Talmudists do at their beards. He spoke Lithuanian Yiddish, of course, which I used to think an affectation. How the following conversation began and ended I do not remember. It remains in my mind's museum, along with other disconnected exchanges and incidents, like a fragment of a cuneiform inscription.

Uncle Moritz was, it seems, disconcerted by the sudden realization that Abraham's all-welcoming tent must have been constructed in the form of a cross, dread emblem of our persecutors which Jews must scrupulously avoid, even to the extent of never laying a knife and fork crosswise on the table. Then, as suddenly bethinking himself: "Aha! Of course! There were no Christians in Abraham our Father's day. Besides, the Torah had not yet been given at Sinai, and the only commandment he had was about circumcision. *Emess?* True?"

"Not true at all, if you'll forgive me," answered Lamport, "and you, having been to *cheder,* should know better, for it is written in the Pentateuch that God blessed Isaac because Abraham had observed all His commandments, statutes, and laws. You've forgotten."

"By no means," retorted Uncle Moritz. "The Torah is not mentioned in that passage. Commandments, statutes, laws, but it doesn't say Torah. We had no Torah yet."

Lamport's voice went into a singsong, his chin wagged together with the hand that clutched it. "So—we are becoming pedantic! Then let me tell you: it is written clearly in the Midrash that Jacob our Father studied under Shem and Eber. What do you think he studied?"

"How should I know? There are many things they could have studied," said Uncle Moritz, sharply. But he was uneasy.

"Certainly, certainly. But tell me, my very dear Mr. Acker, can you imagine that Jacob our Father was such a *goy* that he studied many things but not the Torah?"

"*Gevald!* Help!" cried Uncle Moritz. "I don't imagine

105

anything unbecoming to Jacob our Father. I only know the
Torah came a long time later."

"Came where? The Torah was ready, black fire on white,
a million years before it was handed to us at Sinai, a million years before the world was created."

"That stands written?"

"And how! But I will ask you another question. Do you
think Abraham our Father ate pork?"

Uncle Moritz was stunned. "God forbid."

"Why not, if he didn't know the Torah and all the six
hundred and thirteen commandments?"

"Because it doesn't make sense," said Uncle Moritz.

"Moreover," continued Lamport, "the Fathers were all
prophets, and even if the Torah had not yet existed they
would have foreseen its contents and lived according to
them."

"They were prophets? That too stands written?"

"It stands written, it stands written," and Lamport
quoted chapter and verse.

A light had come into Uncle Moritz's face, and he ral-
lied. "I believe you with all my heart. You are not the kind
to mislead a simple Jew." And, smiling sarcastically: "So
you will please let me go back to where I was. *If* Abraham
our Father was a prophet, and *if* he foresaw, as he must
have done, that Christians would come into the world, why
did he build his tent in the form of a cross?"

"That," said Lamport blandly—and it was clear that he
had been stalling while he cast about for the answer—"that
is an entirely different matter. It happens to be one of the
Teccou questions."

Teccou! Blessed refuge of the baffled intellect! The
proper transliteration is *Teiku*, but I have made it *Teccou*
so as to transpose the acronym into English. The word is
composed of the first letters of a Hebrew phrase which in

free translation would read: *T*ill *E*lijah, *C*oming, *C*larifies *O*ur *U*nderstanding. For in the folklore Elijah the Prophet is the most multifarious of benefactors. While the present world order endures, he is the comforter of the poor, the sick, and the oppressed; and when this order draws to a close, he will announce the coming of the Messiah. But perhaps most important of all to a highly disputatious people, he will solve all the unanswerable intellectual riddles that have tormented it since its beginnings.

I know now that Lamport often poked fun at us; he passed off on us hoary jokes that were current in his part of the world but not in ours—the consecrated academic pleasantries of the learned Litvaks, chiefly of the question-begging variety. Thus, Uncle Leon once asked him why God had chosen to liberate the Jews precisely on the wonderful festival of Passover, to which Lamport replied: "Exactly! *Because* it is the most wonderful festival. God knows what He's about." To the question: "Where is it written that a Jew must always keep his head covered?" he was shameless enough to come up with the ancient chestnut: "In the Pentateuch itself, in Genesis: 'And God said unto Abram: "Go! Get thee out of thy country." ' Can you imagine Abraham our Father going about with uncovered head?"

Behind Lamport's playfulness there was solid learning and a deep meditative streak. I cannot forget what he once said on the subject of "nothingness." Whether it was Uncle Moritz, or Uncle Leon, or my father who had raised the immemorial problem of the *yesh m'ayin,* the creation of the world out of nothing, I do not remember. I remember, however, Lamport's swarthy, prematurely wrinkled face, dead earnest, and his eyes suffused with a dark glow as he exclaimed: "Nothingness, eh? You utter a word and you don't stop to reflect what it means. Nothingness! A simple matter, you fancy. You, a creature of flesh and blood, point into what you call empty space, and you say: 'Nothing is there! And out of nothing you can make nothing.' But I tell you that there is no such thing as nothingness. *Our* nothingness is to God's nothingness as night is to day. The human eye cannot see it, the human hand cannot touch it, the balance cannot weigh it—but in God's nothingness all creation lies dissolved, everything is there, asleep for us, awake for Him, ready at his word to become visible and tangible to us." Lamport, though trained in the rationalist Talmudic school of Vilna, was talking the mysticism of the Chassidism and Cabbalists.

Uncle Leon was greatly drawn to Lamport, and since his warehouse was only a few doors away from Uncle Moritz's shop, he would come over at odd moments "to snatch a human word," as he put it. In fine weather Lamport would be squatting in the yard sorting his rags; on rainy days he worked in the cellar by the light of a kerosene lamp. I would be present occasionally, but only by chance, perhaps waiting for my cousin Mick, perhaps on an errand. I had no relish for these conversations, for this was about the period of my sharpest rebellion against Jewish things; and yet, marvelously enough, what I heard accidentally, indifferently, or with disdain, sank in, so that I am repeatedly astounded, as I come across traditional Jewish stories or sayings or anecdotes, to feel a sudden start within me, a resurrection: "Why, *Rebbe* said that once!" Or my father, or one of my uncles. It is not difficult for me to accept the theory that once an idea or impression passes through the gates of consciousness it takes a permanent residence there, far more securely fastened in than the substance of the body, which is replaced several times between birth and death.

It was from Lamport that I first heard of the *Maggidim,*

the wandering Jewish preachers of East European Jewry, those fabulists and moralists and sayers of parables and popular educators who were to the Jews of the ghettos and *Shtetlach* what the minstrels and *vagantes* and minnesingers were to the medieval European masses, the one difference being that the *Maggidim* were of a strictly religious cast. The most famous of them was the *Maggid* of Dubno, and his name was forever on Lamport's lips, for, said Lamport, there was not a human problem or situation that the Dubno *Maggid* had not resolved or illuminated in one of his countless parables.

Uncle Leon once voiced to Lamport the plaint of the Prophet that the wicked prosper while the righteous suffer, and Lamport answered that this was only fitting and proper and in the nature of things. Uncle Leon began a tirade: such a point of view was incomprehensible, an affront to the Ruler of the world and to the intelligence of man. Lamport held up a hand.

"*Kocht sich nit*—take it easy, Mr. Rothman, and I will tell you how the Dubno *Maggid* explains it, so that the simplest soul may understand. For the Dubno *Maggid*, his memory be a blessing to us, spoke to the common people, but in such a way that even the wise could learn. There were once, he tells us, two men who loved each other dearly, and whenever they met they exchanged the most affectionate salutations. But one morning, as they encountered each other on the street, one of them fell upon the other with such curses and insults as only the lowest men and the bitterest enemies bestow on each other. The victim of the assault was at first astounded, then indignant, but out of his love he remained silent; he did not raise his hand or his voice, he did not defend himself, he uttered never a word, but went home, saying, as you have just said: 'This is incomprehensible.' But he also said in his

heart: 'There must be a reason for it. I cannot see it, but
the reason is surely there.' Some time later the two friends
again met in the street, and to the utter amazement of
the one who had been insulted, the other greeted him
with the customary expressions of affection. 'What is this?'
asked the insulted one. 'Why did you treat me so villain-
ously the other day? What cause had I given you?' 'None
at all,' answered his friend. 'This is how it was. Shortly
before I met you I was cursed and vilified on the street
by an evil man whom I had never harmed. I was filled
with indignation, but I held my peace, thinking: "If I
answer him as he deserves, he will become more offensive,
and who knows how it will end?" Then I came face to face
with you and I let my indignation boil over, and I poured
it all out on you, knowing you would not answer lest you
provoke me to still greater rage.' That is the *moshel,* the
parable, my dear Mr. Rothman, and now I will give you
the *nimshal,* the application of the parable. God sees the
wickedness of the wicked, and He hears their insults, but
He will not argue with them or punish them in this world,
for that would only drive them into greater wickedness.
So He turns from them and pours out His indignation on
the righteous, who so love Him that they endure their unmerited afflictions without complaint. Thus they are God's
partners in saving the wicked from complete destruction,
and this is what constitutes their righteousness. Now do
you see?"

It was thus, or approximately thus, that I heard the
parable recently, and I was carried back as in a vivid wak-
ing dream to Uncle Moritz's yard, and the heap of rags,
and Lamport and Uncle Leon. I cannot tell whether Uncle
Leon "saw," for the rest of the conversation has sunk to
lower levels, perhaps never to be plumbed in this life. I
surmise that he had his objections and that in the end

Lamport fell back on his *Teiku,* as so many others have done on this haunting and tormenting problem.

Another and somewhat fuller evocation was granted me when I heard from an old *Maggid*—the breed is almost extinct—the parable of the King and the Expert. The *à propos* was a remark by Uncle Leon that even a fool could make big money and a deluded world would forever stand in awe of his cleverness. "On that point," said Lamport, "he of Dubno disagrees with you, and he proves that sooner or later the fool comes to grief. Listen and learn. Once upon a time there was a king who was a passionate lover of rare and precious stones. The king's jeweler, who built up his collection for him, was the greatest expert of his time, and since even jewelry experts are only mortal, this one, too, stretched out his feet one day and took himself off to the place where there is no buying and selling and no eating of *beigels.* Great was the consternation of the king. Where was he to find another expert? And how was he to set about it? A wise old councillor, himself no jewelry expert, came to the king's rescue. *'Adoni ha-melech,* my Lord the King, take the most costly of your jewels, and give it into the hand of one of your trusted servants, and let him go into the city and offer it for sale at auction. The rest will follow.' The king took the advice of the old councillor, and a servant went into the city with the gem. Now it so happened that in this same city there was a rich man, a fool, whom everybody considered very clever. He too was a lover of jewelry, but because he was a fool, he thought he knew everything and never made use of experts; his collection therefore consisted of diamonds with flaws and even of pieces of glass cunningly cut to look like diamonds. When the servant put up the king's gem for sale, the bidding began at a high level and the fool, hearing the figures go up, was duly impressed and said craftily to himself: 'This must be a wonderful stone. Whatever they offer, it must be worth more, for the buyer surely intends to resell.' So he entered the bidding and raised every offer by ten per cent. The dealers at last dropped out, and the fool remained the buyer. When it came to paying, he brought out his rubbishy collection of flawed diamonds and pasteboard pieces and said: 'Choose! Here is more than enough.' But far from being enough, you understand, it was so short that all the other possessions of the fool could not make up the difference. So not only did he have to pay a heavy fine, but at one stroke he lost his reputation as a clever man. Now do you see?"

This time Uncle Leon "saw." He closed his eyes in a spasm of delight, he rubbed his hands as if he had just done a good stroke of business, and exclaimed: "Gold, Mr. Lamport, pure gold! But tell me, who became the king's expert?"

"The dealer who made the last bid before the fool."

Uncle Leon sighed: "Ah! Not for nothing do they say that learning is the best merchandise."

It was from the *Maggidim* that my people learned to exercise their imagination in the folklore. Their treatment of certain Biblical characters was, as I have indicated, arbitrary, and I have my own *Teiku* questions on some of the results. Why, for instance, did they always say "drunk as Lot" and never "drunk as Noah," or Ahasuerus, or Nabal, the brutish husband of Abigail? Of all these it is told that they became drunk on at least one occasion; but it was Noah who planted the vine, and he was the first of all mortals to get drunk. Similarly, they said "Balaam the wicked" and "Haman the wicked," but never Pharaoh the wicked, though they held Pharaoh to have been wickeder than either Balaam or Haman. Balaam had been hired to pronounce a curse on the Jews, but he choked on it and pronounced a blessing instead, to the astonishment and fury of his employer, Balak, King of Edom. Haman had planned to liquidate only a part of the Jewish people—that which lived in the Persian Empire. But Pharaoh's plans had been directed against the Jewish people in its entirety; nevertheless, he remained plain "Pharaoh," or, formally, "Pharaoh, King of Egypt." On the other hand, one cannot but approve of their characterization of Ahasuerus as the *melech tippesh,* the royal dope. But what did they have against Vyzoosoo, the youngest of Haman's ten sons, who were hanged together with their father on the gallows, fifty cubits high, which had been prepared by Haman for Mordecai? Vyzoosoo (Vyzatha in the standard transliteration) is just one name in a string of ten; neither he nor his brothers are ever mentioned again, and he alone has been singled out, without rhyme or reason, for everlasting disparagement. In the shadier part of the Yiddish vernacular a Vyzoosoo is a special kind of fool, the kind to whom "liberal shepherds give a grosser name."

I pick out faces and names at random. Their ever-presentness to us obliterated the centuries that separated them. They come before me in ones and in groups. There is Eleazar ben Azaryah, out of the Passover Hagaddah; at the age of eighteen he stood first among the scholars of Israel, so that they elected him Head of the Academy of Yabneh, that center of the spirit which enabled the Jewish people to outwit and outlive their Roman conquerors. Young Eleazar ben Azaryah found the honor acutely embarrassing. How was he, a beardless youth, to stand before his elders expounding the Law? But God came to his rescue, and the night before his induction caused him to sprout a septuagenarian beard, a face-saving beard, and none of us asked whether the rest of him was transformed to suit. There is Rabbi Akiba, another master of the

Torah. He is the opposite of Eleazar ben Azaryah, for until the age of forty he was an illiterate shepherd, with a brutish hatred of scholars. He could not see one, he confessed in later years, without wanting to "bite him like an ass." Then, with the encouragement of his bride-to-be, a young woman of noble family who foresaw his illustrious future, he began to study, and by the time he was eighty he ranked for knowledge of the Law with Moses our Teacher. He married, and taught for another forty years, and at a hundred and twenty he died a martyr in the Hadrianic persecutions. Near him stands his pupil Bar Kochba, the leader of the rebellion against Hadrian the Destroyer whose name is never mentioned, to this day, without a fervent "May his bones be broken," as if they have not been dust this many a century. And there are the sages of B'nai Brak, who once sat out a Passover night expatiating on the wonders of the exodus, so that their pupils had to break in on them respectfully with: "Gentlemen! The time has come for morning prayers." There, also in the Hagaddah, is the gentle Hillel, a man incapable of an impatient word even under the grossest provocation. A low buffoon once undertook, on a wager, to put him into a rage, and one night called him repeatedly out of bed to ply him with ridiculous questions, but Hillel answered him sweetly throughout, and in the end was rewarded with a curse for his imperturbability. "Better," finished Hillel softly, "that you should lose your wager than I my temper."

Every member of the supporting cast on this enormous, timeless stage is clearly limned, and no matter how minor his role and to what age he belongs, he is indispensable; the *dramatis personae* would be incomplete without him. We felt about them in the irrational way one feels about the members of one's family—that we would have missed them if they had never been born. But it was with the greatest figures that we felt most at home; and just as we turned Abraham the revolutionary into a lovable, kind-hearted grandfather type, we domesticated Moses into the apotheosis of the homey *rebbe*. We acknowledged the awesomeness of his deeds, we saw him confronting Pharaoh, and commanding the waters of the Red Sea, and descending from the lightnings of Sinai with the tablets of the Law; but we treated him as the children of a home-loving Prime Minister might treat their father. His greatness belongs to his business hours. They are proud of his official standing, but to them he is predominantly the paterfamilias, worrying over their schoolmarks. Had we contemplated Moses as the Bible presents him, we would have been terrified by him. As with Abraham and Moses, so with Elijah the Prophet. He was to us no wild man of the desert, no slayer of false prophets, no rebuker of kings; he put off those functions when he came to us as the consoler and helper of the poor, and as the herald of the Messiah.

The ever-presentness of the fathers of the clan, their contemporaneousness with us, was consistent with our awareness of a past so immense that it dwarfed into nothingness the historical time-span of other peoples. *We* moved tacitly among the millennia, while *they*, powerful, majestic, but evanescent, were cramped into the centuries. That was how my *rebbe* put it, and I objected to the ten-to-one proportion. I reminded, or rather informed, him that our history was, at most, only twice as long as England's. I expected him to deny it, or be taken aback, but he answered with a tolerant smile: "Peasant brain! If your grandfather is a venerable ninety and mine a miraculous hundred and eighty, there's actually no comparison at all!" That left me speechless.

115

At the Passover table my father used to interpolate into the service a Yiddish song I have never heard elsewhere, nor have I been able to trace it to its source.

> Full four hundred years did Pharaoh
> Bathe himself in Jewish blood,
> Till the day of retribution—
> First-born slain and Red Sea flood.
> Israel, mocking, calls to mind
> What befalls him and his kind.
> Psalms of David, words of sages,
> Guarded us across the ages.
> What can kings and tyrants do
> In their rage against the Jew,
> God's word holding firm and true
> Through eternity.

Kings and tyrants could of course do much against the Jew, and had done it, as my people very well knew. What, then, did my father mean? In part, that we were losing all the battles and winning the war; but, more than that, he used the word Jew to indicate an indestructible pledge. My people saw their Jewishness as a pledge given by their ancestors at Sinai, binding on subsequent generations till the end of time. Jewish history, Biblical and post-Biblical, revolved about this pledge, around repudiations of it, around repudiations of the repudiations, and on its fulfillment depended the fate of humanity. God would keep His word if the Jew kept his. Hence, the prayer "Thou hast always saved us from enemies stronger than we" really meant: "Thou hast always saved a remnant of us, so that the pledge might not be lost." What a megalomania of responsibility! But it is after all only the kind of megalomania which election posters seek to awaken in the individual citizen. It was as if a finger were forever pointing at my people from a celestial hoarding: "*Your* vote can change history!"

They could neither live up to the pledge nor get rid of it. They knew themselves to be unworthy, but there was no way of disowning the commitment. They simply could not believe that the Jewish people had survived so long to no special purpose, for this would have implied that God had created a madhouse and called it history. So there they were, in Glodorlui, in Macheen, in Lower Strangeways, waiting and believing.

"Believing" was only part of it. "Belonging" is equally important. They belonged to that beloved, densely populated world which stretched back to the beginning. This was their home in the cosmos; it gave them their human form. Loyalty and affection held them there, and, more than that, the terror of becoming utter nullities if they left it. Out of it, they would have nothing to talk about but their suffering and their sordid economic struggles.

The darkest word in their vocabulary was *meshumad* (they pronounced it *meshimid*), literally "the destroyed one," by usage "the apostate," the Jew who had himself baptized. The literal meaning lurked behind the idiomatic; a *meshumad* had destroyed his memories, hence himself. He had turned his back on that which had made him one with the patriarchs and prophets, the kings and saints and sinners and sages and fools among whom Jews had always lived. Nameless and naked he went forth in his perversity into an alien world, where his ancestors were either unknown or mentioned with contumely.

To this attitude, too, I objected strenuously, and in an argument with Lamport the rag dealer pointed out that Christians spoke reverently of Abraham, Isaac, and Jacob, of David and Solomon and Isaiah. "I know it," said Lamport, "I know it. But the Christian thinks of the patriarchs and prophets in his own way. To begin with, he turns them into non-Jews; and he disowns any kinship with them. Does an Englishman talk of Abraham our Father as his ancestor? Does he tell his children that if there hadn't been an exodus they would still be slaves in Egypt? And anyway, the only use the Christian has for our ancestors is that they lived and died in order that Jesus might be born. Where does that leave us for the last two thousand years?"

"Faith," "belief," "credo"—these are words which can be applied to my childhood world only from the outside. My relatives spoke of their "Jewishness," which must be described from the inside. Sometimes I have asked myself whether they would have gone to the scaffold or the pyre rather than apostatize. For the large majority the answer is, certainly, "No." Would they, outwardly denying their Jewishness under duress, have felt desolated, soiled, and debased? The answer is, as certainly, "Yes, all of them." Given the alternative, the same large majority would have preferred exile and beggary to baptism. Given no such alternative, a number would have accepted death.

But who among those I remember had such stuff in him? How difficult to think of such ordinary people as my *rebbe,* my grandfather, my mother, my father, in that exalted role. Still, I know with the utmost certainty that there were some who simply could not have kissed the cross in token of submission. *They could not have done it!* If they had tried, they would have fainted or gone rigid in hysterical paralysis. I hear someone say: "Then it would not have been a question of willing or not willing. It would have been mechanical." And I answer: "They would have been true martyrs nonetheless."

118

CHAPTER VIII

Patchwork

❀

How DID I cram so much into my boyhood years? I
seem to have had time for everything. There was school
five days a week, from nine to twelve and from two to half
past four; there was *cheder* six days a week, from six to
eight on Mondays, Tuesdays, Wednesdays, and Thursdays,
an afternoon session on Saturdays and a morning session
on Sundays. (My poor *rebbe;* he earned his shilling or
shilling and sixpence a week from each pupil.) There were
"the hills," there were the penny weeklies, there was
much miscellaneous reading, and not a little daydreaming.

Until the age of ten and a half I lived vividly in everything except school and *cheder*. A faint echo of far-off
raptures reaches me and makes a stirring in my blood.
"The hills"! That wild expansion of heart and lungs and
imagination when I scrambled up them, oblivious to the
penalties that waited for me at home! In his youth, Heine
felt that he could eat all the elephants in Hindustan and
pick his teeth with the spire of Strassburg Cathedral. I, in
my boyhood, felt that my running feet kept the world
spinning. On "the hills" I was master of an illimitable
present in which I forgot hunger and thirst, home and
school and *cheder*. I forgot them also when I plunged into

the penny weeklies and the doings of Tom Merry and Harry Wharton and Billy Bunter and Arthur Augustus d'Arcy. I would read walking in the street, bumping into lampposts in my addled absorption. I was at St. Jim's, or at Greyfriars, I was making a century at cricket, scoring the winning goal with five seconds to go, discovering and denouncing the rotter from the rival rowing team who had surreptitiously sawed through the oars of our leading stroke.

At school I stayed consistently near the bottom of the class; at *cheder* I was considered a clod. My parents wailed: "It's *de heels*, accursed may they be, *de heels*, and football, and cricket, and little fishes." I loudly exonerated "the hills"; my playmates spent as much time on them as I, and some of them were at the top of the class. My teachers blamed the penny weeklies, and for them I had the same defense; among the top-ranking boys in the class were *cheder* companions of mine who were equally addicted to the weeklies. I was willing to pass for a dolt rather than dock my playtime or change my reading habits.

My early school years have left me only scattered memories. Miss Browne of Standard Three wore green; she was haughty and and handsome; once she wrote on the blackboard:

> Full many a flower is born to blush unseen,
> And waste its sweetness on the desert air

and I whispered to myself: "How true; I'm the only one who understands." Miss Porrit of Standard Two was narky (mean), and accepted apples from the pupils; Mr. Fisher of Standard Four A was "champion," even "bleddy-well champion," but I was in Standard Four B. Mr. George Sharples, the headmaster (he might have sat for James Joyce's Mr. Deasy), was a kind of divinity with a life-pattern all his own. On certain unpredictable mornings he lay in ambush for late-comers; he would station a monitor at the entrance and we were not permitted to proceed down the corridor to class. We would line up, and at a quarter past nine Mr. Sharples would appear, carrying a thin, flexible cane. We would hold out a hand for a single swish; no excuses, no reprimands, just a brief, silent, and tacit transaction. He had a good aim, and would hit us sometimes on the fingertips, which really hurt, and sometimes on the palm, which wasn't too bad. There were fingertip mornings and palm mornings, and whether you were late by one minute or ten made no difference; everyone got the same swishing. We took this ritual to be the duty or prerogative of all headmasters, and when we learned that Mr. Harris of the Jews' School and Mr. Shair of Southall Street School did not perform it as the one or exercise it as the other, we thought the less of them for it. Mr. Sharples had a fat brother William, whom we called Tubby, and who was an ordinary teacher in the same school. Once, for what was called "object lesson," he brought a live rabbit into class, choked it to death, and dissected it for us. A girl vomited.

School was suddenly and completely transfigured for me when I moved up one autumn into Miss Clarke's class, Standard Five. The very building became unrecognizable, as I must have been to anyone who saw me hurrying toward it in the morning, radiant-faced, well ahead of the bell. Never again did I hold out my hand to Mr. George Sharples, and try to shove it forward on fingertip mornings to receive the cane on my palm. Never again did I search the hills for something we called alum, which was supposed to anesthetize the skin. Honor and love to the memory of Kate Clarke; she was one of the happiest accidents of my life.

I worshipped her from the first day, and could only express my emotion—how inadequately!—by rising to the
top of the class. I was glad that I had come to her with a
poor record, with a reputation for slovenliness and in-
attentiveness. I wished the record had been poorer still, to
make the contrast greater. Toward the end of that year I
was haunted by the dolorous prospect of losing her, and
when we heard that she would move with us into Standard
Six, I felt like uttering a prayer of thanksgiving.

Rising to the top of the class was no trick at all; it was
just as easy to be there as at the bottom. I played as much
as before, I read as many weeklies, and I did as badly as
ever at *cheder*. The transformation was exclusively a school
phenomenon; during school hours I was obsessed by a
single need—to please Miss Clarke, to do the best com-
position in the class, to have the right answer when she
called on me, particularly if she had called on others before me and their answers had been wrong. How my excitement mounted as one wrong answer followed another,
how I trembled lest some male or female oaf, who hadn't
a thousandth part of my love for Miss Clarke, should
anticipate the words trembling on my lips; what a sunburst
there was in the room when, still unsatisfied, Miss Clarke
turned the pointer toward me and the right answer came
tumbling out. Correspondingly dark were my moments of
failure; their memory rankled for days.

Once she called me third or fourth to the blackboard to
draw a circle around a triangle. I came forward in a sickly
panic, with not an idea in my head. I picked up the ruler
and compass from her table and turned my back on the
class; then somehow my trembling hands executed, quite
of themselves, the bisection of the two sides, extended the
perpendiculars to the meeting point, and drew the circle.
I had done it! I made blindly for my seat and heard Miss

Clarke say, in a pleased voice: "You'd better leave the ruler and compass with me." But the culmination was yet to come. Dazed as I was, I had wit enough to hand her the compass with the point toward me, and her "Thank you" was for that not less than for my performance at the blackboard. Oh, the flush that went through me, sweeping from the roots of my hair to my toes! What are Nobel Prizes and peerages beside such triumphs?

I cannot judge whether Miss Clarke was an unusually gifted teacher, one of those blessed spirits whose lives are one long, obscure, irreplaceable service to generation after generation of school children. She was not wildly popular, like Mr. Fisher, nor unpopular, like Miss Porrit, but popularity is not the measure of a teacher's worth. Schoolmates with whom I have talked about her in later years do not recall her as a magic influence. I can only say that but for her I would probably have grown up an illiterate.

It was a great moment for me when the news of my transformation reached my home. I was vindicated; I had proved in my person that one could be at the top of the class without taking off time from "the hills," football, cricket, and little fishes. But such crowing as I felt myself entitled to was soon choked off. If I wasn't such a dolt after all, why didn't I do better at *cheder,* reports from which also reached home, delivered in person by the *rebbe* himself? And again, if I did so well at school without giving up "the hills," how much better would I not do if I gave them up? Further, how unbecoming it was for a boy with a good head on his shoulders to behave like a young heathen. The injustice of it! I would have been just as well off at home if I had remained at the bottom of the class; no, better, because before this new and outrageous principle of *noblesse oblige* intruded into my life I had been more or less adjusted to the status of a dolt. It is some measure of my adoration of Miss Clarke that I did not hold her accountable for the backfire from my sudden and unexpected eminence, or so much as dream of returning to a more comfortable ignominy.

Miss Clarke lived in rooms above Chanot's violin shop, right opposite Uncle Moritz. I found that out when she asked me once to carry a parcel home for her, and gave me a penny for my trouble. She slipped the coin so quickly into my hand that I hadn't time to protest, and when I got downstairs I was overwhelmed with shame. Didn't she know that for her I would have lugged sackloads of bricks to the ends of the earth and accounted myself her debtor? I didn't spend that penny. I kept it in a wooden box until it somehow disappeared.

It was Miss Clarke who in the second year suggested that I try for a free-tuition scholarship at the Manchester Municipal Secondary School; suggested rather than urged because she knew we were poor, and I would have to win what was called an Exhibition as well as a scholarship. The Exhibition carried with it five pounds for the first year and would offset part of my forfeited earnings. My parents were hesitant; they suspected that I had begun to use my head too late; besides, "the hills" were still there, and the penny weeklies, habits and compulsions I could not shake off. I was hesitant too, fearing the disgrace of failure. I would have felt more confident if I could have had Miss Clarke as my examiner, not, however, because I would have expected her to favor me unfairly. I wanted desperately to please her by winning, but I needed to please her face to face, immediately, not indirectly and across an interval of suspense. I wanted to see her dark, somewhat severe and old-maidish face light up at my correct answers, while she glanced away with a little smile directed at some invisible witness with the unspoken comment: "I can usually rely on *him*." The approval of strangers, assuming I could get it, was insipid by comparison, and I went forth on the fateful morning as if to be sentenced rather than examined. It was a sensation with which I was to become dolorously familiar.

My miscellaneous reading included, among others, Hans Christian Andersen, Samuel Smiles, Susan Coolidge, the Grimm Brothers, Rider Haggard, Jules Verne, and Rhoda Broughton. Of individual books I recall most clearly *What Katy Did, What Katy Did Next, John Halifax, Gentleman, The Lamplighter, Cranford, King Solomon's Mines, The Hero of Crompton School,* and *Cometh Up As a Flower.* I wept over *Cometh Up As a Flower* and *John Halifax, Gentleman* and *The Lamplighter.* Pictures and phrases still stick in my mind; some I can assign to their proper place, some are homeless; "Rapunzel, Rapunzel, let down your hair," and "Eternity," from Hans Christian Andersen; little Ursula (?) cutting her hand at the door as she struggled with the stern old servant woman who would not let her give a piece of bread to little John Halifax, starving in the snow; Nadin, "the cowardly bully," guilty of the Peterloo massacre of peaceful Manchester workers— that was in *The Lamplighter;* Allan Quatermain in his duel to the death with the Zulu chief, in *King Solomon's Mines;* but whose was the kettle "merrily wobbling on the hob"? And who was it threw a sack of grain out of the upper-floor window into the river rather than let the hungry villagers rob him of it? I have learned not to look into those books when chance brings them my way; I shrink from anything that threatens to spoil the sweet memory of my boyhood reading. It hurt me to find in one of Zangwill's essays a take-off on *Cometh Up As a Flower,* which he re-entitled, cruelly, *Boometh As a Bumble Bee;* and when I was in the country of *King Solomon's Mines* and saw the Zimbabwe ruins and the primitive kraals of the Zulus (they were a shockingly peaceful lot), I refused to associate them with Rider Haggard.

The juvenile section of the Free Library on Cheetham Hill Road did not lend out books in those days; you had to read them on the premises, and I remember happy hours I spent there, though I cannot for the life of me imagine where I fitted them in. We sat on hard benches at long tables, and the librarian was a small, bandy-legged red-whiskered man, Mr. Jones, whom we called Puggy Whiskers. The room was below ground level, and boys would sneak down the steps, open the door, yell: "Puggy Whiskers, your mamma wants you for *kreplach*," and scuttle up the stairs, laughing like hyenas. Mr. Jones would turn as red as his beard, his face would work spasmodically, and he would start up as if a pin had been jabbed into his back. Sometimes he lurked at the door in the hope of laying his hands on one of the miscreants, but always in vain; the wretched man did not know, apparently, that he could be watched from the ground-level windows, and the assault on the peace would be made only when he was behind his desk, from which he could never get to the door fast enough. He once asked me: "What are they shouting? What is *kreplak*?" I told him that *kreplach* were patties filled with meat. He shook his head in disbelief; he must have read into the word a meaning profoundly offensive to himself and his mother, who was probably dead. Forty years ago there was in the Bronx Zoo a gorilla called Baldy, and people used to tease it for the pleasure of watching its gibbering rages. Baldy reminded me of Puggy Whiskers; but I laughed neither at Puggy Whiskers nor at Baldy. In my Puggy Whiskers days I was annoyed by the interruptions and in my Baldy days I was indignant at the cruelty of the public.

I have told how, on winning the scholarship and Exhibition, I dropped the boys of St. Jim's and of Greyfriars as
abruptly, ungratefully, and priggishly as Prince Hal
dropped Falstaff and Poins on becoming Henry the Fifth.
"Never came reformation in a flood/With such a heady
current." Now, the truth is that I have always found it
hard to swallow Shakespeare's story of that complete
dramatic conversion. There must have been, I argue,
twinges of regret, twilight nostalgias, even an occasional
visit, à la Haroun-al-Raschid, to Eastcheap ale houses
where he had not been seen before. That conversation
with the simple soldier Bates during the night before
Agincourt—does it not prove that Henry remained thoroughly at home with the common people, and mingled
with them so naturally that no suspicion of his identity
ever crossed their minds? I therefore will not, on reflection,
take an oath that I never again peeped into the penny
weeklies for a glimpse of the low company I had forsworn,
though the temptation did grow less as I found the same
intellectual and moral values in Kipling and Henty and
Tennyson. Nor did I, in spite of my vow, immediately
abjure "the hills," and football, and cricket, though their
attraction did taper off as new influences came into my life.

On the day we got the great news, my father impulsively
gave me a shilling, which I accepted with stupefaction and
alarm. The vastness of the sum impressed on me the
solemnity of the occasion, and played some part in re-
shaping my outlook on life. I spread the shilling as far as
it would go on second-hand, third-hand, and fourth-hand
books, among them two tattered Blatchford pamphlets and
a coverless astronomy primer almost as old as its subject
matter. Why Blatchford? Why astronomy? The answer is
the cadaverous young Shudehill bookseller, into whose
shop I stumbled more or less by accident, and whose name

I have completely forgotten. God rest his evangelical soul; he has his share in my life's history. What if he had been of a religious rather than a rationalist turn of mind? What if he had been neither and had sold me a job lot of travel books? I am quite sure that in my suddenly aroused passion for self-improvement I would have read them with the same fervor and perhaps with the same lasting effect. As it was, Blatchford and astronomy set their stamp on me in the years that followed.

I did not become an avowed socialist and atheist immediately; the words were so abhorrent in our world that I censored them in my own mind. I accepted all the arguments, I rejected the implication of their sum. Some months still had to pass; I had to become a member of our high-school debating society. I had to discover that I had the gift of the gab, and learn the tingling delight of standing before an audience and delivering myself of daring ideas.

It would have been better for me not to have been provided with an audience at that age. The debating society developed the show-off in me; it encouraged the quick retort and the muddled idea. Nor, in spite of my affection for them, can I think with gratitude of the foolish people who arranged street-corner meeetings for me. They were decent and earnest and, with all their revolutionary slogans, humble; they meant well and they did me no good. The responsibility of indulgent adults in the spread of juvenile delinquency is nowhere clearer than in the case of boy and girl orators and evangelists.

This was the time when the *inner* conflict set in between my two worlds, the Jewish and the non-Jewish, so that I quarreled with myself as well as with the community. The Tom Merrys and Harry Whartons had had nothing to say to my Jewish world; Blatchford had much to say, though indirectly, for I do not recall that he expressed any views on the Jewish question. As a socialist, science popularizer, and atheist, he taught me to see Jewishness as an "effete" (I loved that word) and obstructive phenomenon, an obstacle in the path of human progress. It was, therefore, "Down with Jewishness!"—though of course not with individual Jews, except in their capacity as capitalists, lackies of capitalism, or disseminators of religion, that opium of the masses. There were as yet no real capitalists in my community; there were, I suppose, a number of lackies of capitalism, and practically everyone was a disseminator of religion. Thus, there was no one to benefit by my tolerant distinction. My *rebbe,* and others, logically denounced me as a little anti-Semite; if they had been familiar with the jargon they might have added: "Objectively."

Without knowing it, I happened to be following good Biblical precedent. "Have I any pleasure at all that the wicked should die? saith the Lord God; and not rather that he should return from his ways and live?" But it must be admitted that in the Bible it is often difficult to distinguish between God's hatred of sin and His hatred of sinners; and where His example is so confusing, how can we expect ordinary mortals to keep separate their dislike of Jewishness and their benevolence toward Jews?

It was true that I didn't like being a Jew; on the other hand, I didn't know how to be anything else. Nor could I keep away from Jewish life. Throughout my high-school and college years I was forever joining, leaving, and rejoining Jewish youth groups, Zionist, cultural, and dramatic, and during membership periods I preached socialism, atheism, and assimilation to my fellow-members. I have seen this variety of psychological muddle in others —Jews who satisfy and accentuate their Jewishness by devoting their lives to the demolition of Jewishness in others.

I was a patchwork of contradictions. I pointed my accusing finger at the well-to-do and was ashamed of myself and my parents for not being of them; I despised Kipling the Sahib and would have liked my parents to be English enough to be thrilled like me by *Gunga Din,* that expression of British imperialism on the gutter level; I had fits of patriotism (Blatchford was himself something of a jingo, had been a soldier, and had written Kiplingesque stories of army life), but my people's admiration for England was nevertheless an abject thing in my eyes; under duress I took part in school sports, and was irked because my parents were unmoved by the glad tidings that "our side won"; under no duress, I played cricket with schoolmates and didn't want my parents to know; I was always on the side of the oppressed, but the Jews with their obstinate insistence on being Jewish were responsible for anti-Semitism; I was a pacifist, but the pacifism of my people was one of its outstanding defects, and my father got no credit for being an exception; as a pacifist I grinned at myself for marching joyously in the Jewish Lads' Brigade to the stirring rhythms of bugle and drum (what fun it was!), but I was wounded when my parents smiled.

All this time, at high school, as well as later at college, I read hugely, I addressed socialist meetings, I worked during elections, and I alternated between high exaltation and sullen despair. Life was a marvelous gift, life was an obscene cruelty; mankind was the highest product of the cosmic purpose, mankind was a maggoty crawling on the surface of an obscure planet doomed to early extinction; I was a free-willed participant in the meaningful and endless process of creation, I was a comical little contraption emitting sound waves into the void. The moral law was a built-in feature of the universe—this was crystal-clear to

me in my mystical moments; the moral law was a wretched
superstition—this was crystal-clear to me in my materialist
moments. In its bourgeois form, the moral law was also a
capitalistic device for the befuddlement of the working
classes, while in its general form, as a superstitious heritage
handed down from primitive societies, it turned my high-
falutin speeches on liberty, equality, and fraternity into
the rantings of a comedian.

In my moods of despair I had no argument against any
form of immorality; the universe was indifferent to love
and hate. Theoretically I was ready to lie, cheat, steal, kill;
to the extent that I did not, I was a weakling and a fool;
and I was angry with myself because this limitless permis-
siveness of the universe made me wretched instead of
happy. At the same time, I wanted the fat aldermen who
were guzzling turtle soup while factory girls were starving,
to be in the wrong; but how could they be in the wrong if
there was neither right nor wrong? It was exasperating
beyond words that fat aldermen should in their stupidity
have hit on the sensible course while enjoying the extra
bonus of thinking themselves morally in the right!

My attempts to discuss these matters with Ellen Wilkinson and Walton-Newbold and other fellow-socialists ran
into a blank wall. Their formula was: "Morality is based
on self-interest. If everyone were immoral, society would
disintegrate, and where would you be?" My answer was:
"My being immoral, especially if I'm clever enough to
conceal it, will make only the slightest dent in society, but
it will give me a tremendous personal advantage." Whereupon they said: "You're talking like a lousy bourgeois, not
like a good socialist," and my answer was: "I'm as good a
socialist as you." So I was, or believed myself to be, in my
other moods. It would have relieved me if they had confessed to sharing my misgivings; as it was, I suspected that

they did, and were secretive about it, in which they were being cleverer than I. That, I said to myself, isn't right of them—but what am I talking about if there's neither right nor wrong?

At bottom I knew that my moral scruples derived from my upbringing, which had been Jewish, and this was one of the roots of my anti-Jewishness. I had been made a fool of by Jewishness, as I would have been by Christianity if my upbringing had been Christian.

It all sounds silly and adolescent, but in substance the problems are fundamental; the discussion has been going on for ages, it will go on as long as men think.

CHAPTER IX

Our Shtetl *Roots*

❀

I LOST interest in my father's readings at about the time when I could have stayed up as long as I wanted—an early lesson in the illusions of hope. I had no patience, either, with the homely philosophizing of the grown-ups. Wonderfully and fortunately enough I retained my partiality for my mother's conversation, a circumstance which introduces a puzzle into the development of my Yiddish.

If I had let the language fall into disuse at the age of thirteen, it would have been natural for me to have had only a childish command of it at nineteen, when I met Uncle Berel again. But my mother spoke a rich folk Yiddish, and I enjoyed listening to her. Why did I have to relearn my Yiddish in America? Where was the block?

It is barely possible that I did not really follow my mother's Yiddish word for word and phrase for phrase, but grasped the meaning of the sentences and recalled words and phrases in later years. A second explanation, which could include the first, is equally plausible. I repressed my Yiddish except as a channel of communication with my mother; I wanted to demonstrate my high-principled disapproval of what Yiddish stood for—ignorance, backwardness, poverty, superstition. My mother's Yiddish, however, was exempt from these charges. She disinfected it, as it were, by her personality and her tolerance. She was troubled, of course, to hear me called a socialist and an unbeliever; it saddened her that I wasn't going to be a *"Kreiserrabbiner";* but she took it in the spirit of "we can't have everything," which was remarkable in one who had so little.

My revolt from Jewishness was abrupt, my return to it proceeded by stages. I was becoming dissatisfied with the contradictions and spiritual barrenness of materialism, and it was difficult to hit on an alternative. I was looking for roots; it was inconceivable at first that I could find them in such petty things as my people and its past; and as if their pettiness was not enough, they were steeped in religion, that most lamentable and calamitous of human errors.

Two episodes out of that time played for me, in reverse and less violently, the roles of the Shudehill bookseller and Robert Blatchford. There was a Hebrew teacher in Manchester, Isaiah Wassilevsky, whom Louis Golding has romanticized as Mr. Emanuel. I used to frequent his house during my relapses into Jewish youth groups, and I met Chaim Weizmann there, though not for the first time. But it is not the meeting with Weizmann that concerns me at this point. Toward the end of my college days, Wassilevsky tried to interest me in the Yiddish poetry of Chaim Nachman Bialik. Bialik is primarily a Hebrew poet, a very great one (I shall tell later of my contacts with him), but he has written magnificently in Yiddish, too. My Hebrew being hopeless, Wassilevsky appealed to my imperfect Yiddish, with some success. I was vaguely stirred; there came through to me an echoing of great powers; I was moved to suspect that my contempt for the language was based on ignorance, which in turn was based on willful-ness. But I was less susceptible at nineteen than at thirteen.

And I had a vested interest to protect—my stance and my reputation. The inoculation took, but manifested itself later.

The second episode was the appearance in Manchester of the Yiddish actor Maurice Moskowitz and his troupe, when I served for a week as guest dramatic critic of a local daily, *The Despatch*. The invitation came through a socialist acquaintance I had on the paper. He asked me if I wanted to get free passes and "make a few bob on the side." He did not ask me how much Yiddish I knew, it was enough for him that I was a Jew. Another paper appointed Neville Laski, brother of the more famous Harold. Their father was an alderman and one-time mayor of Salford, twin city to Manchester. I imagine that young Laski's Yiddish was even poorer than mine. What the plays did for him I cannot say; on me two of them made a startling impression quite unrelated to my ephemeral role as dramatic critic. They were Strindberg's *The Father* and Tolstoi's *The Living Corpse*. Strindberg and Tolstoi in Yiddish! Why, they were highbrow (the word had not yet been coined) even in English; and here were my Yiddish-speaking Jews taking it all in with rapt attention. This was something to be looked into.

The snobbery of it! What happened when I got around to the study of Yiddish was that I fell in love with it, and of course not simply because one could be highbrow in it. The lovableness of a language lies in the intimacy of its relationship to a regionalist life-form; the closer the intimacy, the more lovable the language, and Yiddish is so much the alter ego of Yiddish-speaking Jewry, it is so perfect—and indispensable—a replica of that Jewry's life-experience, that one can hardly know the one without the other. One gets out of translations from the Yiddish a smaller proportion of the essential content than out of

translations from French or German, or for that matter
Hebrew—to mention the languages with which I am
familiar.

Yiddish led me back to my people via the *Shtetl,* the
Jewish village community of Eastern Europe. Without
Yiddish I would not have read Sholom Aleichem and Yal
Peretz and Mendelle Mocher Sforim. There were few
translations half a century ago, and these, like the many
translations that have appeared since, my own included,
are at best only good enough to demonstrate that the
original must be much more interesting. They do not
tempt one to a second reading, whereas the originals can
be—and were—read over and over again. Now, it was
obvious to me even as a boy that my Manchester community was a Rumanian *Shtetl* transplanted into the Western world; but what the *Shtetl* had been like *in situ* I could
never have learned without reading the classics and without being at home in the language of *Shtetl* survivors in
America and elsewhere.

Yiddish, then, was my gateway into Jewish life, and
once I was inside, Hebrew followed of itself. True, I became a "Zionist" before I learned Yiddish, but it was an
empty thing (as it still is with many "Zionists"), a gesture,
psychological rather than spiritual. If I turned to the
Bible at the same time, that too was only a self-assertion
and a declaration of purpose. For a long time I thought of
myself as an atheist, for whom Isaiah and Micah and Amos
were moralists and sociologists, magnificent in style and
inspiringly on the right track, though for the wrong reason.
That the Prophets were more than moralists, that Zionism
was more than the demand for a Jewish homeland, that
"Thus saith the Lord" was more than a superstitious
ejaculation—all this grew on me slowly.

But why should I think of the *Shtetl* as the embodiment

of Exile Jewishness? Why not the large Jewish communities, cities and mothers in Israel, with their synagogues, academies, and institutions? The answer lies in the superior cohesiveness of the *Shtetl,* which stood up as an impregnable citadel of Jewishness. The Jewish city had more Jewish life quantitatively, but it also had its large segment of defection. In the city Jews were exposed to worldly opportunity and, very often, an attractive non-Jewish culture; in both these respects, the *Shtetl* was secure. There was, again, a crucial difference between Macheen as the Rumanian *Shtetl* and my Manchester community as a transplanted *Shtetl.* Macheen-in-Rumania had despised the surrounding civilization; Macheen-in-Manchester had admired it. The insulation of Macheen-in-Manchester from its environment was uneven, stronger at some points, weaker at others, differing also from person to person. With my parents and my *rebbe* it was very strong, with my uncles Leon and Moritz weaker; and though at its weakest it was the *Shtetl* spirit that still dominated, there was no comparison with the dominion of the *Shtetl* spirit in Macheen.

With all this, it is essential to know that the Jewish attitude toward the *Shtetl* was and is ambivalent. On the one hand it is remembered sentimentally. From just below the horizon—historically speaking, the *Shtetl* died only yesterday—it sends up a nostalgic glow for its survivors and for those who have received the tradition from parents and grandparents. It is pictured as one of the rare and happy breathing-spells of the Exile, the nearest thing to a home from home that the Jews have ever known. On the other hand, it is recalled with a grimace of distaste. The *Shtetlach!* Those forlorn little settlements in a vast and hostile wilderness, isolated alike from Jewish and non-Jewish centers of civilization, their tenure precarious, their structure ramshackle, their spirit squalid. Who would want to live in one of them?

The temptation of the sociologist is to strike an objective pose, to say judicially that the truth no doubt lies somewhere between the two extremes. But this is a case in which the mechanically judicial is a falsification; for the peculiarity of the *Shtetl* was precisely that the truth lay, not somewhere toward the middle, but only in the two extremes. The *Shtetl* (I capitalize it everywhere because it was a personality) symbolizes all Jewish life in the Exile; not a mixture which fuses into gray, but a checkered pattern of the exalted and the ignominious.

In The Three, which is the usual manner of referring to Mendelle Mocher Sforim, Yal Peretz, and Sholom Aleichem, it is the first who reproduces in sharpest contrast the extreme of *Shtetl* life; but in this he and the others of the triad, as well as most Yiddish writers, were in the ancient tradition. No other national literature has the schizophrenic quality of the Jewish, from the Bible on. The Jewish people loves and hates itself, admires and despises itself with pathological intensity. According to mood, it is God-selected and God-rejected. Certainly no other people robbed of its homeland, to which it had been directed by God Himself, and sent into exile by nations no better than itself, would go on repeating for two millennia: "Serves us right"—which is the meaning of the prayer: "Because of our sins we were exiled from our land." But then, no other people goes on existing for two thousand years after expulsion and dispersion; and no other people associates its ultimate redemption with the destiny of the human species as a whole.

In the final reckoning, however, the *Shtetl*, like the lost Jewish homeland of long ago, is seen lovingly. Today Jews feel with a special poignancy about it because it was done to death in their own time and, as it were, before their very eyes. The *Shtetl* is a martyr, and if one does not go to a cemetery to dwell on the imperfections of the departed, neither does one remember in a predominantly critical spirit a martyr whose last cries of agony still quiver in the air. Our ambivalence toward the *Shtetl* is there, we cannot rid ourselves of an immemorial national habit, but it is strongly modified by a shift toward affirmation.

Some of the nostalgia clinging to the *Shtetl* is undoubtedly connected with its rural setting, but this too in the paradoxical Jewish way. The *Shtetl* was in the countryside but not of it, as far as Jews were concerned; the earth was the Lord's, but the fullness thereof was for the non-Jews. For the Jew, the fields and forests and open spaces evoked, with their beauty, echoes of a very different time and place. His nature festivals were geared to the Palestinian climate and calendar; he celebrated regularly a harvest which he and his forebears had not gathered for sixty or seventy generations; he prayed for the "former" and the "latter" rains, phenomena of a subtropical climate, indifferent to the needs of his neighbors, whose prayers, more practical than his, pointed to a local agricultural cycle. And Nature as a whole was a rather trivial business to the *Shtetl* Jew.

Mendelle tells us of the education of a Jewish boy: "Little Shlomo had accumulated long before his *bar mitzvah* as much experience as if he were a Methuselah. Where hadn't he been and what hadn't he seen! Mesopotamia, the Tigris and Euphrates rivers, Persia and Shushan, the capital of Ahasuerus's empire, Egypt and the Nile, the deserts and the mountains. It was an experience which the children of no other people ever knew . . . He could not tell you a thing about Russia, about Poland, about Lithuania, and their peoples, laws, kings, politicians . . . But you just ask him about Og, King of Bashan, and

Sihon, King of the Amorites, and Nebuchadnezzar, King of Babylonia! Ask him about the Jordan! He knew the people who lived in tents and spoke Hebrew or Aramaic; the people who rode on mules or camels and drank water out of pitchers . . . He knew nothing concerning the fields about him, about rye, wheat, potatoes, and where his bread came from; didn't know of the existence of such things as oak, pine and fir trees; but he knew about vineyards, date palms, pomegranates, locust trees . . . He knew about the dragon and the leopard, about the turtledove and the hart that panteth after the living waters: he lived in another world."

Such an upbringing was possible in a big-city community too; but there it would have had to hold off, besides a gentile environment, a considerable body of modernizing or half-modernizing Jews, so that its course would have been less tacit and self-assured. The vain-longing for the *Shtetl* is a vain-longing for the security of its spiritual life, in which the Jew triumphed over the will of the oppressor. When the *Shtetl* submitted to non-Jewish cultural values, it took them over, absorbed them in a Jewish or Yiddish form; and this digestive capacity was the secret of its endurance.

Yiddish and its literature were as deeply fixed in the Return as were the Hebrew prayers. Despite the rich non-Zionist, anti-Zionist, and anti-nationalist literature which it developed in the late nineteenth and early twentieth centuries, and despite its revolutionary section, Yiddish meant, overwhelmingly, the tradition.

The language was a holding action. A people which was excluded from history except as its passive object, was waiting to re-enter it on the grandest scale, and the language it used reflected its expectations, based on ancient and beloved documents continuously recalled. The expectations were so long deferred that the will to help in their fulfillment became half paralyzed, but the language and its literature preserved it from complete decay. Yiddish is instinct with the certainty of an ultimate meaning in history; this one learns best from a study of the *Shtetl* in its own language.

CHAPTER X

Time Present, Place Here

❀

I

I MUST break off again, come up for air through the strata of fifty years, and remind myself where I am and at what point of time. I must take my bearings again before plunging back into the past.

The place is the Jewish homeland my people and I dreamed about, the time is the thirteenth year of its independence. The air-conditioned room I am working in looks out on the enchanting terraced garden in front of the Faculty House of the Weizmann Institute of Science. I have traveled up to Jerusalem, Haifa, Tel Aviv, and down to Beersheba; I have toured the populous valley of Jezreel, which was a grisly desolation when I first saw it, nearly forty years ago; I have looked down from the Galilean heights on the village- and farm-studded Huleh Valley, which was then a scummy, shimmering, mosquito-clouded swamp; I have threaded my confused way through distracting crowds in the cities, I have spent solitary hours of contemplation in kibbutz huts overlooking the Jordan or fronting the forbidding northern mountains; and I have returned to my double life here, the mornings and evenings given to the evocation of the past, the afternoons to my belated wooing of the power which is molding the future of the planet.

II

I said of Uncle Berel and my mother—and it could be said of my Manchester-Rumanian community and of *Shtetl* Jews generally—that "they had a deep-rooted if unformulated conviction that the world, with its privileges and triumphs, was not for the Jews until something like a Messianic transformation had taken place in mankind." The Return would not come about, the homeland would not be rebuilt, until the Jews and the world were worthy of them. But what was their dream picture of the reconstituted homeland? I don't think they had one; they had bits and suggestions for a picture that couldn't have been put together this side of eternity; the pastoral and the pious on the one hand; the magnificent on the other—if not the resplendent Temple and its sacrifices, then something like it; a land of peace—still, with its complement of warriors in the style of King David's band, for ornamental purposes, since there would be no wars; a land without poverty or crime, a land therefore without policemen or jails (Jewish jails, Jewish policemen, how utterly unthinkable!)—no thieves or swindlers, let alone, God forbid, murderers; an agricultural land, chiefly (how they yearned over "the following of the plough"!), with vineyards and orchards as well as grainfields, with locust trees and a few camels; a land of learning and, of course, rich Jewishness. As to the how, the manner in which this homeland would arise, well, they were vaguest about that; not being fundamentalists, they did not expect the literal intervention of the Messiah; all the same, their thinking was a secularized Messianism.

What would Uncle Berel say at an Independence Day

143

parade of the Israeli army, with its tanks and planes and its smart, arm-swinging ranks of men *and women* and its frantically cheering crowds of spectators? I am afraid that on this point I cannot vouch for his consistency. He would stare for some minutes open-mouthed, he would begin to chew his overhanging mustache, he would mutter into it something like: "I suppose you've got to have those things," and he would finish up by joining in the cheering like a regular *goy*. I find it harder to conjure up the reaction of my Manchester folk and of *Shtetl* people generally to the following excerpt from an Israeli newspaper:

"The lucky 40,000 soccer fans who managed to get tickets for the Italy-Israel world cup match, and the many thousands more who heard the running commentary on their radios Sunday, had holiday in their hearts for 87 minutes of the 90 minute game. For that long it seemed that Israel's amateur David would down the multimillion Italian soccer Goliath. In the 14th minute Israel surprised all by scoring first, and after 38 minutes the unbelievable happened—Israel was 2-0 up. That was at half time. In the 53rd minute the Italians crept up a point, but that only from the penalty spot, and many here still believed and prayed Israel's amateurs would hold out. But the professional training of the Italian footballers told in the end." (The tragedy of it!)

Harder still is it to picture their bafflement on finding out that all of the young people (and quite a number of the older ones) speak not a word of Yiddish. How can that be? Hebrew is the national language? Certainly! In the Holy Land it is fitting that everyone should speak Hebrew. "But our Yiddish! Our beloved *Mamme-loshen* (mother tongue)! We learned the Torah in Yiddish, we suffered and died and were faithful in Yiddish, we kept Jewishness alive

144

in Yiddish! A Jewish boy or girl in the Jewish homeland ignorant of Yiddish! It doesn't make sense."

They would find it hard to acclimatize, my old Manchester folk and the *Shtetl* Jews generally. They would have to realize that the Messiah hasn't come, and this is not the land of their dreams. It has its grainfields and orchards and vineyards and locust and date trees, but it also has its cities and factories, its criminals and policemen and jails. It has its sports and its modern army, its parliament, its diplomats, its spies, its wrangling political parties, its atheists and its religious fanatics. Sometimes I wonder whether my *rebbe* would have joined the Neturei Karta, that group of thrice-ultra-orthodox zealots which, living in Israel, is opposed to the idea of the Jewish state, unsponsored as it was by the Messiah himself, and would like to see it dissolved until his advent. On the whole, I think not; my *rebbe* was a kindly man.

But however difficult they would find it to acclimatize, they would be proud of the Jewish homeland, particularly if they had learned how it had been wrung out of adverse circumstance, and what it had done for hundreds of thousands of refugees. They would resign themselves to the panoplied choreography of statehood, the flags and parades and saluting and standing to attention, which had always seemed a little childish to them. They would adapt more or less to certain incongruities, the gasoline station that announces by its name the entrance into Samson's territory, the subway that leads to the summit of Carmel, the supermarket that is today the glory of Jerusalem.

I imagine myself taking my long-dead relatives on a tour, and there would be some incomprehensible disappointments. They would want to look on the oak of Mamre, under which Abraham sat and near which, no doubt, he erected the four-doored tent which was such a

145

sore problem for my uncle Moritz; I would have to tell them that the oak is gone and the location not identifiable. As for the cave in which the patriarchs and three of the matriarchs are buried, that is in hostile territory; so is Bethlehem, the little town to which Naomi brought Ruth the Moabitess one day in the barley season to become the wife of Boaz and the ancestress of King David, and therefore of the Messiah; so is the grave of the fourth matriarch, the most beloved of all, Rachel, who weeps for her children and will not be comforted. As for the Wailing Wall, the remnant of the Temple at which Jews prayed and wept for so many centuries, that is in a part of Jerusalem itself that is not ours.

But I would take them to the summit of Carmel where Elijah, after his contest with the prophets of Baal, heard—inaudible to everyone else—"the sound of abundance of rain" foretelling the end of the three-year drought, and bent himself to the earth and prayed mightily, and sent his servant seven times to look toward the sea, till he returned with the immortal phrase about "the cloud no bigger than a man's hand"; and I would point out to them —the smoke from the oil refineries permitting—the very spot in the valley below, where Elijah had slain the prophets of Baal who had slain all the prophets of Israel except himself. I would take them to the Valley of Ayalon where (to paraphrase Gibbon) God suspended the laws of nature for the benefit of the Israelites and caused the moon and the sun to stand still while Joshua completed the rout of the Amorites (but God was always suspending the laws of nature hereabouts, and the land is as full of miracles as a pomegranate is of seeds); and to Jaffa, the ancient Joppa, whence Jonah took ship for Tarshish and made an unscheduled submarine return to become the grudging savior of Nineveh.

But we could spend many days in godly folk reminis-

146

cence without stirring more than a stone's throw from my workroom above the garden; for the laboratories are built more or less on the site of that famous Yabneh Academy in which Yohanaan ben Zakkai and Eleazar ben Azaryah (he of the miraculous, face-saving beard) created for the Jewish people the technique of disembodied survival. A thousand years or so before them the Philistines lorded it in these parts, but having no Yohanaan ben Zakkais and no Eleazar ben Azaryahs, they perished with their physical overthrow. Samson was of course a frequent visitor here, a lover of Philistine women and a slayer of their men; King David too, but hereabouts only as fighter, never as lover. By the singlemindedness he displayed in this locality he broke the back of the Philistine power, but because he was such a shedder of blood, not even his psalms could wash him clean, and he was forbidden to rebuild the Temple on which he had set his heart.

But if they would delight in these evocations (hampered a little by blaring klaxons, screeching brakes, factory whistles, radios, plane propellers, and jets) they would delight even more in the countless Sabbath evening strollers, young and old, on roads between villages, on sea- and lake-shore, in *kibbutz* and *moshav* and city. Golden hour when the air is alive with freedom, and Jews laugh, not with the wry, sophisticated laugh of Sholom Aleichem, but with unshadowed and spontaneous laughter which declares tacitly: "We are home!" But since my ghostly tourists are after all of the Exile, their delight would be tinged with a sad musing, and not only because of memories, but of a partial, nagging awareness of extrusion.

III

I have always known of this awareness and of its cause, but they were never as clear to me as this morning, after a night of intolerable dreams and equally intolerable awakenings and fitful note-taking. For yesterday I went up to Jerusalem for my first visit to the Eichmann trial—it will certainly be my last—and it will be some time before the effects sink into their proper place.

I went, thoroughly *à contre-coeur,* and after long resistance. What for? I asked myself. Do I have to have the horror-story spelled out for me again in all its viscera-convulsing, mind-searing details? Do I have to look at the wretched thing in the glass cage, and try to reconcile a human appearance with a mephitic monstrosity? It is for others, not for me; for the millions who let it glide by them with a donation, or a sigh, or perhaps with a crafty head-shake of incredulity. Weeks and months I kept putting it off, telling myself nevertheless that I ought to go, since I so easily could, and that some day I might regret not having gone and perhaps learned something to impart to others.

But I learned nothing from it; that I am prone to nightmares I already knew, and that the story must never be forgotten I already believed. The thoughts I want to order and set down have been running through my mind for a long time, some of them for years, some since the capture of Eichmann, some since my arrival here shortly after the trial opened. In America and here I have listened to, I have read, countless discussions. I have heard untrained laymen argue hotly on the legality of the case and the competence of the court; I have heard those who conceded both object nevertheless to the way the trial was conducted. It should have been thus and so; the indictment should not have been directed solely against Germany; the nations which did so little to thwart the genocidal enterprise should have been included. The Jews themselves are not exempt; they too did less than they might have done. The trial should properly have been an indictment of the human species. The prosecutor and the judges were not equal to their task; they should have—they should have—I am not clear as to what was expected of them; perhaps a grandeur of moral utterance surpassing anything in the Bible, something that would shake the world as the Prophets themselves have failed to do. The court should have risen above the Jewish tragedy; it should have heard crying from the ground the blood of all the butchered minorities. It should have—there is no end to it.

It would be foolish to try to deal with these pretentious dissatisfactions. But there is one which will bear discussion. It did not arise from the trial; here in Israel loudly, elsewhere more softly, it was heard before; the trial brought its utterance to a focus; and it has become, it remains, a moral issue of a kind. It is concerned with the victims, not with the criminals. Why did they go like sheep to the slaughter? Why did so few of them—and these few so late —stand up like men and, knowing themselves doomed, at least exact a life for a life where they could, "take one of the butchers with them" (that is the favorite phrase)? It might not have saved any Jewish lives, but it would have cost the murderers a good many; and under such circumstances the death of the victims would not have been so ignoble, their memory not merely and not so humiliatingly pitiable.

The reproach sometimes cuts deeper. Why did the Jews "collaborate" with their destroyers? Why did they furnish lists? Why did they not simply stage, everywhere, a sitdown strike, thus making it harder (some would aver impossible) for the universal butcher to carry out his plan? As armchair generals refight, victoriously, the battles lost by generals in the field, so these critics of Jewish behavior under Hitler tell the dead what they should have done. The capacity of the Nazis for torture is ignored: that they could have placed women and children on the rack, or shot them down in the presence of husbands and fathers, or simply closed all foodshops to the Jews, makes no difference; neither does the unbelievability, at the time, of the total intention of the Nazis. "I'll tell you what you should have done. . . ."

On the part of a Jew such an appraisal may be rooted in a number of sources, all of them discreditable in some degree. His predominant feeling may be that he has been badly let down by the six million unheroic fellow Jews who perished in the camps; or he may be totally alienated from Jewish knowledge or at least the significance of the two thousand years of Jewish exile. But nowhere does this appraisal come to more revolting expression than in the slanted analysis of the ghastly tragedy offered to the public by Miss Hannah Arendt. One recoils with a quiver of pure disgust from the interpretation of the "facts," which makes the leaders of that trapped Jewry look like a scummy lot, and which leads to the general conclusion that when cowardly people are murdered they have mostly themselves to blame. Bewildered, one contrasts this stony and heartless attitude with the sensitivity and understanding of Mr. Hersey's *The Wall.*

It must however be conceded that Miss Arendt's views as expressed recently are consistent with those she expressed in 1951, when the horror story was still fresh and before she had the "facts" as presented in the Hilberg study on which she seems to rely implicitly. On persecution at large she delivered this dictum:

> Persecution of powerless or power-losing groups may not be a very pleasant spectacle,* but it does not spring from human meanness alone.

* A curious way of putting it, at once tough and mincing. I did not quite get the spirit of it until this book was in press and I read Mr. George Steiner's review of Miss Arendt's *On Revolution* (*The Reporter,* May 9,

and on the persecution of the Jews:

> Just as anti-Semites understandably desire to escape
> responsibility for their deeds, so Jews, attacked and on
> the defensive, even more understandably do not wish
> to discuss under any circumstances their share of the
> responsibility.

Hence, when we press for the outlawing of genocide, let
us not forget, when a case of genocide does occur, to look
carefully into the character of the annihilated people for
their share of the guilt. It might possibly be larger than
that of the annihilators!

Aldous Huxley tells somewhere of a devoted priest who
ministered to kidnapped Negroes on a slave ship, and reminded them of their sins. His motive was noble; he
wanted the wretched victims to feel that even in their
horrible plight they were still human, still capable of a
choice between good and evil; but it does not appear that
he regarded their sins of the past or present as a contribu-
tory element to their misfortune. The word "persecution"
loses its meaning if it is tinged with the notion of punishment—the only ground I can conceive as justifying the
suggestion that persecution does not spring from human
meanness alone. The persecutor may, and nearly always
does, consider himself the instrument of retribution,
divine or historical ("We shall be stern, but just," said Hitler), but he is not concerned with the moral improvement
of his victims. To take the contrary view in the case of the
Jews—one could say the same thing of the Armenians and
the Turks—is, however unladylike it sounds, to spit on
the grave of six million victims of human bestiality. And

1963). He says of it, *inter alia:* "Throughout this brilliant but oddly cruel
book the heart is damned." This is one of the kinder things one could
say of Miss Arendt's articles on the Eichmann trial and the murder of the
six million Jews.

lest the reader suspect, as he must, that I quote Miss Arendt out of context, let him turn to the first chapter of her *The Origins of Totalitarianism* (New York, 1951).

As to what I have called a total alienation from the significance of two thousand years of Jewish exile, let us evaluate two thousand years of Jewish exile nonresistance in the most utilitarian terms. Jewish communities knew that to resist, to rise against the oppressor, meant to be wiped out, whereas the refusal to hit back or even to take aggressive measures of defense, meant the survival of some. But the survival of the few, of "the remnant," was not an end in itself; it was the condition for the perpetuation and the continuance of the faith. Wretched and repulsive as this behavior must strike an outsider, the insider—and the rare outsider—will see in it a valor that is of the spirit as well as of the flesh.

A clear glimpse of this exile ethos is afforded by the revolt of the Warsaw ghetto when *all* hope had been wiped out. Were the Warsaw ghetto fighters (to take but one instance) of a different breed from the rest of the Jews? If so, why did they wait till there was nothing to be lost or gained before they rose on April 21, 1943? There is only one answer: until that date they accepted, though with mounting impatience, the bitter strategy which had served the Jewish people for two thousand years.

How startling it is that a non-Jew, and a German at that, should have shown the keenest and most sympathetic understanding of the Jewish exile dilemma. In his magnificent saga-Midrash, *Joseph and His Brothers,* Thomas Mann has clarified forever its nature and resolution; and to those who are troubled by it I recommend a reading and rereading, in its fullness, of the Jacob-Eliphaz episode in the first volume, *The Tales of Jacob.*

Jacob is in flight from his brother Esau, whom he has

"swindled" out of that paternal spiritual blessing which Esau would have had no use for. Eliphaz, Esau's high-spirited son, sets out in pursuit, determined to wreak venegeance on the thief. Well-armed, overwhelmingly at-tended, he overtakes his uncle, and we read:

"What happened then had touched Jacob's pride and honour more surely than anything else in all his life; it was calculated to undermine and would have undermined for-ever the dignity and self-confidence of another man. He was obliged—if he wanted to live, and that he did at all costs; not, we must remember, out of common cowardice, but because he was consecrated, because the promise and the blessing handed down from Abraham lay upon him—to try to soften by entreaties the heart of this lad, his nephew, so much younger than himself, and so much lower in station . . . to reach him through self-abasement and tears and flatteries, through whining appeals to his mag-nanimity, with a thousand pleas and excuses, in a word, by thoroughly demonstrating the fact that it was not worth Eliphaz's while to turn his sword against such a grovel-ling suppliant. He did it, he kissed the lad's feet like one frenzied, he flung whole handfuls of dust into the air to fall back on his head; his tongue ran without stint . . ."

Thomas Mann extends himself on the unpalatable scene, sparing neither Jacob nor the reader, till the latter asks: How can a man sink so low, lick the dust so enthusi-astically? Is there anything that can justify it?

We learn further how Eliphaz, half in disgust, half in embarrassment, turns from the babbling, sniveling, pros-trate figure, and contents himself with stripping Jacob of all the treasures his mother had sent along with him to win the favor of his uncle Laban in Syria. But—

"He had saved his life, his precious covenanted life, for God and the future—what were gold and cornelian to set against that? For life is all; and young Eliphaz had been even more brilliantly swindled than his father—but at what a price! Above and beyond the valuables, it had meant the loss of the whole man's honour, for how could one be more shamed than Jacob was, having bowed his head in the dust before a stripling, whining, his face smeared with dust and tears? And then? What happened straightway after the degradation?"

That happened which is unforgettably recorded as Jacob's dream of the ladder to heaven and the ascending and descending angels, for the place was Beth-El, and here Jacob lay down to sleep . . .

"Then it was that high matters came to pass; then truly, toward midnight, after some hours of profound slumber, his head was lifted up from every ignominy, even to the countenance of the Most High, wherein mingled all of the royal and of the divine which his soul had ever compassed in its imaginings; which that soul then, humbled, yet smiling privily in its abasement, erected for its own strengthening and consolation in the space of its dreams . . ."

I am not suggesting, even remotely, that all Jews who vainly or successfully have licked the boots of their murderous oppressors have been Jacobs; it is enough to consider how for two millennia a people endured, between precarious respites, all the cruelties and humiliations that man can endure, and set its teeth to survive *together with its dream*. To thousands of Israelis, and particularly to *sabras* (the native-born) the Exile, the bi-millennial stretch between Bar Kochba and Ben Gurion, is something to be "repressed"; it offends their honor. *They* fought against immense odds, put the life of the new homeland to the hazard, and won. They do not reflect that the chances in a declared war, a challenge taken up, in the Exile, were not one in a million. They forget that they owe their existence to the obstinate passivity of their forefathers who, cringing, ran the gauntlet between rows of murderers, hugging under their coats the precious burden which they delivered at its destination in the fullness of time.

Many *sabras* despise Yiddish as a language because it is the symbol as well as the creation and mirror of the Exile and its long disgrace; of Yiddish as the custodian of the Jewish idea they have no concept, and of the richness of experience distilled into it no inkling.

There was a time, thirty and forty and fifty years ago, when young zealots in the evolving homeland demonstrated against Yiddish, rebuked users of it in public places, bade them use Hebrew or presumably, if they knew only Yiddish, to be silent except when at home. There was no objection to the use of other languages; Yiddish represented the traumatic memory to be effaced. It is true that the climate in the country has changed; Yiddish speakers are free from molestation, Yiddish periodicals—among them *Die Goldene Keit,* one of the best we have ever had—are common, Yiddish theatrical performances are frequent. But the attitude toward exilic Jewry, past and present, remains, among many of the young, and some of the old, negative and impatient; and the achievements of exilic Jewry are squeezed into insignificance between the grandeur of ancient and the pride of modern Israel. There is tolerance of Yiddish only because Hebrew is so firmly established; but what Yiddish represents is contemptuously dismissed.

This belittlement of the travail of sixty generations may be linked to a passing hubris; if so, it need not trouble us. But if it is the symptom of a growing division in the identity of the Jewish people, the spiritual purpose of the re-creation of Israel may be long obscured and perhaps suffer permanent eclipse. The Exile is as meaningful a part of Jewish history as the Homeland; to assume that it was an aberration, a nightmare without values, is to lop off more than half of Jewish history and to declare that Jewish persistence was nothing more than an incomprehensibly extended exercise in low cunning which it would be decent to forget. A Jewish state which does not absorb the affirmative part of the Exile is not true even to the remote past in which it purports to find its justification, for that remote past foretold the Exile and bade the Jewish people learn from it.

Hence the touch of reserve on the faces, the reflective hesitance in the voices, of my imaginary visitors. In their inarticulate way—for I am thinking still of *amcho,* the plebs—they feel that they were not nobodies and nullities. They had something which derived from Sinai and the Prophets, and that something, defaced as it was, they conserved for the Homeland-to-be. The Homeland-in-being is a wonderful thing surely; but there were and are Jewish moral values in the Exile which the Homeland can ignore only at its peril. And as I take my bearings now, looking back over fifty years of Israel's growth, I imagine that the humble plaint I am formulating for my relatives is the crucial spiritual problem before Israel.

PART 2

❊

Cities and Men

CHAPTER XI

The Eruption

❀

HE CITY of Paris has been a recurrent marker in
my life. I was there first from my fifth to my sixth year in
transit to England with my family; a second time in the
summer of 1914; a third from 1919 to 1920, during and
following the negotiations of the Versailles peace treaty;
a fourth in the summer of 1939, at the outbreak of the
Second World War. These are the sojourns with significance; there have also been many brief visits.

I give the first place to my 1914 sojourn, which occurred
in my twentieth year, when I left Manchester for Paris
because I was going to be a Writer. I did not make the
decision to be a Writer; it had made itself in my boyhood,
probably in Miss Clarke's time. I could of course have
been a writer anywhere, but a Writer only in Paris. What
kind of Writing was I going to do? Well, poetry, novels,
essays, short stories, plays—I was good at everything. I was
prepared to wait for recognition, even anxious to; immediate success would have been a reflection on my genius.
I did not, however, aspire to the supreme tribute of lifelong starvation and obscurity; a year or two in a garret
would satisfy my self-esteem and add the indispensable
cachet to my life story.

From this point of view the beginning was inauspicious; I did not come within hailing distance of starvation. The day after my arrival in Paris in June 1914, with two shillings or so in my pocket, I was able to write home that I was profitably employed not by one newspaper but by two, and under conditions—which I did not describe— the most conducive to my literary freedom. I was, in fact, selling the Paris editions of *The Daily Mail* and The *New York Herald* mornings at the Gare St. Lazare where the suburban trains brought in the American and English commuters. I cleared seven or eight francs a day for an hour's work (nearer three with the coming and going), and the rest of the day I was free to read, write, gulp in life, invoke the ghosts of Murger and de Musset and con- gratulate humanity and myself on our successful rendezvous. The sinister omen escaped my attention: selling newspapers in one's youth *might* be the prologue to the acquisition of great wealth, the tradition did not link it with high literary achievement.

Thirty-five to forty francs a week and no work on Saturdays and Sundays! It was more than a competence in the Paris of that time; it was affluence. At 33 rue des Ecoles, just off the boulevard St. Michel—beg pardon, the Boul' Miche' (and where else would I be living?)—I paid seven francs a week for a room on the fifth floor, and had my shoes shined every morning, no doubt to their great astonishment, unaccustomed as they were to more than a flick of the brush every week or two. Breakfast, a buttered croissant and coffee, was fifteen centimes; lunch eighty, with tip; supper a franc ten, *pain à discrétion* (all the bread you wanted). Total, rent included, three francs five centimes a day, leaving me with a discretionary surplus, as I think they call it, of over two francs a day. Newspapers cost me nothing, I read my own. But there was in the France of those days a kind of Haldemann Julius enterprise, the French classics in newspaper form at ten centimes each, and I bought and devoured three or four a week. What else did I need? Writing paper and pencils and, yes, a bottle of *pinard* (cheap table wine) daily, at seventy-five centimes. I could also afford an evening *apéritif*.

Every morning, after work, I wrote; and every afternoon, except when it rained, I lay in the grass in the Jardin du Luxembourg and read, and sipped, and made notes, or broke off to meditate, or to watch the puppet showman delight an audience of juveniles in the charge of mothers and nurses with a performance of *Jean le Redoutable*. I would have liked to come close enough to enjoy the show itself, but I was ashamed to betray my infantile taste, and I would have had to drop something in the puppeteer's hat. On rainy days, I was perched in my garret—infinite room in a nutshell. And there were times when I needed infinite room, when I felt I was about to explode with sheer joy into the dimensions of a sizable nebula.

There was a history behind that onset of euphoria. I had just finished college, that is, I had come to the end of the three-year scholarship awarded me by the city of Manchester, and I had not taken a degree. Not that I had been wanting in application; it was only that I had applied myself with immense if unsystematic industry to anything but the subjects I had enrolled for (French perhaps an exception). I had learned by heart scores of pages of poetry, not one page of physics formulas; I had read Shaw, Wells, Bennett, Galsworthy, Conrad, Rolland, Hamsun, Hauptmann, instead of *Beowulf* and Langland. I had had fits of Plato, Kant, Bradley, Hume, and there was my political activity. All this not because physics or

Beowulf bored me, but because I was in reaction from competitive study.

From my thirteenth year on, when I got my scholarship to high school, I had hounded myself for good marks because there was no other road for me to an education. At fifteen I had been awarded a "bursary" of fifteen pounds a year for two years; without that six shillings a week I might have had to leave school. I used only one year of the bursary, for at sixteen I won the *Grand Prix* of our junior academic world, three years at the University with sixty pounds a year, enough to keep me and pay for my books. By that time my soul had become warped with the anguish of waiting for examination results.

This is not an exaggeration. When even today I read of a student committing suicide because of failure in an examination, a throb of retroactive terror goes through me. I remember coming home from important examinations, creeping upstairs and lying down on my bed sick in all my body. Or I would walk for hours in unfamiliar streets, muttering. I had failed! My papers had been starred with idiotic answers, and they sprang up before me the moment I left the examination hall. On bad nights I still have nightmares of a peculiar kind which have their origin in that post-examination misery, and I come out of them in a sweat. When, a few years ago, I saw a similar experience portrayed with great skill in *Wild Strawberries,* I trembled with terror.

I did not actually fail at the university; it was simply that my credits did not add up to a degree, and at the time it seemed a terrible thing to me that I should have to go through life without a B.A. after my name. Against this, however, and overwhelming it completely, was my graduation into freedom. I was no longer a schoolboy, watched and weighed and graded at regular intervals. The world was my examiner now, and I didn't have to be *better* than anyone now; I just had to do my best.

There was another reason for my happiness, deeper, revealed to me later. I was coming out of the phase of philosophic materialism I have described, alien to my type of mind. I had never accepted it completely or consistently, but there had been enough of it to bring on periodic depressions. My love of poetry was one expression of my rejection of it. I was going to find my spiritual roots before long, but for the time being I was at large, bursting with unchanneled mental energies and reacting to intimations of approaching self-discovery. Some years were to pass before I committed myself to Jewishness, much nourishment had to come up from the roots; I had to learn much in the way of Yiddish and Hebrew and Jewish history, subjects in which I was an illiterate. Thus, my first published books were not on Jewish themes; those waited for almost a decade.

When I look back at those 1914 summer months in Paris, it seems to me that all unsuspecting I was acting out in person a charade of the general self-deception of the time. I was living blithely in a world that was about to burst apart, never to be reassembled. Under our feet tremendous pressures were at the detonation point, and not the slightest tremor reached our consciousness. There were of course criers of doom; but there always are, and one never knows when the cries are timely. There are always Columbuses, real and fake, and they look alike. If you pick out a real one it is largely by luck, which you later represent as shrewdness, or vision. So one plays it safe, one closes one's ears, and as a rule one is of course right. It seems that thus far human history has been unable to proceed in any other fashion. Besides, even the Columbuses themselves never know where they are going.

In that fatuous world of June and July 1914, so complacent, so self-assured, in that massively self-deluding world, I was playing my own silly little game of make-believe. Murger and de Musset! Why, their world was deader than a doornail in 1914—that is, if it had ever been alive. The Latin Quarter, like its imitators everywhere, was largely a sham; the streets swarmed with poets, painters, sculptors, musicians, writers; perhaps one in a thousand meant business. As with the Columbuses and the political prophets, there was no distinguishing between the young dedicated artificer and the windbag. I ought to add that five years later, when I was again in Paris, I still believed for a while that to be a Writer one simply *had* to be in Paris.

I have often wondered why my childhood year in Paris, in 1900 and 1901, has left with me nothing more than factual little memories, unattended by nostalgia. We were very poor there, but not poorer than during our first year or two in Manchester. I remember going in 1914 to the rue Joseph Dijon, in the Clignan court district, where we had lived, but I was not stirred. We had occupied a room and a half on the ground floor of Number 23; in the half room at the front my father had worked and slept; in the living room at the back my mother and the four children had slept. My mother used to take in sewing and work late into the night; I can still see the shadow of her hand sweep up and down the wall. Hannah and I used to get free lunches at school (Dora was too young for school) and I loathed them; they made me sick—all except the potato soup, and how relieved I was when that came round.

I must have known a lot of French by the time we went to England, but it faded out; I had to learn it all over again, but as with my Yiddish, there was no doubt a permanent residue. Blocks of meaningless syllables were lodged in my mind, such as my brother Mendel saying: *"Lepattronnaypalla,"* which I have deciphered as *"le patron n'est pas là."* There was a snowfall, and we sang in school:

> *Larnairzher, larnairzher,*
> *Tombofflonker, tombofflonker*

That, I have decided, must have been:

> *La neige, la neige*
> *Tombe en flocons, tombe en flocons*

One look at the rue Joseph Dijon was enough. I cannot recall having gone that summer to the Louvre, or the Tour Eiffel, or the Sacré Coeur, or any other of the sights. My pictures are of the entrances to the Gare St. Lazare, of my tiny room, of the swarming boulevard St. Michel, and above all of the lawns in the Luxembourg Gardens; and all of them are etched in my mind with a surrealistic sharpness which has survived all subsequent returns to them.

When the explosion came, its significance was, as everyone remembers or has read, recognized or guessed at by only a few. War! Ridiculous and unbelievable! All (as we chanted in chorus) because of a shot fired in Sarajevo; because of bumbling, panicky politicians, Austrian, German, Russian, French, English, prisoners of antiquated modes of thought, with antiquated institutions called armies at their command. Hadn't Norman Angell just proved conclusively in *The Great Illusion* that war was an anachronism, as costly to the victor as to the vanquished, and that colonies were liabilities? I myself had made many speeches to that effect to my socialist audiences. This thing was simply inadmissible. In a few weeks, a few months at the outside, the peoples would come to their senses; the damned foolishness would be over by Christmas; the workers would rise in their might; we would take up where we had left off. You couldn't stop the world's progress, you know.

My indiscriminate memory retains words, phrases, scenes, incidents. At street corners crowds on their way to work in the early morning would stop for a short song-fest (a lovely Parisian custom) led by a man on a box selling sheet music. One of the instantaneous successes of that time is still with me.

> *Un bruit frappe l'espace,*
> *C'est celui du canon,*
> *Qui vient avec audace*
> *Troubler les nations.*
> *Vont-ils longtemps,*
> *Ces Allemands,*
> *Nous entraîner vers la fournaise?*
> *Mais sans broncher*
> *Sachons marcher*
> *Quand retentit la Marseillaise!*

On the wall of the Sarah Bernhardt theater someone had scribbled in chalk:

> *Aux abeilles les fleurs,*
> *Aux Français l'honneur;*
> *Et pour ne rien perdre*
> *Aux Allemands la m——.*

A paroxysm of war fever gripped the country, or at least the city, which I was able to observe at first hand. Good God! What was happening to common sense, to the working class, to civilization, to my *Vie de Bohême?*

On the evening of August 2 I sat at an outdoor café

166

on the boulevard des Italiens. I had been sitting at another café nearby, a day or two earlier, when I heard the shot that killed Jean Jaurès, the great socialist, one of my idols, for his opposition to the extension of the conscription period. On that second evening I was remembering the agitation that boiled along the streets, the incredulousness, the rage—and with them the consolatory cries: "This does it! This will show the world what kind of people warmongers are. Jaurès! With your martyr's death you have crowned your life work. There will be no more war!" This I was remembering, and war was here.

A black, roaring mass came down on us like a flood from the direction of the Porte St. Martin. It stretched from wall to wall, sweeping back the traffic, upsetting, smashing, and trampling on chairs and tables, carrying along those who did not escape into doorways or side streets. A tremendous rhythmic howling went up from it:

Hein-hein-hein! Hoo! Hoo!
Hein-hein-hein! Hoo! Hoo!

(The rhythm was that of *Al-gé-rie Française!*)

I was not among those that escaped. I wanted to know what this thing was, and what the howling meant. I found myself linked arm in arm with two young Frenchmen, of whom I remember only the one on the right, an undersized boy, with thin face and bulging eyes.

The

Hein-hein-hein! Hoo! Hoo!

resolved itself into:

A Berlin! Tous! Tous!

and out of politeness, out of timidity, out of whatever it was, I began to chant with them, feeling like a fool.

167

A Berlin! Tous! Tous!

As we drew close to the Place de l'Opéra, another chorus swelled on us from behind, mingling with ours and overwhelming it. At first it sounded like:

Ombébého! Ombébého! Ombé:
Ombébého! Ombébého! Ombé!

That resolved itself into:

Conspuez Guillaume! Conspuez Guillaume! Conspuez!

A curious and beastly tickling of excitement, which made me feel like an even bigger fool, was manifesting itself in my viscera. The boy on my right flung his head from side to side. In another minute or two, I thought, I too was going to have a fit. As we turned off into the rue Royale, a third chorus was sent forward to us from the rear:

C'est l'Alsace et la Lorraine,
C'est l'Alsace qu'il nous faut!
Ah-ah-ah-oh!

Other crowds, converging from the Left Bank and down the Champs Elysées, joined with ours in the Place de la Concorde, and a wild demonstration was staged before the statue of Strassburg, which had been in mourning for over fifty years.

I had been at demonstrations before, election crowds and political rallies. I remember how, when it was a question of increasing the Royal Navy by eight battleships, there was great agitation, and at one very large political rally a speaker who opposed the increase was silenced for several minutes by an audience which chanted nothing but:

We want eight!
And we won't wait!

I remember other, similar occasions, but I had never
known anything quite like this. The beastly tickling in
my stomach was spreading through me; it threatened to
develop into a maniacal seizure. I fought it down, I fought
it back, repeating to myself something like: "Idiot! You
need Alsace and Lorraine like a hole in the head!" And
it was amazing how this obvious fact refused to stay put
in front of my mind, how it kept wriggling away out of
my grip, as if it suffered acute anguish when it was looked
at.

The mob! That was where I first met it in its naked
form. The mob! At its most "useful" it is like a gangster
whom we hire to rid us of another gangster, and who
takes over in his place, remaining a gangster still.

I am prone to read premonitions into my memories; I
may be wrong in thinking that this incident in Paris
gave me my first conscious feel of mob psychology; but
I cannot be wrong in thinking that the incident was to
stand out for me in years to come as the prototype of all
the mob scenes, all the mob forces, that have been involved
in the shaping of recent history. Not that the mob is a
new thing. Moses several thousands of years ago sternly
warned his people against it! "Thou shalt not follow a
multitude to do evil." He did not, by way of balance,
issue the positive command: "Thou shalt follow a multitude to do good." Goodness cannot issue from mob in-
toxication.

Before the twentieth century, mob manipulation had
not become a science, with psychologists and scenarists
at its command. What I saw in Paris that evening was
primitive and, I believe, relatively spontaneous. What we
have seen and heard of since then in the way of mobs is

almost in another category; and what our children and grandchildren may yet see is something we seldom think of; for though there is much proper concern about the feeding and housing of a world population of six billion, or ten billion, little thought is given to guarding against mob psychology when America will have a population of half a billion and China of a billion and a half.

I used to think that creators of mob psychologies—and for that matter nearly all those who held what I considered reactionary views—were consciously wicked men, *salauds* (sons-of-bitches, Sartre's favorite word). I was still of that conviction five years later, during my second long stay in Paris, in 1919, when in American uniform, I was working in the Hôtel Crillon, one of the headquarters of the peace delegations. But I was myself in a mood of mob enthusiasm for Wilson and the League of Nations, and of hatred of Clemenceau and Lloyd George (Orlando made no impression on me). I had a genuine personal hatred of Lloyd George for his Khaki Election campaign, held soon after the victory (Hitler was to write admiringly of Lloyd George as a master demagogue, in *Mein Kampf*). But the chief focus of my fury and contempt was a certain Sir Eric Geddes, one of Lloyd George's lieutenants, because of the powerful slogan he coined at the time: "We're going to squeeze the Germans until the pips squeak!"

That stunned me. I held Germany to be more guilty than the Allies, I thought some reparation was due if only in token of this fact, but I asked: "What kind of man can this Geddes be? What does he think he's up to, and what kind of contribution does he think he's making to the stabilization of Europe and the world after 'the war to end war'?"

These were rhetorical questions. I had the answers; he was a wicked man, a low man. He did not see himself making, he did not want to make, a contribution to the

stabilization of Europe and the world. On the contrary.
. . . I thought: I'd like to get hold of that man; I'd like to
look him straight in the eye and ask him: "What the hell
are you driving at, Sir?"

But there wasn't much likelihood that I would ever get
hold of Sir Eric Geddes; I was a sergeant in the A.E.F.,
and he was a Knight and a Minister in His Britannic
Majesty's Government.

Life, in the peculiar way it has, arranged a meeting. I
had a long and friendly chat with Sir Eric Geddes on
Christmas eve, 1933, in Khartoum. We had flown up together from Johannesburg, and I sat with him for an hour
or so before dinner. He was an attractive and knowledge-
able man. I had been watching him for three days, ad-
miring his massive head, his unself-consciousness, his
graceful carriage. He talked easily, a man secure in achievement and reputation, first about the oddity of the scene—
Christmas decorations near the equator and black men
hanging up artificial holly. "Though after all," he said,
"the Christian part of Christmas originated nearer the
equator than we usually remember." Then he spoke about
Christmases he had observed in other parts of the world.
He boasted pleasantly: "I've been in every one of your
forty-eight states." A man of wide experience, solid intelligence, admirable culture, serious, personable, attractive. A wicked, low man? A *salaud?* Ridiculous! I turned
the conversation strategically to the need of a supranational outlook on world affairs.

"Oh, yes," he said. "We must have a new system."

"Especially in our teaching of the public," I suggested.

"In that above all."

I had my opening. "Sir Eric," I said, "may I ask you a
rather personal question which goes back a number of
years?"

He looked a little astonished. "By all means."

"In the Khaki Election you coined a slogan: 'We're going to squeeze the Germans till the pips squeak.' What were you thinking of?"

He leaned back and laughed delightedly. "You know, I've been asked that question, one way or another, several times. I didn't think I'd meet it in Khartoum."

"And what did you answer, Sir Eric?"

"I answered: 'Yes, wasn't that a perfectly silly thing to say!' "

I didn't know what to make of that. In a way, I still don't. There is something about it so disarming—in the literal sense of the word. I wonder what I would have felt and said if I had got that answer from Sir Eric in 1919.

In those days life and human beings and the course of history didn't look to me as complicated and baffling and recalcitrant as they do now. My optimisms of early 1914 had not only survived the Great War, they were livelier and more self-assured than ever. Mankind had at last learned its lesson. A benevolent supranational organization was going to take over the management of human affairs, the Clemenceaus and Lloyd Georges and Sir Erics and Senator Lodges notwithstanding. Yes, a new era was dawning. Little nations as well as big ones, the Jews and all other peoples, were to have their wrongs righted, their future secured, by a high-minded World Authority. There would of course be an interim period of turbulence here and there, but that was only natural.

Chaim Weizmann was then in Paris, heading the delegation that was presenting the Zionist cause to a sympathetic Peace Conference. He was by then—and would remain for the rest of his life—a world figure. I saw him once or twice at a distance, and my heart swelled with pride. (I did not dare to approach him; I took it for granted that he had forgotten me, and was glad of it.) This man was the architect of the Balfour Declaration of 1917; if the Jewish claim to a homeland was now on the international *ordre du jour,* Weizmann's role in placing it there overshadowed everyone else's. But the homeland was not all. The Jewish minorities of Eastern Europe, like all other substantial minorities, were to be safeguarded by international law in the enjoyment of their cultural identities. What more could one ask?

To be sure, there had been murderous outbreaks against the Jews in Poland, and it made one sick that after more than a century of foreign occupation and oppression a country should celebrate in this fashion the new-found freedom which others had bestowed on it. But I was willing to allow for a turbulent interim period. Pockets of unregenerate prewar viciousness, backwardness, and stupidity were bound to linger here and there. They would soon be flushed out by the triumphant forces of progress. I wince as I set down this bombast; but that is the way I thought and talked.

Two important episodes belong to that Paris time: a seven-week spell as secretary-interpreter on the Polish Pogrom Commission headed by Henry Morgenthau senior; a twelve-month spell as interpreter on the Reparations Commissions in Berlin and Vienna. The visit to Poland fell within the period of my army service; on the Reparations Commissions I worked as a civilian. Each Commission separately strengthened me in the conviction, long since abandoned, that the world's troubles come solely from the wickedness of men at the top.

I was demobilized in Paris in September 1919, and together with an army buddy opened, at 19 rue St. Roche, a secretarial service called The Franco-American Public Stenographer. Paris was then full of American businessmen, and we made good money. The stenography I learned for the enterprise came in handy when I got a job as interpreter on the Reparations Commission. Simultaneous translation over a transistor system was of course unknown then. Each speaker at an international conference had his say, in shorter or longer pieces; the interpreter took it down and gave it out in one of the official languages. It was exhilarating work, full of rapid-fire and tricky linguistic challenges; it was also very well paid.

But that was not why I took it on. The writing for which I had had myself demobilized in Paris had come to a dead end. The Left Bank, which was then assembling its expatriates of the American "lost generation," had become tiresome. I was fed up with the blather at the Coupole and the Café du Dôme. My experience with the Polish Pogrom Commission—which I shall describe in detail—had shaken me up badly; I was beginning to feel that the Jewish problem, like many others, was not by a long way on the point of solution: the wickedness of men in power symbolized a far greater obstacle than I had imagined, and Lord Acton had been only too right. My experience on the Reparations Commission confirmed my pessimism.

The officials whom it was my duty to interpret for in French and English were not in the front rank of the famous. I never heard again of Sir Philip Goodenough of England, or of Dr. Zaghradnik of Czechoslovakia, or of M. Tsouderos of Greece, unless the last is the one who became Prime Minister. They were intelligent men; their work was important; but my memory and my notes do not testify to a single exchange of views that could by a generous estimate be considered on a level either with their capacities or with the seriousness of the time. I recall much squabbling over the allocation of loot, precedence, and credit for victory. I recall an atmosphere of excessive

nationalist sensitivity, and of an indifference to the condition of the vanquished. And I recall a certain M.
Klobukowski.

M. Klobukowski was an elderly, pink-faced, white-
mustachioed French Assistant-Minister who came to us
from Paris to discuss an Austrian petition for a downward
revision of the costs of the Reparations Commission. M.
Klobukowski summed up his refusal with Gallic Charm:
*"Messieurs, j'ai essayé de mal dîner à Vienne, mais je n'ai
pas réussi*—I have tried to dine badly in Vienna, and I
have failed." The Austrian kroner had climbed to the ten-
thousand-per-dollar mark and was poised for its subsequent flight into the billions; at the Bristol Hotel, at flashy
cafés like Tonello's and Sacher's, the hangouts of the
Schieber (black-market profiteers) and foreign correspond-
ents, one did indeed fare luxuriously for next to nothing
in foreign exchange; but the streets of Vienna swarmed
with beggars, and a blight of hunger and hopelessness lay
on the city. M. Klobukowski had *tried* to dine badly in
Vienna, and had failed. It was not the refusal of the petition that horrified me; it was the blasted wickedness of
the form. I choked when I had to interpret.

The last of my significant contacts with Paris was in
August 1939, not a sojourn but a five-day pause in transit.
The New York *Post* had commissioned me to write, from
on board, the story of one of the boats laden with Jewish
refugees which were crawling over the Mediterranean,
forbidden to make port in Palestine or anywhere else. I
got to Paris the day the Hitler-Stalin pact was signed, and
my assignment collapsed. Nobody would be interested in
the story. There was barely time to run down to Basle,
where the Zionist Congress was closing its sessions, and
to get back to London via Paris.

In the Paris of August 1939 there were no demonstrations like those that flared up in 1914, no *hein-hein-hein hoo! hoo!,* no madness. Even before the blackout was ordered, no evening crowds congregated in the boulevards or the Place de la Concorde. I saw only little knots of people, for the most part silent, before the offices of *Paris Soir* and *Le Matin,* scanning the bulletins. I saw scrawlings on the walls: *Mieux vaut Hitler que Blum*—better Hitler than Leon Blum." In London no singing of Tipperary. 1939 was reaping what the years since 1918 had sown.

I go back to fill a hiatus. From my Paris visit of 1914 I returned to Manchester late in August, when the Germans were at the Marne and the government was preparing to evacuate to Bordeaux. (It got there in 1940. Bordeaux! It was only a name to me then, but I was to spend the better part of a year there, 1918–1919, attached to GII, counterespionage.) I managed to get on one of the last trains permitted to leave Paris for the north, and during the go-stop-go-stop journey I saw the beginnings of that hideous phenomenon which has since then become a universal commonplace—a population in flight ("fleeing from the foreign faces and the foreign swords"), desperate men and women, weeping children, jammed railroad stations and carriages, and bundles, bundles, bundles, baskets, pillows, bottles, pots and pans and kettles and toys. A dissolving world—but only a miniature of what was to be a quarter of a century later. And in Calais I saw the famous London buses being rushed to the front. Some of the buses had advertisements running along the top, *Potash and Perlmutter,* Montague Glass's play, the hit of that season; and crowds lining the streets of Calais cheered them on with: *"Vive Potash! Vive Perlmoutaire!"*

In the Paris of August 1914, I also saw the beginning of something as symptomatic of later calamity as the refugees, namely, the bigger and better queues. Oh, that waiting in loathsome *couloirs,* that going from office to office, that subjection to jack-in-offices! I learned a new law: Put a man behind a desk and he'll want the world to stand in line.

Three miserable months ensued for me. It is easy to say: "I was a pacifist and refused to join up." It was not so easy to sustain the refusal. I doubt whether my "principles" were determinant; a powerful deterrent was pride, the dread of ridicule: "Look at him! The socialist-pacifist, the Norman Angellite! One drum roll and he's off!" Self-ridicule and the ridicule of others. I was therefore the more scornful of fellow-socialists who defected. And all the time there was a tug at the heart to take the irrevocable step, to be done with the suspicion that I was simply a coward. And then again, on the other hand: "It'll all be over by Christmas anyhow."

And, oddly enough, I was becoming more Jewish in my feelings all the time. There was no road-to-Damascus conversion, only a steady deepening of conviction, or pre-conviction. I won't try to psychoanalyze myself; I only make a guess that in the big upset my fundamental values were beginning to assert themselves.

I got a clerical job. September and October passed. "Next spring" took the place of Christmas as the terminal of the war; I grew more restive, more irresolute. My mother urged me to go to America; my father said: "The sons of the noblest English families are lying in the trenches." There was discord in the house. I quarreled with my father, argued socialism with him in my pidgin Yiddish, and exchanged insults with him. My quarrels with my father had something to do with my final decision.

177

My father was no longer a shoemaker. He had opened a shoeshop on Bury New Road and had failed; he had opened a grocery shop on Sussex Street and had failed; now he was working as a presser in a large clothing factory in which my two older brothers were the managers. The factory was flourishing on war orders, and my father, now in his fifties, was making more money than ever before in his life, but under a terrible physical strain (all the members of my family have been addicted to overwork). He very much wanted to have a son of his in the army, a renewal of himself. When I came home on leave from France in December 1919, in my American uniform, he could not take his eyes off me. He kept repeating, dreamily: *"Der serjent, der serjent."* He would not believe that I had seen no fighting, that in France I had been transferred from the infantry to Intelligence. He would have it that I was suppressing, lest it come to my mother's ears, participation in desperate melees from which—since there was no evidence of a wound—I had emerged miraculously unscathed.

Well, then, I left for America on the S.S. *Adriatic* on November 14, 1914. Incredible as it may sound today, all I had to do was buy a ticket (third class, five pounds—a little less than thirty dollars) and get on the boat; no quotas, no interviews, no forms, no consulates, no passport, no visa. I was to be in America for a few months, a year at the outset. Then I would come back and take up as if nothing had happened. I did not come back, except for visits over the years.

CHAPTER XII

Chaim Weizmann

❀

I

THE MANCHESTER of my boyhood was the world-
renowned center of the cotton-goods trade. "Cottonopolis"
it called itself, and was; its overseas rivals, in New England
and Japan, were only flexing their muscles in those days.
In the factory areas of Manchester and of the towns ringing it you could hear, mornings and evenings, the rush of
the cataracts of wooden clogs—the weavers going to and
from work. It was said that on a clear Sunday morning
ten thousand factory chimneys could be counted from the
top of the Town Hall tower in Albert Square; the grimi-
ness of the tower, as of every other building, was strong
supporting testimony.

But Manchester had cultural eminence, too. It was the
home of the famous Horniman Repertoire Theatre, the
joint product of Horniman's Tea and Miss Horniman's
passion for the stage; it was the home of the Hallé Con-
certs, of *The Manchester Guardian,* second in reputation,
if second at all, to *The London Times,* and of Manchester
University, the roster of whose faculty carried names
which still echo in the world of science and the humanities.

Ernest Rutherford taught physics there, and Niels Bohr
was his assistant. Henry Moseley, the young genius who

was killed in the First World War, had also worked there under Rutherford. Flinders Petrie lectured on Egyptology, and James Frazer of *The Golden Bough* came over occasionally from the sister university of Liverpool to lecture on anthropology. Samuel Alexander taught philosophy; he was already a name, though he had not yet published his *Time, Space and Deity*. Arthur Schuster and Chaim Weizmann and the younger Perkins taught chemistry, and Horace Lamb mathematics.

I can always cause a little flutter in scientific company by mentioning casually that I studied physics under Ernest Rutherford ("And did you once see Shelley plain?"). True, Rutherford taught the old, classical physics; the revolutionary experiments he was then conducting on the structure of the atom were too new to be offered to his students; Einstein's Special Theory of Relativity had already been published, but not his General Theory; the Bohr model of the atom (itself now called classical) had not yet been given to the world; the quantum was known, but quantum mechanics was still a long way off. And yet —physics under Rutherford! Something must have rubbed off on me. I am not believed when I deny it. But Rutherford was one of my many lost opportunities. All I have of him is a personal recollection: a burly, genial man, easily moved to laughter, and a superb teacher, holding, with a single exception, the attention of his large class by force of personality and ingenuity of exposition. I have tried to explain the source of my resistance to him, perhaps too kindly; but there it was. To top it all, I was chosen by the class to express its pride and gratification when he returned from receiving his knighthood (he became Lord Rutherford later); a more incongruous choice could hardly have been imagined.

Perkins and Schuster I did not meet; if I heard Frazer lecture, as is likely, I have forgotten him, and of Flinders

Petrie I have only the dimmest recollection. I attended one class under Horace Lamb with no benefit whatsoever, and I remember a mild and gentle spirit detached from this world and from his students, who complained that he confided his expositions to the blackboard, not to them. My English teacher, Herford, is also a remote figure, but Samuel Alexander, whom I met once or twice, stands, or rather walks and rides, clearly before me. It was more a shamble than a walk, and the sight of him on a bicycle, familiar though it was, moved the beholders to mirth and solicitude. He was a big, stooping man with a huge beard, and looked like a cross between an old clo'man and a Hebrew Prophet. He rode his bicycle meditatively, on the sidewalk as often as not, miraculous in balance and in escape from collisions. We pointed to him affectionately as our specimen, the finest extant, and the finest in university history since Hegel, of the absent-minded professor. It was told of him that a policeman once asked him gently to ride off the sidewalk onto the traffic level, and was waved off with the dreamy reply: "Not now, I have just found God." It was also told that he was the owner of a metaphysical dog by the name of Griff, short for the German *Begriff* (concept).

I could have known him better, for he was accessible to all students, but I was too raw and too conceited to use the opportunity, which never came again. Another opportunity which I neglected at the time, and which came my way again, to my life's enrichment, was Chaim Weizmann.

II

I made my first contact with him when I enrolled in one of his chemistry courses, and at the interview I was too nervous to retain a clear picture of him. He examined me briefly and suggested that I sit in on one or two of his lectures. I remember, however, my astonishment that a man with such a heavy Russian-Jewish accent should be a chemistry professor. I was not thinking of discrimination; I just could not reconcile Yiddish with chemistry or anything else modern and scientific. I must have supposed that an adult mind tinctured with Yiddish had been permanently affected. I could not follow his lectures and I put it down to his accent, which, curiously enough, was no obstacle to the other students. At his suggestion I changed to physics under Rutherford, whose accent was colonial but otherwise impeccable; as we have seen, this linguistic improvement was not reflected in my phvsics studies.

I met Weizmann again two years later in the house of Isaiah Wassilevsky, the Hebrew teacher who introduced me to Bialik's Yiddish poetry. The memory of this encounter is uncomfortable and uneven; vivid patches alternate with areas faded almost into invisibility. I see the room, the armchair under the window in which Weizmann is seated; I see the bookshelves and the table; I hear his voice, low-pitched, guttural, slyly good-natured. But I cannot remember why I was there, accidentally or by arrangement, and sometimes it is not Wassilevsky who hovers in the background, but Massel, the Hebrew poet, who also lived in that area; and I cannot remember being reintroduced to Weizmann, or even his noticing me, let alone addressing a remark to me. Most vivid is my recollection that I wanted to be rude to him, and, as I already knew him to be a prominent Zionist, tell him that I considered the Zionist movement a paltry, shabby affair, morally indefensible and intellectually beneath contempt. This need not mean that I was then in one of my violent anti-Jewish phases. Perhaps I do not remember being noticed or addressed because I thought at the time that he did not recognize me; and perhaps I thought he did recognize me and was sparing me the embarrassment of a tacit reference to my disappearance from his chemistry class. Whatever it was, I made up my mind to dislike him.

The next time I met him was in 1922, when I was in the employ of the Zionist Organization of America, and by then he was the world leader of the movement. The moment he set eyes on me he said, with a smile that went through and through me: "Why, yes, you're the fellow I chucked out of my chemistry class." It hadn't been quite so, though next door to it; but his manner of saying it made me feel, still makes me feel in retrospect, that he was administering a friendly and facetious rebuke for my sullenness at our encounter in Wassilevsky's (or Massel's) house, ten years or so earlier. Lest this should sound like vanity, I add that his memory for faces, names, and personalities was of unbelievable tenacity; it extended to thousands of individuals in a dozen countries. A one-minute encounter sufficed to make a permanent impression on him, filed away and subject to instantaneous recall twenty or thirty years later. If I was immensely flattered at the moment, I learned to see the incident in perspective after working with him for a few weeks.

When the Organization assigned me to act as his secretary during his stay in New York, I was as happy as when Miss Clarke had smiled on me. The assignment was repeated several times, till I left the employ of the Organization, and I looked forward with increasing happiness to every repetition. My service with the Zionist Organization ran from my twenty-seventh to my thirty-third year; I was not and am not a hero-worshipper; the happiness I found in working with Weizmann was not simply the pride of being on close terms with greatness; it was perhaps partly that, but if so, it was his peculiar greatness, which had immense meaning for me in cultural-spiritual terms; and with this was mingled a deep personal affection.

It was an affection that remained steadfast to the end; my admiration changed, became more thoughtful, more critical, and far more appreciative, as the record of his achievements accumulated. When I left the Zionist Organization to become a freelance writer and lecturer, I maintained contact with him for longer or shorter periods at longer or shorter intervals. We would meet in New York, in London, and in Israel. The last and longest contact—it would have been the happiest had we been less concerned for his health—was in 1947, when I worked with him for some months on his autobiography, *Trial and Error*. He was then seventy-three and at the beginning of the sickness he lingered in for the next five years.

III

For me, Chaim Weizmann personifies, more than any other man I have known, the best that was in the *Shtetl* Jew combined with the qualities of worldly greatness, and the more I ponder the mixture the more intriguing I find it. He was at home among statesmen, but his spiritual home continued to be the townlet of Motol-near-Pinsk, in the Pripet marshes, where, he tells us, "Jews lived, as they had lived for many generations, scattered islands in a gentile ocean; and among them my own people, on my father's and mother's side, made up a not inconsiderable proportion." He spoke many languages well, he was most himself in Yiddish. He had a commanding and arresting presence; when he entered a room it became his; relaxed, among intimates, he was still the center of attention, but by virtue of a Sholom Aleichem warmth and wit. He was a scientist of international repute; but to him, as to my people in Manchester, the Bible was the supreme source of life, and its figures were his contemporaries. He had been brought up with them. Science was his instrument for the rebuilding of the Jewish homeland; the Bible was his inspiration. "Inspiration" is somewhat misleading; it suggests perhaps an exalted remoteness where there was a homey familiarity as well as reverence. He was familiar with Abraham, Moses, and Isaiah in a spirit of neighborliness. So were my people; so was Sholom Aleichem's Tevyeh the Dairyman.

He loved and hated the *Shtetl* just as Mendelle Mocher Sforim had done. He loved it for the vision it had guarded for him, he hated it for the formlessness of its life, its surrender to meanness and self-pity and *shlimihlishness*. He was, supremely, the man of form. Whether in submitting a memorandum to the British Foreign Office, or in planning his Rehovoth home, he had a perfect instinct for the right stance. He prepared carefully, but could improvise brilliantly. I am tempted to say that he knew all the tricks of being enormously impressive, and yet there was no trickery; his impressiveness flowed from uncalculated total commitment and immense intellectual capacity. At the same time he was amused, even tickled, by the decorative superfluities that often went along with "being impressive." The skeptical *Shtetl* Jew peered, grinning, over the shoulder of the impressive statesman, and both were genuine.

I pick at random, from memory, from notes, from earlier accounts, illustrative incidents and scenes of which I was the witness. I have described in more detail elsewhere his appearance in Jerusalem before the UNSCOP (United Nations Special Committee on Palestine) in the summer of 1947, when I was working with him on his memoirs.

The session was held in the YMCA building, and the trip to Jerusalem was a strain on him. He was no longer the magnificent figure I had known in the early days; he was to outward appearance only a sick, shuffling old man whose sight was failing him. He had to be escorted carefully on to the platform, and we who watched from the auditorium were filled with apprehension, for his voice was so low that it barely carried to the committee members before him. We could not hear what he was saying, and we knew that some of the members—particularly the Indian—were hostile; thus we were horrified when we saw him put aside the prepared statement (it had been printed for him in half-inch type). In a few moments we were at ease, for it was obvious even at a distance that he had established his old ascendancy. The faces of the most hostile smoothed out, their questions were respectful, almost deferential; they knew themselves to be in the presence of greatness.

That evening (July 8, 1947) a small group of us accompanied the Weizmanns to a performance of the Israel (then the Palestine) Philharmonic Orchestra in Rehovoth, and late that night I made the following notes:

> It's like accompanying royalty to a command performance. The cars sweep up to the door after everyone has entered and been seated. The concert is held up. We come in from the side, and before our coming we sense a stirring in the audience, which rises as we enter. We advance slowly to our places in the front row; the orchestra also rises and plays the *Hatikvah* (the national anthem). All that, and the military guard at the gate of the Weizmann house (with its grounds and gardens and winding drive), and the military guard at the concert, and Weizmann's personal bodyguard, heighten the effect. I feel a bit silly in

this *galère*. Applause as we enter, the heartier because
of W.'s performance before UNSCOP.

Weizmann feels and believes himself to be demo-
cratic. So he is—in the way a benevolent "good" king
is: laboring for his people, making no distinction between high and low, thinking of the poor, sharing
their problems, planning for the amelioration of their
condition, opposing the rapacity of the rich, the ex-
ploitation of the masses by demagogues or men of
wealth, supporting the labor movement, feeling a
deep and organic kinship with the *kibbutzim,* keeping an eye on all elements of growth in the people,
concerned for spiritual values, fighting the deterioration of the Jewish spirit, loathing terrorism more for
its effect on the Jewish character than for the deaths
it brings, feeling himself part of every creative effort
(university, music, drama—and of course science and
the Weizmann Institute now in the making). In short,
the touch of the "ideal" king comes from this univer-
sality in relation to all that is part of Jewish life. But
there is the "kingly" about him, suggestive of a court.
Such a man must be wealthy, and live accordingly,
with taste. W.'s house is distinguished; we call it "The
White House" (also because of its color): flowers,
paintings, books, cultivated talk, all sorts of people—
labor leaders, British government officials, dignitaries
of all countries, discreet and devoted servants, *haut
ton* (much is the work of Mrs. W.).

At the same time, *heimishness* when the pressure
is off; we are all on the simplest terms with him.

Much that is childish (?) in W. Eats up praise and
must have it continuously. Makes him feel good and
enables him to work better. All the same, isn't bam-
boozled by it. Knows when what he's done is good,

and when it isn't; not the fool of flatterers. Doesn't relish praise—even merited—from people who don't like him. When he has done well at a public appearance, will sit and purr, and wants to be purred at. It can grow tiresome; but we go along, we realize he's just recharging.

Impressive consistency and persistency in his life's activity. Quite unable to be dishonest toward the fundamental, but can be wary, evasive, crafty, though in reality not a first-rate politician. Enjoys comfort, order, good cooking (not so much now!), tapestry, garden and trees, which he delights in showing off.

Considers himself so much *the* Jew of this generation that his ejection from the Zionist Presidency in 1931 and again now, 1947, made him aghast. Who *dares* pretend to his place? And indeed all the others *are* small beside him (which is perhaps the best reason—and the one they necessarily can't have the sense and courage to give—for changing. We can't have political life thus dominated by one individual).

IV

If Weizmann's oustanding quality was his sense of form, his outstanding spiritual characteristic was his identification with the folk; he confirmed in me the link between me and my people; I do not mean here the Jewish people in the abstract, but the group I have described, the group which gave me life. Because of him I became clear as to its meaning beyond the framework of a particular time and place; for he was representative of the Jewish people as a historic whole, continuous in many displacements through some thousands of years.

He loved the masses in Abraham Lincoln's way; he loved

188

the shoemaker, the carpenter, the shopkeeper, the peddler, while hating from the depths of his soul the formlessness of their lives. Pomp and circumstance as *Narrishkeit,* foolishness, was one thing; form as the craftsmanship of life, in science, politics, social relations, physical surroundings, morals, aesthetics, manners—that was something else. It was what the Jewish people had to acquire, and Weizmann was its teacher in personal and public life. Theodore Herzl, the founder of modern Zionism, had understood that, too, but there was a profound difference between Herzl and Weizmann which is illustrated by a Chassidic saying: "To help a man you must get down to where he is." Herzl was the avatar type, but the task called for a *Shtetl* man, flesh of its flesh, bone of its bone, a *Shtetl* man who had made the transformation in himself—it needed such a man to initiate the transformation, still so incomplete, in the people. He had to draw from the *Shtetl* the power to overcome, against the inertia of centuries, the *Shtetl's* ingrained disdain of order and system, which it had come to regard as an essential ingredient of Jewishness. To the *Shtetl* man form was a *goyish* thing; it had to do with uniforms, governments, *olam ha-zeh* (this-worldliness). But *olam ha-zeh* was the very point. Our exclusion from the national essence of *olam ha-zeh,* namely, a homeland of our own, had warped the Jewish outlook, and the straightening out of this warp in the Jewish people as a whole was for Weizmann an integral part of the reconstruction of the homeland.

Weizmann was a great teacher as well as a great leader. He was particularly concerned with the unhealthiness of the Jewish attitude toward the non-Jewish world. He was himself completely at ease among non-Jews, he felt no discomfort and occasioned none. He did not—as consciously assimilating Jews often do—put his hosts under a strain

practicing and tacitly requesting evasion of Jewish subjects. One of his favorite phrases was: *"C'est à prendre ou
à laisser,* take it or leave it."* He attributed the lack of
natural self-confidence, which expressed itself in overcon-
fidence and submissiveness, to the Jewish sense of abnor-
mality rising from the lack of a homeland.

When I served as his secretary I used to accompany him
to his mass meetings and take notes of his speeches (he
always spoke extemporaneously). Here are some typical
excerpts:

"You will always be treated as a guest if you too can
play the host. The only man who is invited to dinner is
the one who can have his dinner at home if he likes. . . ."

"Among the anti-Semites none is more interesting than
the tender-hearted variety. Their anti-Semitism is always
based on a compliment. They tell us: 'You are the salt of
the earth,' and there are Jews who feel themselves extra-
ordinarily flattered . . . Yet I do not consider it a compliment to be called 'the salt of the earth.' The salt is used
for someone else's food, it dissolves in that food. And salt
is good only in small quantities. If there is too much salt
in the food, you throw out the food and the salt with
it. . . ."

"We are reproached by the whole world. We are told
that we are dealers in old clothes, junk. We are perhaps
the sons of dealers in old clothes, but we are the grandsons
of prophets. Think of the grandsons, and not of the sons."

It was good to see—literally see—an audience catch at
these points; there would be an appreciative turning and
nodding of heads. The listeners knew that he had overcome these psychological handicaps of the Jews; they delighted in the obvious fact that when he ridiculed the
assimilated Jewish notables, he could not be suspected of
of envying their status among non-Jews; his was indispu-

tably higher. He could laugh at the Jewish merchants, writers, and financiers who kept repeating: "We have risen above the ghetto thing called Jewishness. We are moderns."

I too benefited greatly from his talks and from his general attitude. A fast-moving world has forgotten how the idea of a Jewish state was, not too long ago as history is reckoned, regarded as a poky, hole-in-wall oddity, classed with Rosicrucianism and the lost ten tribes. I am, in fact, not completely accustomed to the new situation; I still expect to hear: "You believe in the possibility of a Jewish state? How very interesting, you must tell me about it," meaning: "Oh Lord, how did I get into this?" How easily "What on earth is he talking about?" has become "But naturally." So forgetting, the world cannot appreciate what a long and stony road Weizmann had to tread from his dreams in Motol to the State of Israel. He called it his forty years in the wilderness, but it was longer.

v

The stoniness of that road is known only to those who accompanied Weizmann along part of it. There were large segments of the Jewish people in ideological opposition to the Zionist program; assimilated or assimilating Jews of the bourgeoisie and of the left; non-assimilating Jews who wanted to see Jewishness rooted in the Diaspora without a homeland in Palestine, and these might be extremists in religion (Orthodox *and* Reform) or secularist nationalists; other non-assimilating Jews wanted a Jewish homeland but at all costs anywhere but in Palestine. There were segments which dreaded any kind of publicity about the Jewish people, and there were segments which were indifferent. In that large segment which listened sympathetically to Weizmann there was, predominantly, the inertia I have described in earlier chapters, and it comprised the lower economic strata—transplanted *Shtetl*-Jews and their offspring. They had, on the whole, neither the will nor the means to be effective; a generation had to pass before that was changed.

Among these, Weizmann did one part of his labors, a part the more difficult because while he taught he had to raise funds; he had to be master-teacher and master-mendicant simultaneously, a double role at once spiritually rewarding and humanly humiliating. Sometimes there were well-to-do prospects among the sympathetic, and they had to be nursed and catered to. There were receptions in private homes, to which I went along with Weizmann, and some of those evenings still make me shudder. Amid vulgar and ostentatious surroundings, this man of exquisite taste and subtle intellect endured stupidly obstructive questions and coarse admonitions in the style of the *Shtetl nogid* (wealthy man), in the hope, frequently deceived, of obtaining a few thousand dollars for the pioneers in Palestine. He would come away with a sick look, saying: "You have to bow to every idol on the road to Palestine."

His patience was inhuman. He had to inspire, cajole, scold, and teach. The Zionist position was paradoxical. To prove to the world that they were capable of building a homeland (for few believed they were) the Jews first had to have an opportunity to build; but to be given such an opportunity they first had to prove that they were capable of building. It was the classical problem of the beginner and "job-open—only-the-experienced-wanted." A vicious circle of this kind can never be broken; it has to be eroded; and it calls for undiscourageable self-confidence on the part of the applicant. But in the Zionist case there was little self-confidence among Jews at large; the masses didn't really believe in the capacity of the Jewish people to build a homeland.

All this Weizmann understood, and he accepted the consequences. But there were Zionist leaders who thought otherwise. They denounced his gradualism as timidity and lack of vision. As far back as forty years ago their cry was: "A Jewish state *now!*"—which in effect meant a Jewish state with practically no Jews in it. Weizmann's reply, obstinately repeated a thousand times, was: "A Jewish state cannot be created by decree, but by the forces of a people in the course of generations. Even if all the governments in the world gave us a country, it would only be a gift of words; but if the Jewish people will go and build Palestine, the Jewish state will become a reality."

Among his opponents in the Zionist movement were men of distinction. Max Nordau, the author of *Degeneration* and *The Conventional Lies of Civilization* (all but forgotten now, they made a great stir in their day), demanded, soon after the end of the First World War, that half a million Jews be transported immediately into Palestine—sink or swim; there would be enough survivors to ensure success. Vladimir Jabotinsky, breaking with Weizmann, created the Revisionist Movement—so named because he conceived it to be a return to the principles of Theodore Herzl. Herzl, too, had dreamed of a dramatically sudden *creatio ex nihilo*—an international charter to the Jews, and rapid immigration under international law. There was opposition of quite another kind, headed in America by Justice Louis D. Brandeis, who believed that the time for Zionist teaching and propaganda was past, and the work was straightforward, a businesslike affair. Thus, the movement split twice—in America, with Brandeis leading *his* dissident group (he did this through deputies after he was appointed to the Supreme Court), and in the world Zionist movement with Jabotinsky leading *his* group.

Through all this, Weizmann had to negotiate with statesmen and politicians as *the* leader of the Zionist movement. He did it by the force of his personality more than by the solidity of his immediate backing. We read today of Israel's representatives being received by this or that president or foreign minister, and accept it as natural, which of course it is. But there was no of course about it in Weizmann's case; without a state's bargaining power, or at least its acknowledged right to be heard, he had to rely, for his introduction, on his official status, which was constantly challenged. His personality had to do the rest. Nor was it simply his charm, adroitness, and sincerity that won him a respectful hearing; it was the weight he carried as the concentration of Jewish history. That was his effective backing.

VI

Working with him on his memoirs in the summer of 1947 was like reliving his life with him. He was in poor physical condition, but his mind was as vigorous and supple as ever, and it was amazing to hear him pour forth his recollections and reflections for an hour or an hour and a half at a time, in ordered paragraphs, with witty and pungent interpolations. I would take it all down verbatim on the typewriter, then we would go over it, pruning and mending, before I carried the material away for final polishing and retyping. When we came to some particularly murderous sideswipe at someone, I would ask: "You don't really want that to stay, Dr. Weizmann, or do you?" His face would light up. "No, Maur-r-rice, I think we can do a little p-r-runing." Then he might add, in Yiddish:

"He was, to be sure, a *mamzer*, but that wasn't his fault."
"*Mamzer*," bastard, is figurative in Yiddish too, but it has
a wider range than in English; it may imply grudging
admiration of a clever rascal or semi-rascal, as well as detes-
tation of a low, mean character. Weizmann would use it
in either sense, or in an intermediary one, and the key to
his feeling was the context and his voice. He would of
course have softened or deleted these passages without my
suggestion, but he liked to hear me pick them out. He
had a great sense of public dignity and of the responsibility
of his position; in private he allowed himself outbursts of
petulance, and some of his remarks were cruel, and occasionally unjust.

He had suffered much from the enforced propinquity
of men he disliked or despised but who were useful to the
movement. He took it out on them in the first draft, but
like a man writing an abusive letter which he knows he
is not going to mail. Where he writes positively and affectionately of people, as he often does, he is genuine. There
were many companionships and friendships which were a
deep source of joy to him.

He indulged in another kind of private savagery in the
first draft, directed at political opponents with unchal-
lengeably honest motives. He would pour out his old re-
sentments; the heat of long-since fought-out battles would
return to his blood, and he would remember his frustrations. Then, the emotion having subsided, he would wink,
adding: "He was—or is—a decent fellow, you know." His
most derogatory noun for a man was monosyllabic, Yiddish, and obscene. His English, which he had learned in
his thirties, was excellent, calling for few stylistic correc-
tions. Most of the work lay in the rearrangement of the
material. None of the merits of *Trial and Error* can be
credited to me, and I feel free to say it is a remarkable

work; but what a pity that no copy of the first draft exists.

When I think back to the circumstances under which he produced the greater part of the book, I marvel again at his will power, his reserves of energy, his flexibility, and his capacity to switch his concentrated attention from one task to another. He was, at the time, preparing the Jewish case for presentation to the UNSCOP—not merely his own address, but the general policy. He was also absorbed in the development of the Weizmann Institute of Science, which had begun three years earlier. There was a constant coming and going of men and delegations at the house. And if this were not enough for an ailing man, there was the terror which was being conducted against the British by a small, desperate group of men who held themselves accountable to no one but themselves, and a campaign of insane vilification against his person and leadership. Scurrilous leaflets accusing him of having sold out to the British, for money or honors, were circulated throughout the country; walls were daubed with denunciations of "Weizmann-Pétain"; and hardest for him to bear, there was the terror itself, blind, ferocious, and demoralizing.

Weizmann writes how he saw "here and there a relaxation of the old, traditional Zionist purity of ethics, a touch of militarism, and a weakness for its trappings; here and there something worse—the tragic, un-Jewish resort to terrorism, a perversion of the purely defensive function of Haganah [the national army, clandestine till 1948]; and worst of all, in certain circles, a readiness to compound with the evil, to condemn and not to condemn it, to treat it not as the thing it was, namely, an unmitigated curse to the National Home, but a phenomenon which might have its advantages."

The terrorists were a mixed lot: idealists whose minds had become unhinged by the multimillion extermination of Jews in Europe and the calculating, callous attitude of the British rulers of Palestine; adventurers with killer instincts in search of justifiable employment; morally disoriented youngsters. Their backers, in Palestine and America, were an equally mixed assortment; the most curious element among them consisted of Jews who had never before manifested the slightest interest in Jewish affairs and who, when the homeland had been established, reverted to their former indifference. Here too there was a wide range of characters, from the genuinely intellectual type like Arthur Koestler to the squalidly picaresque Hollywood type like Ben Hecht. They were fired suddenly by the idea of "the fighting Jew"; the thinking Jew, the building Jew, the Jew who had endured and come through with unscarred psyche was and is meaningless to them. They hated Weizmann, and their campaign against him has not come to an end with his death. The supporters of the terror, to whom history assigns no role in the creation of the Jewish state, still raise their voices from time to time, not to further the work that remains to be done, but—"noteless blots on a remembered name"—to vent their frustration in continued vilification of the greatest Jew of modern times.

VII

I return from this digression to the summer months of 1947. The two or three hours I spent daily with Weizmann were of course the smallest as well as the most enjoyable part of my labors. The collating, the excision of repetitions, the verifying of dates, and so on, took much longer. Some of this was mechanical, none of it was wholly dull, for throughout I was gripped by the unfolding of a fascinating record as dictated by the man who had lived it.

What moved me most deeply I have referred to in one of my notes made at the time: "Impressive consistency and persistence in his life's activity." The irrevocable commitment began in his childhood, and curious recurrences of theme confirm like echoes the unity of purpose, the straight line of destiny.

As a *cheder* boy in Pinsk, little Chaim Weizmann wrote a Hebrew letter to his *rebbe*, affirming his faith in the rebuilding of Zion and prophesying that England would play the major role in it. The letter might have been written by any imaginative youngster who had grown up in a Zionist home and who had heard his grandfather tell and retell how Sir Moses Montefiore (a legendary name among Jews), held in honor by the Queen of England, had come to Russia to try to alleviate the condition of Russian Jewry, and how the Jews of Vilna had unharnessed the horses and dragged the carriage in tumultuous procession through the streets of "the Jerusalem of Lithuania." By itself a moderately interesting childhood incident, the letter is, in conjunction with the man's development many years later, an extraordinary one. For Weizmann tells how, in 1913, having been denied at Manchester University an academic promotion he thought himself entitled to, he almost left England to become a professional Zionist in Berlin. He recounts:

> Whether, left to my own counsel, I would actually have taken this step, I do not know. But it was my wife who put her foot down. She disliked Germany; so for that matter did I. I cannot help thinking she was guided by something more than personal considerations, either for herself or me. In any case, I shudder to think of the possible results if I had yielded to the importunity of my friends (in Berlin) and my own momentary impulse.

He tells also how, as a boy in Pinsk, he used to take part during the Purim holiday in the money-box collections for Palestine:

> Purim always came in the midst of the March thaw, and hour after hour I would go tramping through the mud of Pinsk, from end to end of the town. I remember that my mother was accustomed, for reason of economy, to make my overcoats much too long for me, to allow for growth, so that as I went I repeatedly stumbled over the skirts and sometimes fell headlong into the icy slush of the streets. I worked late into the night, but usually had the satisfaction of bringing in more money than anyone else. Such was my apprenticeship for the activities which, on a rather larger scale, have occupied so many years of my later life.

"Rather larger scale" was British understatement, which Weizmann liked and employed effectively. The organized campaigns and "drives" of the later Zionist movement have dwarfed into insignificance the collections of thirty or forty years ago, when two or three million a year from American Jewry was the limit, but Weizmann in his day was the greatest individual mendicant in Jewish history and perhaps, considering the economic strata among which he did his main work, the greatest in all history. I asked him once what difference he had found between soliciting on the ten-kopeck and the ten-thousand-dollar levels. He answered that you heard the plea of poverty more frequently on the ten-thousand-dollar level. "It's usually after an elaborate dinner for twenty; you look around at the furnishings, the tapestries and the pictures, and you feel like returning the dinner—on the spot. When a poor man is mean he makes no bones about it; he slams the door in your face, a swift and painless operation. I can remember certain houses in Pinsk where I was regularly refused with: 'I've already given.' It was a lie, as we both knew, but it was a time- and energy-saver. I liked best the man who answered coolly: 'I don't give, I'm a swine that way.' I had no quarrel with him. The rich aren't straightforward, they keep you dangling, they make a pleasurable game of it, they like to see you with your tongue hanging out. And when they do give they make you sweat for it.' But he had encountered much generosity among the rich, too, and remembered it gratefully.

His apprenticeship in this field of mendicancy served him well in another field, the political. In a sense he begged his way to the Jewish state at the doors of chancelleries. There too he knew what it meant to be kept dangling, with tongue hanging out, but there too he remembered with gratitude acts of generosity and understanding. He was contemptuous of Zionists who accused him of lack of firmness when there was nothing to be firm with. "They want me to go to Downing Street and bang on the table. I could get in, and I could bang on the table once, and that would be the end of it." He used to call Downing Street his *Via Dolorosa*.

To understand the consistency of his life, one must realize that he was not a Zionist by conviction any more than one is a human being by conviction. There was nothing else for him to be. Thus, whatever vicissitudes and changes he went through as a person, the Zionist idea worked in and through them. As a child in Motol, as a youth in Pinsk, as a student in Berlin and Geneva, as a chemistry teacher in Manchester, as director of a British Admiralty laboratory in the First World War, he was Weizmann the Zionist. When he came to full leadership in the Zionist movement, he had passed through all the intermediary stages; the boy, the youth, the man had lived his essential life in preparation, at meetings, conferences, congresses, traveling, speaking to handfuls in tiny halls, speaking to large audiences, arguing with individuals.

He had greatness of personality as seen from within, as well as consistency of purpose. A narrow personality united with obsessional persistence and unflagging energy can achieve much. I have known such men; by their persistence and energy they become multiple until they are like a large island of coral-reef insects; they perform wonders by the sheer multiplicity of their small, relentless selves. Nor do I mean by "greatness of personality as seen from within" the power to fascinate, the imposing or stage-filling personality, which was developed to such a high degree in Weizmann, so that people were afraid to meet him lest they be swept off their feet. Lord Balfour, a friend and admirer of Weizmann's, hearing of an anti-Zionist who refused to meet Weizmann for that reason, called the man a coward. I would not wholly agree. The power to fascinate is sometimes nothing more than itself, like the technical ability to hypnotize which I have sometimes seen displayed by trivial and unworthy men, night-club performers for instance. Weizmann had obsessional persistence as well as the power to charm, almost to hypnotize, and these qualities helped to place him on the stage of world affairs. But I can think of him as essentially the same man without these qualities and without his external achievements.

CHAPTER XIII

The Scientist

❀

O N THE WALL of the marble-paved plaza that leads to Weizmann's tomb, these words of his are inscribed:

> I feel sure that science will bring to this land both peace and a renewal of its youth, creating here the springs of a new spiritual life. And here I speak of science for its own sake and applied science.

I have paused many times before this inscription, trying to fit it into the life of the man. Had he not been a scientist, I would not look for deeper meaning; I would pass over it as the sort of thing one says nowadays. But he was a scientist, and this was his scientific credo.

The spiritual value of science seems to have meant to him its intellectual and moral discipline, the maintenance of standards, the conquest of the *Shtetl* handicaps. It meant integrity, modesty, and form. About the founding of the Daniel Sieff Research in Rehovoth—the forerunner of the Wezmann Institute—he wrote:

> The whole experiment of setting up a research institute in a country as scientifically backward as Palestine is beset with pitfalls. There is, first, the risk of falling into the somewhat neglectful habits

of Oriential countries; a second danger is that of losing a sense of proportion because of the lack of standards of comparision. One is always the best chemist in Egypt or in Palestine when there are no others. Also, if one turns out a piece of work which in England or America would be considered modest enough, one is apt to overvalue it simply because it has been turned out in difficult circumstances. The standard and quality of the work must be watched over most critically and carefully. Many of the publications issued by scientific institutions in backward countries are very much below the level required elsewhere, but the contributors to these publications are very proud of them because the local level is not high. I made up my mind that this sort of atmosphere should not prevail at the Sieff Institute, and that it should live up to the highest standards.

There were several ways of combatting the dangers I have indicated. First there was the proper selection of the staff and the infusion into it of the right spirit—that of maintaining the highest quality. Every member was enjoined to take his time over his piece of work, and not merely have publication in view.

But while he was fighting the negative aspect of a *Shtetl* psychology, he still appealed to the affirmations in it. He wrote, on the subject of the *Shtetl* tradition:

Our great men were always a product of the symbiosis between the ancient, traditional Talmudic learning in which our ancestors were steeped in the Polish or Rumanian ghettos or even in Spain, and the modern western universities with which their children came in contact. There is often as not a long list of

Talmudic scholars and Rabbis in the pedigrees of modern scientists. In many cases they themselves came from Talmudic schools, breaking away in their twenties and struggling through to Paris or Zurich or Princeton. It is this extraordinary phenomenon—a great tradition of learning fructified by modern methods—which has given us both first class scientists and competent men in every branch of academic activity, out of all relation to our numbers.

Weizmann was himself a remarkable example of the blend of tradition with modern science. He had never attended a Yeshivah (Talmudical academy), but his Jewish education was thorough. He was not a religious Jew in the formal sense, and like his father—a timber merchant who studied Maimonides in his leisure hours—he had no high regard for clerics, but his Jewish drive cannot properly be described as secular. It was a kind of blend which he did not trouble to think through.

His emphasis on applied science as the key to the renewal of the Jewish homeland needs no explanation nowadays, when the whole world is caught up in the scientific revolution; but there is some interest in observing how his own scientific equipment played into his Zionist commitment. He was a chemistry teacher at Manchester University when he met Balfour in 1906 and won him to the Zionist cause; conceivably such a meeting could have taken place anyhow; but it is doubtful whether he would have met Churchill in 1916 if not for his discovery of a fermentation process for the production of acetone, a chemical badly needed for the conduct of the war. A popular legend has it that the British government "awarded" Palestine to the Jews in return for Weizmann's war services; it is a beautiful instance of the myth at work simplifying and distorting a complicated truth. We meet it again in 1942, when John G. Winant, the American ambassador to Great Britain, invited him on behalf of President Roosevelt to come to the United States and work there on the problem of synthetic rubber. "Mr. Winant advised me earnestly," writes Weizmann, "to devote myself as completely as possible to chemistry; he believed that I would thus serve best the Allied Powers and the Zionist cause. I promised Mr. Winant to follow his advice to the best of my ability. Actually I divided my time almost equally between science and Zionism." Weizmann was too worldly wise to rely on the prospect held out by Winant, however sincere the latter may have been. He knew that in political life a reward must be earned twice, first deserving it, then collecting it, and the second half usually calls for more exertion. Thus Weizmann looked on his services to the British and American governments as opportunities to urge the claims of Zionism in influential quarters, and had he not pursued these opportunities as assiduously and skillfully as his scientific work there would have been no "reward." An obituary notice on Weizmann in an American weekly said: "His vibrant, eloquent voice, lowered for emphasis, cutting deftly through details to the essentials, was one of the greatest one-man propaganda instruments in history." He got some of his most important audiences through his scientific usefulness; what he achieved through them had nothing to do with science. This the myth does not understand.

Another instance of the indirect but creative connection between science and Zionism came vividly to my attention eight years after Weizmann's death. It was here, in the Weizmann Institute in Rehovoth, that the International Conference on Science in the Advancement of New States was held in the summer of 1960. The ceremonial opening in the plaza, under the open sky, was immensely impressive, with its delegates from Ghana and Ethiopia, from Cameroon, Kenya, Liberia, Mali, Nigeria, Iran, Nepal—thirty-odd new Afro-Asian states and a few old ones in process of renewal—its Israeli and foreign scientists, its thousands of visitors. There was festivity in the bright air. The Israelis were proud, and a little awed; born for the most part in other lands before there was an Israel, they had been accustomed in a millennial tradition to the status of guests of uncertain standing; now they were playing host to a newborn world, and not merely as a gesture, but for a highly practical purpose in line with a universal need. The practical side had two facets. Israeli specialists had already been at work in the Afro-Asian countries, and contingents from these had already been receiving instruction in Israel's schools, co-operatives, and *kibbutzim*. There were valuable political results for Israel, honestly come by; and it was the expansion of the Weizmann tradition. While it would be absurd to say that a similar tradition would not have been founded without him—Herzl had already laid down the principle that without science a state cannot be created in modern times —Weizmann's example and name added to it the fruitful element of an eponym.

There were two weeks of lectures, seminars, papers, discussions, proposals, resolutions—to what degree immediately useful it is hard to tell. Scientific conferences, I am told, are usually showpieces and marking-points, their value lies in personal contacts, also in what comes before and after. With luck a conference becomes memorable by virtue of some phrases, and one such phrase, in this instance, made a lasting impression on me, and not at all in a "scientific" way. A very commonplace phrase it was, too, a cliché thrown out, I imagine, without awareness of its peculiar relevance to the time, place, and occasion. The delegate from Belgian Congo, called on for a few words, spoke in French, thanked Israel for having been the first country to send a group of doctors and nurses to his country, and closed with: *"Vive la République d' Israël, vive l' Afrique libre."* I started; I could imagine the spirit of Weizmann called up from the nearby tomb, like Saul's by the witch of Endor, but not reluctantly, not to reproach and foretell disaster, smiling, rather, to hear his country's name linked with the latest of humanity's efforts to break the bonds of the past. The sons of the *Shtetl* had come a long way; through them the Jewish people was re-entering world history as a recognized contemporaneous force.

With all this, I keep looking for other meanings in the inscription: "Science . . . creating here the springs of a new spiritual life." It has a special poignancy "here," where a spiritual life developed long before the beginnings of science. Will Israel make a comparable contribution to the solution of the science-and-humanism, science-and-religion problem? During the last few years, and particularly during this long Sabbath-summer, I have been preparing myself for the examination of this problem by a consistent effort to learn at least the elementary language of science; but it is a problem with which Weizmann himself was never occupied.

He was not a philosopher of science, and wrote nothing about its epistemological aspects, like a Mach or a Bridgman. He was a scientist-humanist, naturally, as it were, never troubling himself about a justification. His outlook was spiritual-practical; science was a practical matter and also a discipline in truthfulness. He was concerned with truthfulness, not absolute Truth. Even so, he shied away from certain relevant questions: Are the skills of science transferrable to the humanistic field? Are scientists, in their non-scientific relations, truthful, more honest, more "spiritual on the whole than laymen"?

Other, "deeper" questions seemed to trouble Weizmann even less. He was not concerned with the widespread popular complaint that modern science is making the world unintelligible to common sense. I do not, for myself, share this view: or rather, it is my view that the world was *never* intelligible to common sense. The "common-sensicality" of Newtonian physics, of matter composed of discrete particles moving about in absolute space, was a popular delusion. Newton himself was completely baffled by the phenomenon of gravitational "action at a distance"; it didn't make sense to him; he died a baffled man. The new explanation, the "curvature of space," and matter "naturally" moving along the shortest available line, is called, conceptually, complete nonsense. Conceptually speaking, it is not greater nonsense than action at a distance. It just happens to be new, and when we have got used to it (without understanding it, of course), we shall think it just as common-sensical as we thought the classical physics to be. (What we call an explanation is usually a restatement of the new un-understood in terms of the old un-understood.) But we can say that the science of the last half century has jolted us again into an apprehension of the unintelligibility of the physical world in terms of everyday common sense. The very big and the very little, inter-galactic space and intra-atomic space, do not conform to anything conceivable—in the sense of picturable—by us. We make "models" of the atom, but they are no more like an atom than a railroad time-table is like a journey. Religion asks us to believe what we cannot prove, and science proves what we cannot conceive. Of the events in the sub-atomic world we may say with Goethe:

Das Unbeschreibliche,
Hier ist's getan—

even though it is to a large extent *beschreiblich* as corresponding to calculations.

To Weizmann the world and life were intelligible and manageable. With all his subtlety, he was in a sense *simpliste,* which makes him the more complex. His scientific bent and his spiritual intuitions were in complete harmony, and whether this was so in symbiosis or by balance was unimportant to him.

CHAPTER XIV

Founding Fathers

❀

MONG the men who stood close to Weizmann there were two whose influence on me was second only to his. They were, like him, products of the *Shtetl,* but as different from him as they were from each other. One was Shmarya Levin, whose memory as a dazzling orator is cherished by a dwindling old-time Yiddish-speaking generation; the other was Chaim Nachman Bialik, whose poetry will be read as long as Hebrew lives.

Shmarya Levin was in America when I arrived in 1914, and whenever he made a public appearance I was in the front row. I followed his addresses with difficulty at first, then with increasing joy as I acquired intimacy with the language by dint of reading, of frequent visits to the Yiddish theater—those were the great days of Maurice Moskowitz and Jacob Adler—and of conversations with Uncle Berel. My first translations were of Levin's articles in the now long-defunct Yiddish daily, *Die Varheit.* In the Yiddish phrase, I served my barber's apprenticeship on his beard. Years later I translated his three-volume autobiography. From Levin I first learned that Zionism was something more than a nationalist-political movement or a philanthropic refugee undertaking; he introduced me to the philosophy of Achad Ha-am, whose disciple he was, together with Weizmann, and to the Biblical, folkloristic, and spiritual roots of the movement. I have many reasons for remembering him with gratitude.

Levin was a man of great gifts and little discipline; he wasted much of his life at chess, and was the unfortunate kind of addict who plays poorly and hates to lose. Even I used to win a game from him now and again, and I might have won oftener if he had not had the habit of taking back moves—which he always did in a high state of indignation and resentment, as if some invisible and stupid *kibbitzer* had forced his hand. On my visits to Palestine in later years, I would always find him at the Café Vienna, in Jerusalem, absorbed in a game of chess. At Zionist Congresses he sometimes had to be dragged away from the board almost forcibly to attend to serious business in the *plenum*. He played in what we call the Yeshivah manner, accompanying his moves with audible singsong meditations on Talmudic aphorisms. He confesses in his memoirs that two arts, as he called them, chess and smoking, played an altogether too important part in his life, adding that in both of them he reached his peak early and registered no advance with the passing years. I sympathized with Levin; I too am by nature indolent, but unlike him have become reconciled to the fact that you can't beat work for getting things done.

In appearance Levin suggested a stage Mephistopheles: he was tall and lean, with a long, dark, furrowed face, brilliant eyes, the right one with a strong outward cast, a small pointed beard, and something like horns—a peculiar growth of hair standing up at the corners of his temples. On the platform he dominated an audience by his appearance, his intensity of manner, and his brilliant oratory. His Yiddish was at once formal and racy, colorful with folk allusions and quotations from Bible, Talmud, and Midrash; when I translated him I had to go round many of the passages; their point depended so much on intramural intimacies, on exegesis, and tradition familiar only to *cheder* and *Yeshivah* Jews. He made the Bible alive by finding in it parallels or contrasts with current affairs; for him, as for my people, the Bible covered all possible human situations.

It was a common practice to refer to the Russian Czar as Pharaoh, oppressor of the Jews, the only difference being that the Czar was willing to let them go. Like Pharaoh, said Levin, Nicholas II kept making promises and breaking them; he called a Duma and dissolved it, called another and dissolved it. "He promised and retracted, promised and retracted," said Levin, "till the Red Sea swallowed him up."

One of his most famous parallels went back to preWorld War I Zionist history. A number of wealthy Jews in Germany were ready to contribute toward the development of a technical school in Palestine (it has become the famous Haifa Technion, Israel's M.I.T.) as a purely philanthropic enterprise on condition that the language of instruction be German, not Hebrew. In this they were acting as patriotic Germans supporting Germany's imperialist *Drang nach Osten*. Their spokesman was a Dr. Paul Nathan, head of the Union of German Citizens of the Jewish faith, an organization analogous to the American Council for Judaism today. Levin, denouncing him, made a great play on the David-Bathsheba story and the denunciation of David by the Prophet Nathan. He cited the parable of the rich man with many flocks and herds and the poor man with only one litle ewe-lamb "which he had brought and nourished up, and it grew up together with him and his children; it did eat of his own meat, and drank of his own cup, and lay in his bosom, and was unto him as a daughter." "We have one little ewe-lamb of a school in Palestine," cried Levin, "and Germany has a thousand schools. Like the rich man who forebore to take of his own flock to entertain a visitor, Germany with her thousand schools wants to take away our one little school. But who is the villain of the story today? Not David, but the false prophet. Nathan, *thou art the man!*"

Levin had a biting wit, not always under control, and some of his sallies must have been costly to the Zionist movement—but how refreshing they were! He made his first visit to America in 1907, and in spite of his identification with Zionism was invited, as a Jewish celebrity, to the home of Jacob Schiff, the anti-Zionist philanthropist. The host, anxious to make his position clear, stated it in the following terms: "I want you all to know that I consist of three parts: I am an American, I am a German, and I am a Jew." Levin, asked to address the assembled guests, wanted to know how Mr. Schiff effected the division; was it perpendicularly or horizontally? And, if horizontally, which section did he allocate to the Jewish people? There were hopes that Schiff would some day become, if not a Zionist, at least a contributor to Palestinian charities, and Levin's question was not helpful.

Levin was on friendly terms with Julius Rosenwald, another famous philanthropist who, somewhat less violently anti-Zionist than Schiff, helped Levin in a publishing venture in Palestine, as a gesture toward Jewish culture, of course, and not, God forbid, to promote Zionism. Rosenwald twitted Levin: "The most I'll do for you in a personal way is to build myself a villa in Chicago and call it Tel Aviv." "You've got it upside down," said Levin. "We want you to build a villa in Tel Aviv and not call it Chicago."

There were many Jews who contributed to Palestine

213

philanthropic funds while disclaiming any intention to promote the building of a Jewish homeland. It was not their fault, they argued, that Palestine happened to have Jews who needed help or offered a refuge for Jews who could not find a haven elsewhere. If in effect the Zionist cause was thereby promoted, let the Zionists bear the blame. Levin, whose humor often ran to ribaldry, likened these good-natured people to a man who sleeps with a woman out of sheer kindness and washes his hands of any unintended consequences; and, in less Rabelaisian vein, to an atheist who is outraged because the only place available to the victims of a flood happens to be a synagogue.

Of a very distinguished American rabbi whose activities were multifarious, Levin said: "He's a big man; as big as the Woolworth building, and if you look closely you'll see that he too is made up of nickels and dimes." His favorite Yiddish word for a fool was the same as Weizmann's, but Levin improved on it and coined the *"yam-fool." Yam* is Hebrew and Yiddish for "sea," and Levin explained that this variety of fool was not to be found on land; his habitat was the ocean deep, among the other primal monsters. Thenceforth, in Zionist circles, so-and-so was a *yam,* without the indelicate addition. *Yam* could also designate a low type of person. There was, many years ago, a Yiddish journalist writing under two names for a New York daily. That he was an anti-Zionist was the least of his defects; he was equally cynical, scurrilous, and boastful under both names. When Levin discovered that the two men were one, he was overjoyed. "Thank God! One *yam* fewer in the world."

Levin was an unhappy man, knowing that his impatience and his indolence, in both of which he differed so greatly from Weizmann, were harmful to himself and

214

to the cause. He lacked also Weizmann's spontaneous
liking for simple people. But in spite of these limitations
he was a great popular force. He lifted Zionist exposition
to a new plane, and he was loved by the masses because
he never spoke down to them. I learned from him a
principle of the utmost importance to a professional
lecturer: You may assume that an audience is uninformed
in your field, but never assume that it is stupid.

The lifelong friendship between Levin and Weizmann
began in Berlin in the late eighteen-nineties. They were
both members, though not at the same time, of the *Jüdisch-
Russisch Wissenschaftliches Verein,* a Berlin group of
students who long before the coming of Herzl were advo-
cating the creation of a Jewish State. It was in effect a
group of Zionist founding fathers, extraordinary men who
dreamed the maddest of dreams; for if Zionism looked
freakish and harebrained in the early nineteen-hundreds,
what must it have looked like twenty years earlier? By
1914, when I became a Zionist, famous men like Max
Nordau and Israel Zangwill had declared for the movement. Herzl had left his indelible stamp on it. The En-
cyclopaedia Britannica of 1911 devotes two whole pages
to it—and, incidentally, not much more to Communism.
There were dozens of Jewish colonies in Palestine. But
in the eighteen-nineties there were only the faintest beginnings of colonization, and in the Western world the
movement, which was not yet a movement but an obscure
and formless, though powerful, folk agitation, must have
looked correspondingly madder. Yet there they were,
these Russian Jewish students, nearly all of them penniless,
sublimely self-confident, sublimely sure of their historic
mission, talking big, but big, about the Jewish state-to-be,
about international diplomacy, the alignment of the
powers, the buying off of Turkey. "Mad" must be taken

literally here. When Theodore Herzl showed the manuscript of his *Judenstaat* (The Jewish State), the classic
document of modern Zionism, to a friend, he was implored
to seek medical treatment. No doubt, similar counsel was
given more than once to members of the *Jüdisch-Russisch
Wissenschaftliches Verein.*

The brilliance of these men and their apparent nor-
mality outside their one obsession must have strengthened
the suspicion of mental derangement. All of them were
gifted in various fields. Herzl was political reporter for
the *Wiener Neue Freie Presse, The Manchester Guardian*
of Europe, attached to the French Chamber of Deputies.
He was an engaging feuilletonist and playwright, a man
of address and wide reading, the kind of man one calls
civilized, until suddenly, one day . . . And so it was with
Weizmann, Levin, and others. If you kept Levin on Russian politics, for instance, or German literature, you
could listen for hours with profit; but if you should happen
accidentally to touch on the Jewish problem—"Good
heavens," you thought, "what a pity!" And in a sense
these men were in fact *déraillés.* That many of them forfeited distinguished worldly careers was to be expected
and is not to their discredit: but in their Zionist fervor
they also neglected to follow a systematic training which
would have enhanced their usefulness to the movement.
The impracticality of the *Shtetl* clung to many of them
throughout their lives. Weizmann writes of them:

> At first I was greatly overawed by my fellow-stu-
> dents, among whom I was the youngest. Fresh from
> little Pinsk, with its petty collections and small-town
> discussions, I was staggered by the sweep of vision
> which Motzkin and Syrkin and the others displayed.
> There was also a personal detail which oppressed

me at the beginning. I was only a student of chemistry; they were students of philosophy, history, economy, law and other "higher" things. I was immensely attracted to them as persons and as Zionists; but gradually I began to feel that in their personal preparations for life they were as vague as in their Zionist plans. I had brought with me out of Russia a dread of the "eternal student" type, the impractical idealist without roots in the worldly struggle, a figure only too familiar in the Jewish world of forty and fifty years ago. I refused to neglect the lecture hall and the laboratory, to which I gave at least six or seven hours a day. I acquired a taste for research work. In later years I understood that even deeper motives impelled me in those days to attend strictly to the question of my personal equipment for the life-struggle . . .

The deeper motives which underlay Weizmann's systematic approach to his life problem were connected in part with those characteristics which turned him into an able scientist; in part they were connected with his belief in himself, only tacit at the beginning, as a "man of destiny." The Weizmann archives here in Rehovoth reveal how early Wiezmann began to keep copious records and copies of correspondence. He probably did not foresee that they would some day be historical documents; he did not foresee, of course, that he would be the first president of the Jewish state; he was only obeying an impulse, but the "deeper motives" were already there.

There was no such subconscious *arrière pensée* in Levin's makeup. Not that he was without ambition or suffered from modesty; and he was as organically committed to Zionism as Weizmann, and was equally convinced of the inevitability of a Jewish state. I doubt whether the sharpest insight would have picked out the superior figure between these two Berlin Russian-Jewish students; but Weizmann became a world figure, while Levin's reputation is confined to the Jewish people, and even among them he is being forgotten. There was a time when he was better known than Weizmann, and not just because he was a few years older. He was a member of the Russian Duma when Weizmann was a struggling chemistry teacher in Manchester; he attracted large audiences in Europe and America. But his achievements came by fits and starts, not only because of his laziness but because his high opinion of himself was not geared to greatness. Every movement knows such men, gifted, useful, devoted, but lacking in a kind of inexorability. They don't "take hold" of history, they are not predestined leaders, their impact on people fails somewhere. Levin was admired or disliked; Weizmann had his fanatical followers and his fanatical enemies.

The third of my teachers in Zionism and Jewishness, the poet Chaim Nachman Bialik, began to mold my thinking some years before I met him in person. When I had mastered Yiddish in America, I turned again to the poem Wassilevsky had read to me in Manchester— Bialik's own translation of his Hebrew *City of Slaughter,* a bitter cry of outrage and despair wrung from him by the Kishinev pogrom of 1903. Later, when my Hebrew was good enough, I translated some of his poems from the original, and the Zionist Organization issued a small volume of my translations in 1926, on the occasion of Bialik's first visit to America. It was then that I got to know him in person. Still later I saw much of him in Palestine, especially when I lived two doors from his house on the street named after him.

I have not met or read of a poet who looked and talked less like one than Bialik. He had the round face of a clever moujik, and the build of a medium-sized but hefty butcher. He must have had in him the blood of Khazars, the medieval Tartar converts to Judaism. From his appearance you expected sound, pithy, earthy conversation, and you were not disappointed. You also expected him to be a good businessman, and he was. He had run a large and successful printing plant, first in Odessa, then, after the Bolshevik revolution, in Berlin, and finally in Tel Aviv. He was completely without literary affectation; but when you got him on to the subject of books he blazed into unquenchable enthusiasm. His Jewish erudition was enormous, and he was widely read in other literatures. Once launched, he was not to be stopped, and one listened fascinated by the range of his knowledge and the luminousness of his observations; and still, never a hint that he was a poet of the first magnitude, with few equals in the modern world and none at all in Hebrew since the time of Yehudah Halevy nearly a thousand years ago.

Shmarya Levin was his partner in the publishing house of Moriah, which issued a standard set of the Hebrew classics, edited by Bialik. To be in their company when the conversation veered from business to literature was a fearsome and unforgettable experience; one got a living illustration of the riddle of the immovable body and the irresistible force, for both of them were enthusiasts and tremendous talkers. One of them would be off on a streak, the other interjecting desperately every minute or two: "But let me say . . ." only to meet the ferocious response: "Don't interrupt!" The torrent continued till the speaker, pausing to catch his breath, would suddenly find himself on the outside, vainly interjecting in his turn: "But let me say . . ." The bystander, of course, didn't have a chance and didn't want one. Levin revered Bialik as one reveres a prophet, but the compulsive talker is not his own master.

In company there was a perpetual good humor about Bialik which was utterly incomprehensible when one remembered certain of his poems which could only have issued from a deeply tormented soul. In his 1926 visit to America I traveled with him to several cities where he addressed audiences in Yiddish, I in English. I was prepared, when we set out, to have a moody genius on my hands, and I braced myself for an exercise in tactfulness and understanding. It was, instead, a jolly experience. He was fascinated by the American scene, general and Jewish, and his observations, usually directed at the contrast between America and Jewish Palestine, were ingenious. I showed him, as a typically American product, a copy of *The Saturday Evening Post,* which sold for a nickel in those days. It consisted of two hundred pages, more than half of them advertising. He said: "In opulent America the problem of a magazine is: how low can we price it without losing our advertising value? In poor Palestine it is: how high can we price it without losing our readers?" "I've noticed," he once remarked, "that here in America you say: It's so many hours from this place to that. The land is so big that distance loses its meaning. In little Palestine we speak of kilometres; every one of them counts." He was vastly amused when he listened to my English addresses; he understood not a word of them, but every now and again his name would bob up, and it sounded to him like: "Mumble-jumble-bumble—BIALIK—mumble-jumble-bumble—CHAIM NACHMAN BIALIK—mumble-jumble-bumble . . ." As the distinguished visitor, he always spoke after me, and he would comment in various ways on his impressions. "I have just heard my friend Samuel conducting me through long and lightless corridors." "I felt like a cat in a sack being beaten from time to time." "I felt like a swimmer on a stormy sea; now and again I came up for air, most of the time I was drowning." He had a quick eye for comical situations. I once came across him, during an all-night session of a Zionist Congress, contemplating with fascination a fat delegate who had jammed himself into an armchair in the lobby and had fallen asleep. Bialik pointed at him and murmured in my ear: "A chairful of Jew."

There was no clue in his personal bearing to the misery and destitution of his childhood and boyhood. Weizmann and Levin had been born into what by *Shtetl* standards were well-to-do homes. They had never known real privation of any kind, and they had been immersed in warm and happy families. Bialik was born into grinding poverty, and at the age of seven he had been sent away to live with a stern, pious, and scholarly grandfather so that his mother would have one mouth less to feed. His earliest memories were of a wretched inn kept by his sensitive father for peasants whose rude and boisterous ways he could not endure. The inn failed and the family moved to the outskirts of Zhitomir, where his father tried his hand at various occupations, never with success, so that one by one the household possessions were sold, down to the family candlesticks—that last symbol of Jewish respectability and piety—and the mother had to make the Sabbath eve benediction over candles stuck into clay. Then the father died, and the mother peddled fruit and vegetables from door to door to feed herself and her seven children. In the nights she mended their garments and one night a week she baked bread for them; and as she kneaded the dough and implored God to help her feed her little ones, she wept into the dough, so that as Bialik tells, her children literally swallowed her tears.

A cycle of Bialik's poems is dedicated to these oppressive memories. In one he asks:

> Would you know
> From whom I have my heritage of song?
> A singer settled in my father's house,
> A humble, lonely soul who hid in corners,
> And comforted his frailty in the shadows.
> He had one song, and only one, to sing,
> The same words always, set to the same tune.
> And when my heart was frozen into silence,
> My tongue hard-cleaving to my throbbing palate,
> My stomach empty, and my cry choked back
> By my unyielding throat, his song would wake me.
> He was the cricket, minstrel of poverty.

If you knew nothing of the man's history, you would declare from this and the other poems in the cycle that childhood misery had set its stamp on him—were it not for another cycle in which he celebrates the life of the Jewish village with such charm and gaiety that you are ready to declare: "No, *this* is the experience, the other is painful imagination and empathy." In the end, unable to reconcile the authenticity of the two extremes, you give up the quest for "internal evidence." Equally irresoluble is the contradiction in his attitude toward the disciplines and sacrifices of the classical Talmudic education: in one place a lyrical glorification of the Jewish will to learning and its meaning for the preservation of the people, in another a cry of lamentation for the cruelty and waste of it. He sounds these opposite notes in his poem, *Ha-Matmid,* in which he describes the life of the dedicated young Talmud student, who is fastened to his books as the Cossack is fastened to his horse in wartime.

But the battle is one of self-conquest, and it is not fought out under the open sky, but in a dim, candle-lit corner of a musty Yeshivah. Of the day's four quarters, three are given to combat, one to the body's needs—brief sleep and meager rations. Outside, the fields are magic with summer green or winter white; the boy's eyes are fixed on the ancient text. A seductive wind steals in through the window; he does not even feel it lifting his earlocks.

> An eremite whose corner is his cave!
> With pallid face tight-drawn and puckered brows
> He keeps his incommunicable watch.
> And in the Talmud under him his soul
> Is lost and locked, forever and forever . . .
> Granite is yielding clay compared with him,
> A Jewish boy unto the Torah vowed.

There are other students in the Academy, each devoted in his degree, but he is the *Matmid,* the fanatic of learning. Hunger and thirst and aching eyes have no power over him. If his mind wanders a moment from the text, it is to glance at the glory of great scholars shining across the centuries of the Jewish past, to remember how

> in the chastity of poverty
> The people and its sons have kept the faith . . .
> He tastes the prize
> He pays for with the gold of youthful days.

Is the victory worth the sacrifice? Bialik, himself once a *Matmid* in the Yeshiva of Zhitomir, stares back into the past and his mind becomes clouded.

> I in my boyhood was a listener
> Among those voices, and my youth was passed
> With those wan sufferers whose wrinkled brows
> And staring eyes implore the world's compassion.

And every wrinkle spoke to me in silence
Of passions stifled and of fires extinguished . . .
My fate denied I should be lost with you,
Unhappy ones! and to the hearth you knew
Long, long ago I said my last farewell . . .
The times are changed; far from your boundaries
In alien places have I raised my altar . . .
All, all of you do I remember still—
The hungry childhood and the bitter manhood,
And my heart weeps for my unhappy people . . .
How burned, how blasted must our portion be
If seed like this must wither in its soil.

Once again, the ambivalence of the Jew, here expressing
itself in acceptance and denial of his traditional values. It
is as though the poet were involved in a love which he
recognizes as the source of his strength but knows to be
destructive. Sometimes the love is on the intellectual level,
as in this poem, sometimes on the homely level, as in his
bewitching *Songs of the People*.

In all these qualities, and by virtue of his mastery of
language, Bialik surpasses every contemporary in verse or
prose, but they do not exhaust his greatness and com-
plexity. One aspect of him introduces a second duality. This
product of the *Shtetl* detaches himself completely from his
time and place in a great Miltonic poem, *The Dead of the
Wilderness*. The subject is drawn from a Midrashic legend
which tells that the Jews who left Egypt with Moses and
were condemned to perish in the desert rose in rebellion
and tried to storm their way into the Promised Land
against the divine decree. They were thrown back and cast
into a deep slumber from which they awaken periodically
and renew the attempt, again to be cast into slumber. Between the spasms of fury their gigantic bodies lie in dis-

order on the burning sands, the black rocks surrounding them, the hot sun beating down on their matted and monstrous faces, on the weapons paralyzed in their clenched fists, on their silent tents. It is a universal poem of man's refusal to accept the decree of fate, and the splendor of the imagery matches the grandeur of the theme.

The scenic descriptions are overwhelmingly powerful. Those who have read *The Dead of the Wilderness* and have looked on the desolation of the Sinai Peninsula are filled with wonder at the evocative imagination of a ghetto Jew who had hardly strayed outside the limits of his world; he has caught the primal terror of the desert as if he had been its prisoner for many years, as if his soul had been recast by it. I once asked Bialik how these images had come to him. He said: "Outside my father's inn there was a little hill. I used to lie on it face down, thinking myself into the desert."

Bialik spurred me to the learning of Hebrew as Levin did to the learning of Yiddish; nevertheless, Bialik was a greater master of Yiddish than Levin. He could do in poetry what Sholom Aleichem did in prose—portray the lovableness of the ordinary human being; but he also had powers beyond the reach of Sholom Aleichem—a nobility of style which at one time I thought alien to the spirit of this folk language. There is much talk today of the decline and approaching death of Yiddish; it is, I think exaggerated; but whenever I hear it I think with a pang of the lovelinesses that must be locked away forever in forgotten languages.

CHAPTER XV

Of an Old Tragedy and a Bitter Farce

❀

I

T IS WONDERFUL to see how, when a special life-pattern is forming, the necessary accidents come along to fill it out. To be sure, something is given, an initial pattern issuing from parents and early environment; after that, life is full of accidental events and encounters, and a man takes his pick of them, letting this one affect him more, that one less, a third not at all. But there are indispensable accidents so improbable, and so contingent on preceding accidents, that we stand puzzled as before a conspiracy.

The two months I spent in the late summer of 1919 as secretary and interpreter for the Morgenthau Pogrom Investigation Commission to Poland had a permanent effect on my already developed Jewish interests. But how did I happen to get a place on that Commission? Did I hear of its formation and put in an application? Not at all. I knew nothing about the Commission till I was offered the job. It so happened that the commanding officer of my GII unit had elected to defer his demobilization and stay on in Paris and, being on hand at the center of things, was asked if he would like to go along with former Ambassador Morgenthau to Poland; he answered he would like it very much, whereupon he was empowered to find himself two secretaries; he selected me and the friend with whom I later operated the stenography office in Paris.

It might be assumed at this point that I was chosen because I knew Yiddish, the language of Polish Jewry, which would not have been an accident. But my knowledge of Yiddish had nothing to do with it; I wasn't even asked about it. Like my friend, a non-Jew, I was taken along on general grounds, and when my knowledge of Yiddish was discovered I became more an interpreter than a secretary.

But how did I happen to be in GII to begin with? When the reader last heard about my military career I was in the infantry; the fact is that I went across with the infantry, and I was already in the advanced zone, expecting to be at the front in a matter of days, when our company was drawn up and all those who could speak French were ordered to fall out. Some twenty or thirty responded, a circumstance which would be surprising in a New York outfit but was not at all surprising in the outfit to which I now belonged. For after my training with the 307th Infantry in Camp Upton I was transferred to Camp Green, near Charlotte, North Carolina, and assigned, for no particular reason, to the 103rd, originally the First New Hampshire Infantry, which had had a contingent of men who spoke Canadian French; and when GII headquarters in Paris was recruiting its personnel it sent round to the Louisiana and Northern New England regiments for candidates. Of the twenty or thirty men in my company who were examined half a dozen or so were chosen, I among them. We were sent up to Paris, fitted out in civilian clothes, and distributed to various points in France.

That was how I got into the Bordeaux unit of GII, and what we did there for nearly a year by way of counter-espionage I never found out. We lived in private lodgings, and went every weekday to an office on the rue Esprit des

Lois. Evenings and Sundays I used to take Hebrew lessons from a Palestinian medical student at the local university. (I continued these later in Berlin and Vienna, when I was attached to the Reparations Commission. In Vienna I had an office in the huge Kriegsministerium, and there I did my first translations of Bialik, under the noses of Austrian generals in effigy.) But how was it that my French was good enough to get me into GII? Well, it was the only subject I did well at as a student. That, in turn, was undoubtedly due to the fact that as a child I had spent a year in Paris. My childhood year in Paris, too, was an accident. When we left Rumania in 1900, our destination was, at my mother's inflexible insistence, England, the country without military conscription, and we stayed on in Paris as long as we did only because my father had two half-brothers there. Also, I mightn't have gone to Paris in 1914 if I hadn't already felt at home in the language.

Such, in brief, was the series of accidents which along a meandering route of twenty years dovetailed to land me on the Polish Pogrom Investigation Commission and fill out an important area in my life-pattern.

I was thrilled by the prospect of a sojourn among the Jews of Eastern Europe, and, let me add, elated by the privilege of working on an official body headed by a man of ambassadorial rank, with whom I would surely have occasional contacts, in however obscure a capacity. An ambassador was a romantic and awesome figure to me, far more so than a prime minister or a secretary of state. These were politicians, immensely able perhaps, but politicians still, men of the hustings, exploiters of mob psychology. An ambassador was of a different breed; he was appointed for his knowledge of men and history, for his *savoir-faire,* his subtlety and charm. Dishonest and devious he might be, but these qualities would be marked by distinction, adroitness, and wit. I was twenty-four years old.

My knowledge of Yiddish brought me into more frequent contact with Ambassador Morgenthau than I had dared to anticipate. Morgenthau spoke German, but not Yiddish, and in spite of a widespread belief to the contrary, there is a great gap between the two languages. The vocabulary of Yiddish is, indeed, nine tenths of German origin, but the spirit and the idioms of Yiddish are its own, and what with its admixture of Hebrew words and its pronunciation, which varies from section to section of East European Jewry, it can be quite unintelligible, except for the most primitive exchanges, to one who knows only German. Similarly, formal German can be unintelligible to one who knows only Yiddish. Morgenthau would often call me in when he found the going hard with some particular delegation; he would make part of his address in English, and I would interpret. I got to dislike these occasions intensely because of the curious things Morgenthau said. I did not mind interpreting for General Jadwin or Mr. Homer Johnson, the other top members of the Commission; they did not think it part of their duty to make speeches.

The question before the Commission was not whether violent outbreaks against the Jews had taken place in newly liberated Poland; there was no denying that they had; hundreds of Jews had been killed, thousands wounded; thousands of Jewish homes had been pillaged and destroyed. Whatever the official statement, the real terms of reference of the investigation had, at least for me, a wider purpose. Were the "outbreaks" a symptom of a deep-rooted national condition, or had they been, as the Polish government loudly protested—while minimizing their extent—random mob explosions in a lawless time of transition? Were they merely part of that "turbulent interim period" which I had accepted as the inevitable but brief prelude to the universal reign of law? And if anti-Semitism was indeed an organic element in Polish life, what was the attitude of the Polish ruling classes? Were they fighting it, or were they exploiting it?

From beginning to end the investigations were bitterly discouraging; anti-Semitism revealed itself immediately as a national disease, and Polish officialdom was as widely infected as Russian officialdom had been before it. Yet from beginning to end Morgenthau kept talking to Jewish delegations as if he had undertaken to compose an unfortunate and essentially senseless quarrel in which there was as much to be said on one side as on the other: for the solution of the problem nothing more was needed than a bit of horse sense and some mutual concessions.

In soothing, fatherly speeches he counseled Polish Jewry to take an example from America, where Jews and gentiles got along in perfect harmony because the Jews didn't insist on too much Jewishness. He earnestly admonished Polish Jewry to forget the unhappy past—that was the only way to prevent it from recurring. "All citizens of Poland," he repeated again and again—and he incorporated the advice in his report—"should realize that they must live together" —as if the pogroms had been two-sided. There had been, he conceded, unfortunate incidents, but the future was bright. He was particularly fond of a metaphor which became a nightmare to me because I had to translate it so frequently. "Look at the doughnut, not at the hole." Every time I had to mention the *beigel*—the nearest Jewish equivalent to a doughnut—and the *loch,* the hole, I stammered and squirmed and blushed. The word *loch* unfortunately had a coarse connotation in that context; I could not avoid it because it is also the German word, and Morgenthau, in love with the metaphor, insisted on a literal translation. I was too timid to explain the source of my embarrassment.

That Morgenthau meant what he was saying was unthinkable to me; it was too driveling. As the weeks passed and the work—and the speeches—went on in various cities, I wavered for a time between two theories. According to the first, Morgenthau was biding his time; he would, while temporarily offending and perplexing the Jews, avoid antagonizing the Polish authorities, whose co-operation he needed, until all the facts were in; then he would speak out. That was diplomacy in high gear, crafty and patient, uncomfortable to watch, but understandable. According to the second theory, also understandable but appalling rather than uncomfortable, the Ambassador was "doing a job" for the American and Polish governments. He was, on instruction, playing the situation down for the sake of friendly relations between America and Poland, and his report would be of a piece with his speeches. What the ultimate effect would be on the position of the Jews of Poland was secondary; perhaps it did not even come into the picture; the real purpose of the Commission was to gloss things over and hope for the best, while Morgenthau's overriding purpose was to win for himself the reputation of a gifted manipulator on the international scene, a Jewish Metternich, a new Disraeli.

If the second theory was right, the man was, I thought, a villain. On that theory, he would of course still have to testify to certain facts, those which stared the personnel of the Commission in the face; he would, however, conceal others, less concrete but of wider bearing, without which the reported facts would lack the proper framework and lose most of their significance. He would obscure the fundamental issue by hints and double talk, so that public opinion would be more confused than ever.

In the event, it turned out that both of my theories as to the character of the man were wrong, but I held on to the second for a long time. I discarded the first before the work of the Commission was completed. "This is a wicked man," I said to myself. "He is going to sell the Jews out." I was so firmly convinced of Morgenthau's wickedness—though I ought to mention that he treated me with great kindness—that I did not want to see the report when it was made public by the American State Department in October 1919. It was when I returned to America in 1921 that it was thrust on my attention; and if I ultimately changed my views as to Mr. Morgenthau's character, my anticipations as to the character of the report were completely confirmed.

I may be asked why I am hashing up these old and half-forgotten matters. They are, it is true, part of my personal record; they wove themselves into my life. But is that reason enough to revert to them when it were best that they should be forgotten altogether? I shall try to show, however, that even with all that has happened since, with all those horrors which have made the Polish pogroms of 1918–1919 look trivial, the Morgenthau Commission and its report have an enduring interest for us.

Now, with regard to the bare facts of the pogroms as such, the Morgenthau report is honest enough. But I remember that when I first read it I was immediately struck by a curious sentence in the introductory remarks. "The use of the word 'pogrom' has purposely been avoided, as the word is applied to everything from petty outrages to premeditated and carefully organized massacres." "Excesses" is the word which is regularly substituted for "pogrom." As far as I knew, and as far as the dictionaries know, "excesses" does not have a more restricted connotation than "pogrom." But—and the dictionaries agree—with or without bloodshed a pogrom is an act of riot and pillage and sometimes of murder *instigated or committed by government officials.* The word "pogrom," I at once suspected, was really avoided lest the report seem to reflect on Polish officialdom and the Polish government. The brutal truth turned out to be that Polish officialdom and the Polish government were, by acts of commission and omission, deeply implicated, when not as instigators, then as connivers. The report itself awkwardly and grudgingly reveals as much; and certain facts still verifiable today are even more revealing in this respect. We shall see that Morgenthau's foray into semantics was motivated by something other than literary fastidiousness.

Eight pogroms are listed in the report. The first, at Kielce, occurred on November 11 (Armistice Day). Four Jews were killed and many wounded. "A number of civilians have been indicted for participation in this excess," says the report, issued nearly a year later, *"but have not as yet been brought to trial."* (My italics here and in the following quotations. M.S.)

The second pogrom took place at Lemberg (now Lvov) and was prolonged for three days, November 21–23.

> Sixty-four Jews were killed and a large amount of property destroyed. Thirty-eight houses were set on fire . . . The synagogue was also burned and a large number of the sacred scrolls were destroyed. The repression of the disorders was rendered more difficult by the prevailing lack of discipline among the junior officers to apply stern punitive measures. On December 24, 1918, the Polish Government, through the Ministry of Justice, began a strict investigation . . . 164 persons, ten of them Jews, have been tried for complicity in the November disorders . . . *Forty-four persons are under sentences ranging from ten days to eighteen months. Aside from the civil courts the local*

233

*court-martial has sentenced military persons to con-
finement for as long as three years for lawlessness during the period in question.*

The third pogrom took place in Pinsk on the afternoon
of April 5, 1919. In this particularly beastly incident one
may reasonably challenge the use of the word "pogrom,"
since there was neither riot nor civic disorder attached to
it.

Some seventy-five Jews of both sexes, with the official permission of the town commander, gathered in
the assembly hall at the People's House . . . to discuss
the distribution of relief sent by the American Joint
Distribution Committee. As the meeting was about
to adjourn it was interrupted by a band of soldiers,
who arrested and searched the whole assembly, and
after robbing the prisoners marched them at a rapid
pace to gendarmerie headquarters. Thence the prisoners were conducted to the market-place and lined
up against the wall of the cathedral. With no lights
except the lamp of a military automobile, the six
women in the crowd and about twenty-five men were
separated from the mass, and the remainder, thirty-
five in number, were shot with scant deliberation and
no trial whatsoever. Early the next morning three
victims were shot in cold blood as soon as life revealed
itself in them . . . The women and the other re-
prieved prisoners were confined in the city jail until
the following Thursday. The women were stripped
and beaten by the prison guards so severely that several of them were bedridden for weeks, and the men
were subjected to similar maltreatment.
*It has been asserted officially by the Polish authori-
ties that there was reason to suspect this assemblage of*

Bolshevist allegiance. We are convinced that no arguments of a Bolshevist nature were mentioned in the
meeting in question . . . We are convinced that Major
Luszynski, the crown commander, showed repre-
hensible and frivolous readiness to place credence in
such untested assertions. . . .

The statement made officially by General Litowsky
that the Jewish population on April 5 attacked the
Polish troops, are regarded as devoid of foundation . . .

*Though there have been official investigations of
this case none of the offenders answerable for this
summary execution has been punished or even tried,
nor has the Diet Commission published its findings.*

The fourth pogrom took place in Lida on April 17,
1919. The city having been taken that day from the Bol-
sheviks,

the soldiers proceeded to enter and rob the houses of
the Jews. During the period of the pillage thirty-nine
Jews were killed. A large number of Jews, including
the local rabbi, were arbitrarily arrested on the same
day *by the Polish authorities* and kept for twenty-four
hours without food amid revolting conditions. Jews
were also impressed for forced labor without respect
for age or infirmity. *It does not appear that anyone
has been punished for these excesses . . .*

The fifth pogrom took place in Vilna.

On April 19 Polish detachments entered the city
of Vilna. The city was definitely taken by the Poles
after three days of fighting, during which time they
lost thirty-three men. During the same period sixty-
five Jews lost their lives. From the evidence submitted,

it appears that none of these people, among whom were four women and eight men over fifty years of age, had served with the Bolsheviki. Eight Jews were marched three kilometres to the outskirts of the city of Vilna and deliberately shot without the semblance of a trial or investigation. No list has been furnished the Mission of any Polish civilians killed during the occupation . . . Over two thousand Jewish houses and stores were entered by Polish soldiers and civilians during these three days and the inhabitants robbed and beaten. Many of the poorest families were robbed of their shoes and blankets. Hundreds of Jews were arrested and deported from the city. Some of them were herded into box cars and kept without food or water for four days. Two of these prisoners have since died from the treatment they received. Included in the list were some of the most prominent Jews of Vilna, such as the prominent writers Jaffe and Niger. *Up to August 3rd, 1919, when the Mission was in Vilna, none of the soldiers or civilians responsible for these excesses had been punished.*

The sixth pogrom took place in Kolbussowa.

For a few days before May 7, 1919, the Jews of Kolbussowa feared that excesses might take place, as there had been riots in the neighboring towns of Rsoszow and Glasgow. These riots had been the result of political agitation in this district, and excitement caused by a case of alleged ritual murder in which the Jewish defendant had been acquitted. On May 5 a company of soldiers was ordered to Kolbussowa to prevent the threatened trouble. Early in the morning of May 7 a great number of peasants, among whom were many former soldiers of the Austrian army,

entered the town. The rioters disarmed the soldiers
and three peasants had been killed. They then proceeded to rob the Jewish stores and to beat any Jews
who fell into their hands. Eight Jews were killed
during this excess. Order was restored when a new
detachment of soldiers arrived late in the afternoon.
*One of the rioters has since been tried and executed
by the Polish Government.*

The seventh pogrom took place in Czestochowa.

On May 27, 1919, at Czestochowa a shot fired by
an unknown person slightly wounded a Polish soldier. A rumor spread that the shot had been fired by
Jews [sic! M.S.] and riots broke out in the city, in
which Polish soldiers and civilians took part. During
these riots five Jews, including a doctor who was
hurrying to aid one of the injured, were beaten to
death and a large number wounded. French officers
who were stationed at Czestochowa took an active part
in preventing further murders.

No mention is made in this section of trial or punishment of the rioters.

The eighth and last pogrom listed in the report (there
were others, but they were minor, and "their detailed
description has not been considered necessary, inasmuch
as they present no characteristics not already observed in
the principle excesses") took place under peculiar circumstances.

On August 8, 1919, the Polish troops took the city
of Minsk from the Bolsheviki. The Polish troops
entered the city at about ten o'clock, and by twelve
o'clock they had absolute control. Notwithstanding
the presence in Minsk of General Jadwin and other

members of this Mission, and the orders of the Polish General forbidding violence against civilians, thirty-one Jews were killed by the soldiers . . . During the afternoon and in the evening the Polish soldiers, aided by civilians, plundered 377 shops, all of which belonged to Jews . . . No effective attempt was made to prevent these robberies until the next day, when adequate officers' patrols were sent out and order established. *The Polish Government has stated that four Polish soldiers were killed while attempting to prevent robberies. It has also been stated to the Mission that some of the rioters have been executed.*

No attempt was made by the Commission to verify these statements of the Polish government.

The Polish government's action on the Minsk pogrom has an interest of its own. The Yiddish papers were permitted to print the story, which was in complete agreement with the report brought back to the Morgenthau Commission by General Jadwin and the other eyewitness members of the Commission. The Official Polish Telegraph Agency, government-controlled, printed a counterreport stating that only seven Jews had been killed, and these either accidentally or deservedly. Side by side with this Polish version appeared, naturally, the usual editorial comment branding the Jewish reports as wild and slanted exaggerations the purpose of which was to traduce Poland in the eyes of the world. The government could of course have obtained General Jadwin's report, which also contained the statement that not a single case of Jews shooting on Polish troops had been observed. Perhaps the Polish government did obtain that report, but in printing its own report as a counterblast to the report in the Yiddish newspapers, it added, as clinching evidence of its own truthfulness and of the mendacity and perfidy of the Jews: *"General Jadwin was an eyewitness of the taking of the town."* It is scarcely necessary to add that when the Yiddish press published General Jadwin's report, corroborating its own, the government and the Polish press ignored it.

In quoting from the Morgenthau report I have italicized those points which bear on the punishment of the pogromists and the official concealment of the facts.

In only two instances was there so much as a *claim* on the part of the Polish government that it had acted with anything like the appropriate severity; and the lenity with which it actually proceeded against offenders in the first five pogroms was mirrored in the connivance of local authorities and much of the military. The report makes some comment in this connection:

> It is [therefore] agreed that a more aggressive punitive policy and a more general publicity of judicial and military prosecutions would have minimized subsequent riots by discouraging the belief among the soldiery that robbery and violence could be committed with impunity.

To anyone who reads the report with attention, this comment is ludicrous in its feebleness. But when additional facts not mentioned in the report are taken into consideration, the word that suggests itself is not "ludicrous" but "cynical." The report states correctly that the Diet Commission set up to investigate the massacre at Pinsk on April 5, 1919, had not published its findings by August 3; it does not state that the Jewish newspapers which tried to tell the story of what happened in Pinsk were confiscated by the government. With a kind of senile gravity the report suggests the advisability of "a more general publicity" when in fact an immense conspiracy of silence and deception accompanied the pogroms. The Polish public, including the intelligentsia, was at one with the government in the conspiracy. Shortly after the pogrom, the poet Leib Jaffe, mentioned in the Vilna section of the report, wrote in his newspaper, *Die Yiddishe Zeitung,* an editorial under the caption "Days of Loneliness."

> What was Polish society doing, what was Polish society saying when the Jewry of Vilna was agonizing in its blood? Where was the Polish intelligentsia? Did the bleeding, humiliated Jews of Vilna hear a single voice of sympathy and protest from the side of the Poles? Some individual Poles did, it is true, come to the defense of certain individual Jews. There were cases, too, of Polish priests defending, at the risk of their lives, the Jews of little villages round Vilna. But where was the Polish social body as such? Where was an appeal to be seen, or a newspaper standing up against these events? . . . Perhaps the hardest thing to bear these days has been the loneliness, the abandoned condition in which we found ourselves.

I met Leib Jaffe in Vilna during the sessions of the Commission, before which he appeared as a witness. He had seen his wife lashed by a Polish soldier, his friend Weiter killed, and Weiter's friend, Madame Sherman, wounded. Together with Samuel Niger, the distinguished literary critic, and others, he had had to run a long gauntlet between two lines of hooligans wielding belts and clubs—a favorite game with Polish anti-Semites. Our meeting in Vilna was official; I got to know him better, years later, in Palestine—a gentle, smiling man, a gifted poet, and a lover of humanity. He was killed, in the land to which he had gone to find a happier life, when the Jewish Agency building in Jerusalem was blown up by Arabs. He was a man incapable of hate or resentment. In another editorial, also published soon after the Vilna pogrom, he wrote:

> One thing must be said these days. The soul of our people is filled with indignation and sorrow, but in it there is no feeling of enmity and revenge. Even at a time like this we can rise to historic heights. We know, we are certain, that the heavy, asphyxiating atmosphere in which we are living will become fresher and freer . . .

Alas for his hopes! They belonged to a time when millions of the oppressed were caught up in the dream of a better world order born of the war to end war. When he wrote those editorials Leib Jaffe believed—so he told me in Jerusalem—that through the Morgenthau report the world would learn the truth about Poland's attitude toward its Jewish citizens, and world pressure would bring about a radical change in Poland. He lost this belief when the report was issued.

But I have not yet touched on the most disheartening and offensive elements in the Morgenthau report. What I have quoted so far is enough, I suggest, to indicate that Morgenthau ought to have known from his own investigations how deeply rooted anti-Semitism was in the Polish masses. But there is more.

> Whereas it has been easy to determine the excesses which took place and to fix the approximate number of deaths, it was more difficult to establish the extent of anti-Jewish discrimination. The discrimination finds its most conspicuous manifestation in the form of the economic boycott. The National Democratic Party has continuously agitated the economic strangling of the Jews . . . Landowners are warned not to

sell their property to Jews, and in some cases where such sales have been made the names of the offenders have been posted within black-bordered notices, stating that such vendors are "dead to Poland." Even at the present time this campaign is being waged by most of the non-Jewish press, which constantly advocates that the economic boycott be used as a means of ridding Poland of its Jews.

And again:

Besides these excesses there have been reported to the Mission numerous cases of other forms of persecution. Thus in almost every one of the cities and towns of Poland, Jews have been stopped by the soldiers and have had their beards either torn out or cut off. As the Orthodox Jews feels that the shaving of their beards is contrary to their religious belief, this form of persecution has a particular significance for them.

A strange sentence, this: I cannot help wondering whether a non-Orthodox Jew who wore a beard—say like Theodore Herzl, or Chaim Weizmann, or even Morgenthau himself—would "feel" less while having it torn out. But the beard was only one of many Jewish characteristics. The Jews of Poland had a life of their own, developed in the course of ten centuries. They formed, with their three millions, fourteen per cent of the population. Their right to their traditional way of life had been recognized at the Versailles Peace Conference, had been contractually confirmed by Poland's representatives. The report notes:

A new Polish constitution is now in the making. The general scope of this national instrument has already been indicated by the special treaty with the Allied and Associated Powers in which Poland has affirmed its fidelity to the principles of liberty and justice and the rights of minorities, and we are certain that Poland will be faithful to its pledge which is so conspicuously in harmony with the nation's best traditions.

But what grounds did Morgenthau have for such certainty, and what encouragement to be faithful to the principles of liberty and justice can the Poles have found in the following passage?

> In considering the causes for the anti-Semitic feeling which has brought about the manifestations described above, it must be remembered that since the partition of 1795 the Poles have striven to be reunited as a nation and to regain their freedom. This continual effort to keep alive their national aspirations has caused them to look with hatred upon anything which might interfere with their aims. This has led to a conflict with the national declarations of some of the Jewish organizations which desire to establish cultural autonomy . . . In addition, the position taken by the Jews in favor of Article 93 of the Treaty of Versailles, guaranteeing protection to racial, linguistic and religious minorities in Poland, has created a further resentment against them. Moreover, Polish national feeling is irritated by what is regarded as the "alien" character of the great mass of the Jewish population. This is constantly brought home to the Poles by the fact that the majority of the Jews affect a distinctive dress, observe the Sabbath on Saturday, conduct business on Sunday, have separate dietary laws, wear long beards, and speak a language of their own . . .

That Article 93 was forced on the Poles by the Allies who had given them their freedom is true; that the Poles would have been less anti-Semitic if the Jews had not

243

claimed minority rights is unprovable and most probably false. When has anti-Semitism lacked a pretext? In any case, the vast majority of the Jews did claim those minority rights, and the reference to the "national declarations of some of the Jewish organizations" is a confused attempt to put the blame on a minority within the Jewish community. But with or without Article 93, with or without "national declarations," the majority of Jews would have gone on living at least for some time as they had lived for centuries: some of them affecting a distinctive dress, wearing beards, observing the Sabbath and the laws of *kashrut*, and studying the sacred books, still more of them in one degree or another cultivating a tradition handed down by many generations; in all of which they would have continued to irritate Polish national feeling. While the report recommends "a more aggressive punitive policy" toward pogromists, it nowhere suggests that something ought to be done about the irascibility of Polish nationalist feeling, that is, about Polish chauvinism. It implies, instead, that it was natural for the Poles to have regarded the Jewish minority as a hateful obstacle to Polish national liberation; and of some deeper significance in the phenomenon of anti-Semitism there is of course no hint.

I return to my observations on Morgenthau's substitution of "excesses" for "pogrom." The reader may have thought them finicky and malicious; perhaps the following will give him a better impression. In 1922 Morgenthau wrote an article for the April issue of the *The World's Work*. He tells there of his meetings as head of the Mission with Polish and other notables, among them Pilsudski, the first Polish chief of state; he also gives us some interesting insights into the frame of mind in which he approached and performed his assignment. I confine myself to a single brief quotation:

"Pogrom?" Pilsudski had thundered when I first called on him . . . "There have been no pogroms in Poland! Nothing but unavoidable accidents."

I asked the difference.

"A pogrom," he explained, "is a massacre by the Government, or not prevented by it when prevention is possible."

It was here, then, that Morgenthau learned to avoid the word in his report, and to think up an ingenious reason for the avoidance. I answered the article bitterly in *The New Palestine* and exposed what I called "The Treachery of Henry Morgenthau." I did not meet him again and of course never heard from him.

II

I shall now tell how I came to revise my opinion of Morgenthau and to clear him in my mind of the charges of villainy and treachery. Many years had passed and I had stopped thinking about the man. It was 1947 and I was in Palestine, working with Weizmann on his memoirs. In *Trial and Error* there is a short and diverting chapter, "Opéra Bouffe Intermezzo," which tells how President Wilson sent Morgenthau to Europe in the summer of 1917 to try to persuade Turkey, the ally of Germany, to make a separate peace, and how Weizmann was sent, unofficially, by the British Foreign Office to intercept him and "talk him out of his mission." A separate peace with Turkey at that stage of the First World War would have meant a pledge to preserve "as is" the rickety, oppressive, and utterly corrupt Turkish Empire, leaving the Armenian, Arab, and other peoples under the misrule they had endured for centuries. This the British government would not accept, for reasons of their own; the subject peoples had better reasons for opposing such a plan. Weizmann writes:

> The British Foreign Office did not attach much importance to the manoeuvre. I did—at first . . . The French, it soon transpired, were taking the American mission seriously. After all, here was an ex-Ambassador who had come across the ocean with the blessings of the [American] President, and accompanied by a whole suite [which included, among others, Professor Felix Frankfurter]. Besides, the wish may have been father to the thought: the French were prepared to consider a separate peace with Turkey on the basis of the inviolability of the Turkish Empire. I, for my part, soon came to the conclusion that the whole business was a *canard*.

It needed only a face to face encounter with Morgenthau, which took place in Gibraltar early in July.

It appeared, continues Weizmann:

> that Mr. Morgenthau had had an idea. He felt that Turkey was on the point of collapse. It had occurred to him that perhaps Taalat Pasha might be played off against Enver Bey, and a peace move considered. I put two simple questions to Mr. Morgenthau. First, did he think the time had come for the American Government to open up negotiations of such a nature with the Turkish authorities; in other words, did he think Turkey realized sufficiently that she was beaten, or likely to lose the war, and was, therefore, in a frame of mind to lend herself to negotiations of that nature? Second, assuming that the time was ripe for such over-

tures, did Mr. Morgenthau have any clear ideas about the conditions under which the Turks would be prepared to detach themselves from their masters?

Colonel Weyl [the French representative] was particularly anxious to obtain a precise answer from Mr. Morgenthau. But Mr. Morgenthau was unable to furnish one. In fact, as the talk went on, it became embarrassingly clear that he had merely had a vague notion that he could utilize his connections in Turkey to some end or other; but on examining the question more closely he was compelled to admit that he did not know the position and was not justified in saying that the time had arrived for negotiations. In short, he seemed not to have given the matter sufficiently serious consideration . . . When I asked Frankfurter, informally, what *he* was doing on this odd mission, he answered that he came along to keep an eye on things!

It was no job at all to persuade Mr. Morgenthau to drop the project. He simply persuaded himself . . . We talked in this vacuum for two whole days. It was midsummer and very hot. We had been given one of the casements in the Rock for our sessions, and the windows were kept open. As Mr. Morgenthau did not speak French, and Colonel Weyl did not speak English, we had to fall back on German. And the Tommies on guard marched up and down outside, no doubt convinced that we were a pack of spies who had been lured into a trap, to be court-martialed the next morning and shot out of hand. I must confess that I did not find it easy to make an intelligible report to Sir Ronald Graham [of the British Foreign Office].

Dr. Weizmann enjoyed redictating this chapter from an earlier draft of his own, and I enjoyed taking it down; but

I thought he was unfair. I had long since lost my awe of ambassadors and ex-ambassadors; all the same, here was a man who, after having done a stint as ambassador, had been entrusted by President Wilson with two important missions. I told Weizmann of my experience with Morgenthau in Poland; he was a bad man, I said, a conscienceless and irresponsible careerist; but surely he couldn't have been the nincompoop depicted by Weizmann. Weizmann smiled and quoted a Yiddish proverb: "If you have money, you're good-looking and clever and a good singer as well." But knowing that Weizmann could be cruelly satirical, I still objected. Not that I minded the unfairness to Morgenthau; I only wanted a more plausible picture of the man. I did not withdraw my objections until 1961, when Justice Frankfurter issued his fascinating volume of reminiscences. *His* version of the Gibraltar episode is even more diverting —and more devastating—than Weizmann's.

"I suppose," he begins, "that there never was a more fantastic mission on which I found myself sent than the so-called Morgenthau mission in June and July, 1917," and goes on to tell how Morgenthau, having been rewarded for his contributions to the Wilson campaign of 1913 by the ambassadorship to Turkey, and finding himself out of a job when America declared war on the Central Powers, went about in Washington "bothering everybody with a great thought he had of detaching Turkey from Germany and Austria."

The idea, thought Professor Frankfurter (as he then was), did not appear, on the surface, altogether harebrained. "There was only the little problem of how it was to be implemented."

Turkey is a far land, and Morgenthau talked glibly of Mustapha Kemal and about people who seemed

248

awfully remote even to those in power. Finally, after some diplomatic negotiations, Wilson got the agreement of Lloyd George and the French Prime Minister, M. Ribot, a long-whiskered gentleman who didn't amount to much, to join in the American-Anglo-French Commission to look into and bring about, if possible, the detachment of Turkey from the Central Powers.

I was then assistant to the Secretary of War, and Baker broached the subject of my going along with Ambassador Morgenthau. I didn't know anything about him except in the way in which we're all influenced by what we hear and read. I assumed he was a considerable personage [I read this with relief. M.S.] but something in me resisted Baker's suggestion. I didn't want to go with Mr. Morgenthau. I finally met him and was puzzled by him. He wasn't my kind of person, in the sense that his talk was inconsequential and not coherent, but loose and big and rhetorical. You couldn't get hold of anything, but I assumed that was just the froth of the man. I didn't realize that the froth was the man.

But Professor Frankfurter got his orders from Wilson and went, "the theory being that they needed an international lawyer . . . I wasn't an international lawyer, knew damn little about international law. I knew where Turkey was on the map and not much more, but as is the way with lawyers I began to study up the case . . . ," and by the time the party was on board, "I knew more about Turkey than Morgenthau had acquired in all his years there because my knowledge was critical and his was general, just hot-air impressions." After a few days at sea Frankfurter also knew much more about Morgenthau than Morgenthau did.

I soon realized that his ego was enormous, insatiable . . . After one or two sessions I couldn't bear it. I forget how many days we were on the water—ten, I think—and I became inaccessible thereafter. At lunch he'd say: "Where were you?" "I was on the upper deck, waiting for you," or the lower, or whatever it was. I really played the game of hide and seek because I soon saw that the man hadn't a brain in his head . . . What gave him what he had? What did he have? Money. He was a great dealer in New York real estate . . . Oh, it was such a boring thing.

For the details of the harrowing experience the reader must go to Justice Frankfurter's own record. I add only two more paragraphs—short ones. After Morgenthau had, as Weizmann puts it, talked himself out of his mission, he went to France to report to General Pershing. "Mr. Morgenthau," says Justice Frankfurter with a deep sigh, "asked me to go along, so I went. But the stuff was so puerile! I remember sitting in Pershing's room and sliding down in my chair with the thought that I could make myself even less conspicuous than my small size inevitably makes me, so that Pershing might not remember that I was even there."

Justice Frankfurter closes the episode with: "I concluded that simply because you can make money in New York real estate doesn't mean that you have an understanding of the relationship of people, or nations, or know the history of forces that made the past and will therefore determine the future."

I have absolved Mr. Morgenthau of villainy and treachery and base political motives in the affair of Polish pogroms. I have come to the conclusion that he just hadn't the foggiest notion what it was all about, his equipment for this mission being of the same order as his equipment for his peace-with-Turkey mission. Those driveling addresses of his to the Jewish delegations—he meant them, in so far as they could be said to have meaning. And he really thought he was serving the best interests of Polish Jewry, as well as of Poland and America and civilization generally.

Morgenthau was, let it be noted, a representative figure —the type of Jew who believes that, on the whole, anti-Semitism is caused by the behavior of Jews. Not, the type adds hastily, that anti-Semitism is ever justifiable; the accusations made by anti-Semites—that the Jews are a bad lot, that they have far more than their permissible proportion of sharpers, arsonists, white-slave traffickers, draft-dodgers and traitors, that Jewish bankers are a sinister world power—are obviously based on a ridiculous prejudice. But—so runs the argument—why feed that prejudice by addiction to Hebrew or Yiddish, and, worst of all, a claim to peoplehood?

This trivialization of a deep-rooted folkloristic malady in the body of Western civilization is itself a result of anti-Semitism. It also turns into a mockery the gigantic tragedy of Jewish suffering. The Jews, it would seem, have suffered massacre and exile not because of their will to preserve, however imperfectly, a meaningful life-view, but because of uncalled for, irritating idiosyncrasies; the six million that were done to death in Europe are a warning against the folly of tactlessness.

My mind runs over the recent history of European Jewry. I look back at the pogroms in Poland which broke out on the day the First World War ended. We did not know that they were a prelude to the ghastliest episode in the history of the Jewish people; but we did know that this was an evil beginning for the "new era." We—I am speaking of Jews who shared my outlook—were embittered not only by the pogroms themselves, but by the anxiety of the world to ignore them. In America the first six Polish pogroms were reported so obscurely as to make no impression. It was only after an immense Jewish protest demonstration had been staged in New York that the American public was roused. The force of the demonstration, wrote *The Maccabean,* the organ of the American Zionists, "can be gauged by this one fact: it has succeeded in breaking through the wall of silence which has been built round the Polish atrocities by the American press. That wall, of course, was erected in pursuance of the policy of pampering Poland. Poland was to be set up as the barrier against Bolshevism."

Germany, too, was to be the barrier against Bolshevism less than a generation later; therefore, German "excesses" against the Jews had to be handled with the greatest delicacy. Morgenthau tells us in his *World's Work* article that Pilsudski was infuriated by the publicity which was finally given to the pogroms. "Excesses? The exaggeration of the foreign press concerning what had happened to a trivial number of Jews had been monstrous." Jews ought not to scream when they are being murdered and robbed; it upsets important negotiations for the preservation of world peace and world freedom. The word the Germans were to use was *Greuelpropaganda*—atrocity propaganda; and in America and England anyone who thought that something ought to be done about the Nuremberg laws was liable to be called a warmonger. Pilsudski, like Russia's rulers before him and Germany's later, was outraged by foreign intervention in his country's internal affairs. What Poland or Russia or Germany did to her Jews was her business and nobody else's. I quote again from Morgenthau's article in *The World's Work:* " 'Why not trust to

Poland's honor?' shouted Pilsudski. 'Don't plead that the article's concessions [referring to Article 93 of the Versailles Treaty signed by Poland] are few in number or negative in character. Let them be as small or as negative as you please, that article creates an authority, a power, to which to appeal outside the laws of this country. Every faction in Poland was agreed on doing justice to the Jews, and yet the Peace Conference, at the instance of America, insults us by telling us that we *must* do justice.' "

Pilsudski was worried by the harm Morgenthau's report might do Poland. " 'These little mishaps,' he said, 'were all over, and now you come here to stir the whole thing up again and probably make a report that may still further hurt our credit abroad.' " Whatever harm Poland's reputation suffered in connection with the pogroms was caused, not by the Morgenthau report, but by the demonstrations and the agitation which led to the appointment of the Commission. They also led to a change in the technique of Polish anti-Semitism. Hot pogroms were too spectacular; the cold pogrom of boycott and economic strangulation was more effective and did not lend itself to dramatization. After 1919, hot pogroms were discouraged in Poland; the cold pogrom was conducted with mounting intensity until the day the country was overrun by the Nazis from one side and the Communists from the other.

‖‖

CHAPTER XVI

Hieroselyma Est Perdita

❀

‖‖

FOR a number of years I kept, irregularly, records of my dreams, setting them down the morning after their occurrence. I still reread them occasionally and I have noticed how, over the years, some of them have died to my memory, so that I have to take my own word for it that I dreamed them, while others have remained alive. I am unable to establish any selective principle. It is not Time. Some dreams dated as recently as 1951, 1954, and 1956 might have been dreamed and recorded by a stranger for all their evocative effect on me now; others, going back to 1941, are almost as fresh as if I had just and incompletely awakened from them. Nor is the selection based on the degree of vividness with which I remembered the dream on awakening. Thus one dream, dated January 5–6, 1954, has the footnote: "Deeply affected," but going over the account, I cannot connect myself with a single detail; while another, dated April 21–22, 1941, with the notation "Mildly affected," is in me from beginning to end.

Thus it is also with individual experiences when I read my notes and diaries and published articles of forty years ago and more. In 1919 I wrote: "Of all those who suffered at the hands of the Poles I got to know best Madame

Philipovka, whose husband and sixteen-year-old son were both murdered on the same day, their bodies being thrown with those of six other Jews into a common grave on the road to Lipuwka, a suburb of Vilna. She came to see me several times in the hotel in connection with her efforts to obtain a pass to Germany. Sometimes she came with her daughter, her one surviving child, and sometimes with a niece, and gradually she told me of her son and of the hopes she had had for him. Once she heard me exchange a few words in Hebrew with her niece, and on the next day she brought me typed copies of two Hebrew poems her son had written at the age of thirteen, and again, on the following visit, a crude twenty-four-page Hebrew brochure, hectographed, which had been got up by young comrades of her son in his memory, containing some of his own poems and fables."

From further notes I gather that I was more deeply shaken by this tragedy than by any other that came before the Commission, and that Mme Philipovka haunted me for some time after her visits: "I can't get her out of my mind!" But it is in vain that I search my living memory for any trace of her. Had I been asked six months ago— that is, before I began to go through these old notes and articles—whether I had once known or even heard of a Mme Philipovka, I would have answered: "I don't think so." If I had been asked: "Didn't you have several conversations with her in Vilna, and didn't you carry away what you called an 'unforgettable' impression?" I would have answered: "Certainly not." And as far as my inner response is concerned, the answer is the same now that the notes lie in front of me. On the other hand, I do remember, down to the details of face and voice and dress, a young woman barely out of her teens whose husband had been killed and who appeared before us only once. It seems to me that if I were shown her photograph, taken at that time, I would recognize her instantly. Similarly, all erased from the tablets of my mind is Mme Sherman, who, I read in my notes, "cried before us like a child" as she told us how she and her friend Weiter were dragged into the street and shot down like dogs, he fatally; but I remember clearly a baffled and outraged little man to whom I had to explain that he could not claim from the American Pogrom Commission compensation for his looted shop. I remember him even though he is not mentioned in my notes.

I cannot account for these mysterious individual caprices of my memory, but I can readily see why the two months I spent with the Pogrom Commission should have become a permanent influence in my life. I was a Zionist before I met Weizmann and would have remained one without him; I had involved myself in Jewishness, in the fate of the Jewish people, in Yiddish and in Yiddish literature, before my visit to Poland, and the involvement would have been lifelong without it; but as Weizmann deepened my response to the Zionist idea, so that strange, fortuitous, direct contact with East European Jewry, attended as it was by its peculiar circumstances, added to my involvement a new element of sensitivity.

Outside of books, my knowledge of the Jewish world had been drawn from our Manchester ghetto and from American—chiefly New York—Jewry. Certainly New York's East Side Jewry was Jewishly vital, but its vitality was not rooted as it were in the landscape, one could not yet speak significantly of its local history, whereas East European Jewry had a majestic historicity, centuries and centuries of it. From Eastern Europe the lines ran back to older sites and through them to long-lost, ever-mourned Judea; but East European Jewry was a great historic phenomenon in its own right, a substantial segment of the immense total trajectory of Jewish history.

Vilna is dominant in my active memory of Poland, though I spent more time in Warsaw, with its larger Jewish community. I was predisposed to that partiality, knowing already that Vilna was the glory of East European Jewry—Vilna, the Jerusalem of Lithuania, as they called it, for Vilna was historically Lithuanian, not Polish, and the Jews were there before the Poles. As it was not the largest, so it was not, by far, the oldest East European Jewish community, but Vilna rose to unchallenged eminence as an intellectual and spiritual center and maintained that eminence down to the end.

Names that mean little to Westernized Jews and nothing at all to non-Jews, but were portents in the Jewish world of yesterday, are linked with Vilna's history. The most illustrious of these names is Elijah Kremer, who is never mentioned by his family name, for which the word *Gaon* has been substituted, meaning Excellency, or Genius. That title once belonged to the heads of certain academies in Babylonia; it fell into disuse with their fall, and was revived for bestowal on Elijah of Vilna. His, in the view of many, was the greatest and widest-ranging Jewish intellect of the Exile, with the exception of Maimonides. His learning was equalled by his piety, and both by his saintliness. Except for some travels in his early manhood, he never left his native city, the fame of which he began to enhance in his boyhood. He was barely out of his teens, a Jewish Admirable Crichton or Pico Della Mirandola, when scholars twice and thrice his age were seeking his opinion on knotty problems of the Law; and the universal reverence accorded him was the more remarkable in that he was an innovator, and in a sense a rebel. He rejected the hair-splitting and casuist spirit still dominant among the

Talmudists of the eighteenth century and moved from the medieval into the modern age, applying philological and rational methods to his studies of Talmudic and pre-Talmudic literature. He was a grammarian and a mathematician, and, in contrast to his contemporaries, held that a knowledge of science was a necessary part of a Jewish education. He left behind him treatises on trigonometry, algebra and astronomy, as well as voluminous commentaries on the sacred books. He lived a modest and retiring life, refusing honors and high official posts and contenting himself with lessons to a chosen group of pupils. His saintliness and unostentatious asceticism were a family tradition. Of his grandfather, the scholar Moses Kremer, it is told that he kept his grocery store open only for as many days as were needed to provide a livelihood for the current week; and if on Sunday he had earned enough, he closed the store till the following Sunday, saying: "The other shopkeepers, too, have to make a living."

The place where Elijah Gaon studied and taught was a little *klaus* (close) or chapel in the Great Synagogue, and the Vilna Gaon's Klaus became one of the sanctuaries of world Jewry. I went there one evening and looked for a long time at the plaque which commemorates the man "who sat here for forty years and spread wisdom till his name became a glory in the world."

In all his long and tranquil life, the Vilna Gaon was involved in only one public controversy, but that a violent and memorable one. He was a *misnaggid,* that is, an opponent of Chassidism, that religious revolt of the humble and unlearned against the spiritual tyranny of the scholastics. The founder of Chassidism, Israel, the Baal Shem Tov, or Master of the Good Name, was born in 1700, twenty years before Elijah Gaon, and died in 1757. The birthplace of the movement was Podolia, and its early and rapid

258

successes were among the Jews of southern Russia. It was
not till some twenty years after the death of its founder
that Chassidism began to make some headway in Lithuania. By then, however, the movement had undergone
much change. Here and there the original simplicity and
mysticism remained, elsewhere there had crept in the
feature called *Tzaddikism,* the superstitious exaltation of
the Chassidic *rebbes,* some of whom lived in regal splendor
on the offerings of their devotees. There had also developed an intellectual Chassidism, the first and greatest
exponent of which was Shnaiur Zalman of Liadi, a man as
saintly if not as learned as the Gaon himself. Whether it
was this brand of Chassidism or another that made the
first breach in Vilna itself, we do not know, but certain it
is that by the seventies of the eighteenth century little
secret conventicles of Chassidism existed in Vilna. Equally
certain is it that the struggle between *Misnagdim* and
Chassidim was long and vicious. The *Chassidim* were formally excommunicated from the body of Israel by the
Misnagdic rabbis. Their shops were declared taboo; their
butcher's meat, though prepared with punctilious attention to the Jewish dietary laws, was declared *treif,* unclean,
unfit for consumption by Jews; marriage with their sons
and daughters was declared as heretical as marriage with
the sons and daughters of gentiles.

It is hard to understand how a gentle spirit like the
Vilna Gaon lent his authority to such rancors. One suspects
that he let himself be carried away by wild reports, for,
having withdrawn into his ivory tower of study, medita-
tion, and prayer, he never ventured forth to investigate for
himself. Nor would he avail himself of the one opportunity
that was offered him to learn the truth at first hand and
from the highest source, namely Shnaiur Zalman, the
Rebbe of Liadi, who humbled himself and sought an audi-

ence with Elijah Gaon. He came as a suppliant to the *klaus* and was refused admittance; he pleaded through the closed door and the man inside remained deaf. Was the Gaon afraid that he might have to recant? Was he by this time, in his fifties, too weary to undertake a struggle with his own followers? Was it enough for him that he had been an innovator in Jewish studies? Whatever the case, that dramatic picture became part of the history of Vilna Jewry, remembered long after the two sects had become more or less reconciled, each recognizing in the other a fruitful branch of the tree of Israel.

Another towering religious figure associated with Vilna is Israel Salanter, of the middle and late nineteenth century, who founded the *Musarist* or Moralist school. He was not a native of Vilna but taught there for a time and left his mark on the life of the city, as, indeed, on much of East European Jewish life. He was, perhaps indirectly, a conciliating element between *Misnagdim* and *Chassidim*. He deflected attention from the barren acrimony of the quarrel by his emphasis on the suppression of egotism in all the subtle forms it takes in the self-deceiving human being. For Israel Salanter, the Law was an instrument for the purification of man in his relations with his fellow-men. Though he was a distinguished scholar, he had no respect for the man of learning who held that his knowledge of the Law set him apart in merit; nor did he respect the blind and rigid observance of the letter of the Law. In his eyes the purpose of the Law was to enable man to live a life of goodness and selflessness; therefore, the Law meant life before it meant anything else, and where it came in conflict with the principle of life it was self-correcting.

He illustrated this once in a startling manner.

It was the Day of Atonement, that awesome point in the cycle of the Jewish calendar, the only day of fasting and self-affliction which can override the tranquillity and happiness of the Sabbath. Even the Black Fast of the ninth of Ab, the reminder of the two Destructions of the Temple, bows before the Sabbath, which must be enjoyed to the full like any other Sabbath even if it falls on that maleficent date; the fasting and the lamentation are deferred to the next day. Now, that particular Day of Atonement fell at a time when cholera was raging in the city, and preaching to the congregation, Israel Salanter pressed the point that the law was given to man to live by; and if by reason of sickness a man might be endangering his life in observing the fast, the spirit of the Law commanded him to break the letter of the Law. To drive home this point the Rabbi, himself not infected by the pestilence, drew from his pocket a slice of bread, held it up, pronounced the benediction: "Blessed art Thou, O Lord our God, King of the universe, who bringest forth bread from the earth," and ate. The worshippers beheld with stupefaction this holy act of sacrilege, unthinkable save in a saint of the first order; and the lesson was never forgotten.

These personalities and stories and many more for which I have not the room here were already familiar to me when I visited Vilna. But the city itself was a legend to me. I saw it mostly by night, driving through it from end to end, the droshky clattering and bumping along under the moonlit and cloud-flecked sky. Sometimes I got out on my crutches (I had broken a scaphoid in a street accident in Paris) and, if the hour was not too late, hobbled with the assistance of my guide into courtyards and buildings. They were crammed with Jewish history; the obstinacy of the Jewish will-to-be was chiseled into their stones. The scholars and saints were only the outstanding representatives of a people's persistence. The Vilna Gaon's *klaus,* famous above all others, was only one of a hundred of its kind. For there were the *klauses* of the trades and professions, the *klauses* of the bookbinders, the draymen, the tinsmiths, the glaziers, the bakers (two such *klauses,* one for the white-bread specialists, the other for the humbler black-bread men), the tailors (similarly duplicate, according to grade), the butchers, the musicians, the coopers, the carpenters, the chimney sweeps, the cobblers, the grave-diggers, and the rest.

Every *klaus* had its teacher or its Rabbi, specializing in a branch of study, and usually its free-loan association and its charity fund. It had its *prushim,* men who had withdrawn from the world and lived out their last years in the *klaus,* studying, eating crusts, and sleeping on the wooden benches. To each *klaus,* but of course particularly to that of the Vilna Gaon, men came with their intellectual or ritualistic problems, and sorrowing women with their supplications for husband and children. As the Vilna Gaon's was *the klaus,* so the Great Synagogue was *the* synagogue, and when the Synagogue Courtyard was mentioned without specification, it could only mean the Courtyard of the Great Synagogue. This, with the houses clustering about it, was the ghetto of ghettos, the heart of Vilna Jewry, the stronghold within the stronghold of tradition.

But as Vilna led in tradition, so it also led in revolt against tradition, and its internecine struggles were a fiery distillation of the struggles within the Jewish people at large. It was in Vilna that the secular Jewish movements found their highest expression. The *Bund,* anti-religious, and revolutionary within the framework of the general Russian revolutionary movement, was founded there in the same year, 1897, that the first Zionist Congress was held in Basle. The Bund was of course anti-Zionist, rabidly, contempuously, unremittingly, but while one section of it stood for the total liquidation of the Jewish people by

262

assimilation into the surrounding peoples, another part stood for Jewish survival as a Yiddish-speaking national minority. Part of the Bund became, after the revolution, the *Yevsektzia*, the Jewish section of the Communist Party, which liquidated a large number of Jews and in turn was liquidated by Stalin. It was in Vilna that Shmarya Levin (*my* Shmarya) preached during his rabbinical years, drawing immense audiences. (I met, in 1919, those who remembered with awe his fiery orations and his exhortations to the revivial of Hebrew as a spoken language.) But it was also in Vilna that the Yiddishist anti-Zionist movement was at its strongest. Of Vilna Sholem Asch wrote, as late as 1939: "It takes the first place in the reconstruction of the Jewish people. Vilna is the center of the Yiddish word. It is here that the new folk school was born, where the Jewish child is given a modern, all-human upbringing in Yiddish. Vilna has become the *Yiddish* Jerusalem."

One stands in astonishment before the spectacle of a community numbering between seventy and eighty thousand souls capable of presenting such a turbulence of ideas and ideals. It calls to mind Renaissance Florence or Periclean Athens; it calls them to mind also by way of contrast. The worship of physical beauty, the delight in the human body which were part of the classical paganism of Athens and the neo-paganism of Florence were unknown to Vilna. Its vitality was exclusively intellectual and moral, and therein it was true to the charge laid upon the Jewish spirit from of old.

Vilna Jewry and Polish Jewry no longer exist; they were systematically obliterated by Nazi Germany; and what is left of East European Jewry as a whole is being ground into enforced assimilation by the Communists. There are those who hope that some day a change will come about in the Communist concept of freedom, but East European Jewry as a civilization is done for; its Jerusalem lies in ashes, and unlike the Jerusalem through the ruins of which the Emperor Hadrian drew the plough, it will not burgeon again with a Jewish life.

There will be no more Vilna Gaons, no more Masters of the Good Name, no more Israel Salanters; no more Sholom Aleichems and Mendelles and Yal Peretzes and Bialiks and Achad Ha-ams and Weizmanns and Shmarya Levins. The city communities and the *Shtetlach* will never be re-created. There is a distinction in ghastliness between the fates of German-Austrian Jewry and East European Jewry. With the former, the Nazis destroyed a high concentrate of genius which was placed directly at the service of the world; there will be no more Einsteins and Freuds and Ehrlichs and Willstaetters. With the latter, the Nazis destroyed a rich form of life; they destroyed a civilization.

It is this aspect of the Nazi crime that has escaped general attention, to some extent understandably. The planned slaughter of six million human beings has such a paralyzing effect on the imagination, the details of the action, the massive organization of it, as for some major industrial enterprise, the regimented rounding up and transporting, the shooting and gasing and incinerating of men, women, and children, lay so crushing a burden on the mind that a conceptual grasp of something beyond the human suffering is almost impossible. The word genocide has become current to denote the wiping out of a people; we have no word for the crime of wiping out a civilization.

It was unforeseen because unimaginable. My experience with the Polish Pogrom Investigation Commission colored darkly forever after my meditations and researches on anti-Semitism, but my darkest forebodings were but the faint penumbra of the black reality that was to come. Even so, I was considered "hipped" on the subject, and what I wrote

on anti-Semitism was widely criticized as morbid and un-
realistic. Would to God that my critics, Jewish and non-
Jewish, had been right! I will not let myself believe that
the world will ever witness again a repetition anywhere
of the Nazi fury against the Jews; I will not because I am
incapable of abandoning hope. But neither will I consent
to the view that warning is no longer necessary.

I read in Gissing's *Ryecroft Papers:*

> Injustice—there is the loathed crime which curses
> the memory of the world. The slave doomed by his
> lord's caprice to perish under tortures—one feels
> that it is a dreadful and intolerable thing; but it is
> merely the crude presentment of what has been done
> and endured a million times in every state of civiliza-
> tion. Oh, the last thoughts of those who have agonized
> unto death amid wrongs to which no man would give
> ear! That appeal of innocence to the hard, mute heav-
> ens! Were there only one such instance in all the
> chronicles of time, it should doom the past to ab-
> horred oblivion. Yet injustice, the basest, most
> ferocious, is inextricable from warp and woof in the
> tissue of things gone by. And if anyone soothes himself
> with the reflection that such outrages can happen no
> more, that mankind has passed beyond such hideous
> possibility, he is better acquainted with books than
> with human nature.

I will go on insisting that anti-Semitism is a specific,
organic disease of Christian civilization; that, wherever it
appears, it is the companion or forerunner of injustice to
others than Jews; and far from ignoring, out of timidity
or a miscalculating prudence, its first public appearance
anywhere, we should—Jew and Christian alike—expose
it at once as a threat to the whole Judeo-Christian world.

CHAPTER XVII

"Writer and Lecturer"

❀

WRITER and lecturer" is the entry opposite "Occupation" on my passport; also on my income-tax form, where the order should be reversed, since my books just about pay the rent, lectures providing the rest. Descriptively, the order is correct; most of my labors go into writing.

But if I did not have to lecture for a living I would be running about offering to do it gratis. I still love with all the passion of my boyhood the feel of an audience and the challenge of oral exposition. I still cannot come across an interesting idea without wanting to tell everybody about it. I am at the opposite pole from the melancholy Jacques with his: "I think of as many things . . . but I give thanks to heaven and make no boast of them"; and it has been my wild good fortune that, unlike most compulsive talkers, I have found people willing to pay to listen to me. If I had had to stay on a regular job, with regular responsibilities, I would have gone to pieces under the pressure of my primary compulsion, that of the writer.

Yet, like some of my betters, I often write when a considerable part of me would rather be doing something else,

for the compulsion is a complicated thing. I used to think
that the hunger for fame was the strongest element in it:

> *Fame.* The adrenalin: to be talked about;
> To be a verb, to be introduced as *The* . . .
> To be forgotten with embarrassment; to be—
> To be.
> It has its attractions, but is not the thing.

Thus A. M. Klein, one of the most unjustly neglected
of our contemporary poets. No, it is not the thing. The
hunger for fame has died, with much else. To become
famous in old age would be like getting cocktails after
dinner. Of course I want my books to sell, but money
apart—I must anticipate the time when the inability to
travel will be cutting into the profits as well as into the
pleasures of lecturing—I am concerned, more than ever,
with giving currency to certain views and values.

This concern mingles with the craftsman's compulsions,
which grow more and more exacting as my taste improves
and my powers wane. I want to see how accurate and
evocative I can make a description, how concisely, grace-
fully, and tellingly express an idea; most troublesome of
all, because here I am weakest, how natural, organic, and
unnoticed I can make the progress of a paragraph, a chapter, a book; and as a protagonist, which I am more than
artist *pur sang,* how proleptic I can make my argument,
anticipating in it the maximum of possible objections.

There are, indeed, times when I sit down and write
furiously for two or three hours. I am "inspired"; the
afflatus has visited me; my spirit's barque is driven far
from the shore, far from the trembling throng; I say to myself, exultantly, modestly, and in Cockney: "This is a bit
of all right!" Such moods are deceptive nine times out of
ten. What I finally accept as passable, often with a grimace,

has been rewritten at least once, sometimes three, sometimes four and ten times, with many deletions, chiefly of the inspired passages. On the whole I work in a spirit of cheerful determination, but black days will come up without warning, without apparent reason; then I write and tear up, write and tear up, and count myself lucky if I break even. For I can get into a howling rage and tear up a week's or a month's work. My gullibility is indestructible; let the afflatus touch me and while it lasts I am certain, each time, that I am at the top of my form. Experience has taught me nothing; I am like the undiscourageable youngster who takes every month's crush for his elective affinity.

To be unable to write when I want—and it does not matter whether the drive is joyous or pleasantly dogged or grimly dogged—turns the whole world awry. There is a conspiracy; I am being persecuted. It happens less frequently now, my days have for a long time been more or less my own. I will not tolerate interruptions except by arrangement—these science lessons, for instance. Even my beloved lectures can become a great nuisance. If one intrudes—fortunately it is almost always in the evening—I strip the obligation down to its essentials of preparation and delivery, though once I am on the platform, my discomforts vanish. "For the duration" I avoid welcoming committees, decline to visit local sights, turn down dinner invitations, excuse myself (with rudeness when unavoidable) from the reception that usually follows a lecture. This for the duration only; when the fit is over, I am as sociable as an ant, curious about people and their individual and family histories, about congregational affairs and communal politics. Thus, I am remembered by some as a morose snob, by others as a most companionable fellow.

I learned early to insulate myself from my surroundings

268

and to work almost anywhere. I traveled—I still do sometimes—with a small portable typewriter which I used on
trains, planes, ships, and even buses. The moment I got
into my hotel room I shifted the table around to get the
best light from window or lamp, took out books and manuscript, and was at it. During the actual traveling I had
wax stopples in my ears; if the passenger in the adjacent
seat addressed me, I would remove the nearer stopple
laboriously and say: "I beg your pardon?" I would answer
briefly and courteously, then replace the stopple with the
same elaborate ritual. I was rarely addressed a second time.

The sharpest and most intractable compulsion is the one
that attends what at the moment seems to be, and on rare
occasions is, the birth of an idea. I must write it down at
once, wherever I am, whatever I may be doing (I may, in
fact, be writing—two compulsions in fratricidal dispute!),
and less from the fear of losing it than from the need to
file it away where it will stop bothering me. If I can sus-
pend the current activity, I will give the newborn idea all
the time it asks for; otherwise I must content myself with
a rapid outline; and if even that much is impossible, I
become distraught. In the army this variety of compulsion
made me a source of hilarity to my fellow-soldiers, and it
got me into a memorable engagement when I was working
in the calender room of the Goodyear Rubber factory in
Akron. My fellow-workers on the night shift looked with
suspicion on my habit of running into a corner, pulling
out pencil and notebook, and scribbling wildly for a minute or so. Finally one of them loudly voiced the opinion
that I was a company spy. I angrily offered to show him
my notes when the shift was over, and a small group of us
gathered before the gate in the dawn light. Far from
allaying suspicion, the notes, codelike, half legible, excited
it the more. One thing leading to another, I called my

accuser a bald-headed son of a bitch. What I meant to say was boneheaded, which, being within the limits of diplomatic exchange, is not a *casus belli,* but he did happen to be partly bald and I was not in complete control of myself. In the ensuing set-to, he proved that he was also what A. E. Housman calls the better man, and I did not return to the factory that evening—or ever again. The worst of it is that these jottings are as unreliable as the longer fits of inspiration; when I reread them later, they are apt to astonish me by their flatness and pointlessness.

The reader is entitled to smile. "What a fuss! He must really think himself a genius." No; that, with the hunger for fame, was *spurlos versenkt* decades ago, though the compulsions remain. Some of my work is well forgotten, some I consider useful, and part of that, good. How good, God alone knows, and the reviewers are not in His confidence. Such reviews as come my way no longer affect me. The unfavorable ones I read with a shrug: "For all the attention he pays, he might just as well have liked it." The favorable ones give me the same mild pleasure as a weighing-machine character-analysis card which assures me that I am a man of inflexible determination. There have been a few exceptions; here and there a reviewer has read carefully, and when he has been dissatisfied for reasons I found valid (and in fact already knew), I have wanted to write him a long, warm letter of thanks.

Even my early delusions of genius had in them an element of pretence; I would not otherwise have endured so many frustrations. I would have turned away from my family: *"Lass sie betteln gehn, wenn sie hungrig sind";* but then, I am myself unable to put up with the privations and humiliations of grinding poverty, as a Dostoevsky did, or be a hanger-on like a Rainer Maria Rilke. How stunning are those rare figures at the very top, a Shakespeare, a

Goethe, who combine supreme genius with worldly *savoir-faire,* and sail through life with reasonable comfort, acceptable to God and the tax collector.

In the days when I got few lecture dates, and those poorly paid, I did an immense amount of translating from Yiddish, German, French, and Hebrew, with Yiddish outweighing the other three combined. This interfered far less with my own writing than the steady job—to be told about in due course—which I held for seven years, for I could fit much of it into my creative schedule. Certain writers, such as Sholom Aleichem, Bialik, Peretz, Shmarya Levin, I felt it my duty to make accessible to English readers; others, such as I. J. Singer and Sholem Asch, were bread and butter jobs. But I never translated a book I did not in some measure respect. I quarreled and almost broke with Sholem Asch when I refused to translate the third volume of his New Testament trilogy, *Mary,* and his novel of our times, *East River.*

When my own work is not hounding me, I can find pleasure in translating; it is a separate craft, with problems and frustrations of its own. I often read masterly translations—Shakespeare in German, Proust in English—side by side with the originals, delighting in particular ingenuities. (The greatest of all translations, the King James version of the Bible, stands apart; how it was done is beyond one's imagination.) Great translators are rarer than great writers (the two never seem to come together) and, alas, I am no more a Schlegel or a Scott-Montcrieff than I am a Shakespeare or a Proust.

Sholom Aleichem I transmitted rather than translated. Supreme among Yiddish writers, he is so drenched in the idiom of the *Shtetl* that every other sentence cries out for a paragraph of explanation—and he par excellence a humorist! I confess that when I read translations by Sholom Aleichem I wince rather than laugh—but I could not have done better myself. I wrote round him, and about him, retelling rather than translating. So, too, with Yal Peretz, who is, however, less of a problem, being more of an intellectual. I waited many years, and lectured a good deal on both men, before I undertook to "render" them into English. Bialik I tackled early because I did not and do not find as wide a gap between Hebrew and English as between Yiddish and English. Shmarya Levin was moderately difficult, I. J. Singer quite easy, and Sholem Asch easiest of all. In substance and style I. J. Singer (not to be confused with his younger brother, Bashevis Singer) is remote from the *Shtetl;* Asch began there and moved away from it. Asch's best book, *Der T'hillim Yid* (literally, *The Psalm-Jew,* translated as *Salvation*), is one of his earliest. It reads poorly in English and was a failure; I was asked to retranslate it, but hadn't the courage to try.

I. J. Singer has done well in English; Asch was of course a tremendous success with and after his New Testament trilogy. To my considerable annoyance, I am better known as his translator than as an original writer, whence obviously—to anticipate trigger-happy amateur psychoanalysts —the moderateness of my esteem for his later work. But I have less disreputable grounds for remembering Asch with distress; he brought a vast amount of still-continuing trouble into my life. As the sales of his books soared, one after another, into the hundreds of thousands, the rumor got about that he owed everything to my genius as editor-translator. There was no truth in it, but the rumormongers were nearly all Yiddish writers with their own standards of evaluation and modes of reasoning. Some of them might admit that Asch was not at all bad as compared with themselves, but he wasn't *that* good; ergo, I had played vis-à-vis Asch the combined roles of Perkins vis-à-vis Wolfe and Scott-Montcrieff vis-à-vis Proust.

It became an article of faith in part of the Yiddish literary world that to get me as translator was to be assured of success, and some considered me such a good translator that they advised me to write in Yiddish and translate my-self into English. Thus, for nearly a quarter of a century I have had to fight off a succession of desperate men in whose minds I was fixed as the only hope. I learned to see in a new and terrifying light Mahomet's classic description of the Jews as "the People of the Book."

"Fight off" is putting it feebly; some I have had to peel away with patches of my skin. As an experienced reader, I need only look at the first few paragraphs of a book or manuscript to estimate the quality of the material; to make completely sure, I pick a few pages at random, and I have never been "disappointed." But what can you do with a man who insists that you read every one of his fifty or a hundred thousand or two hundred thousand words because, he assures you, that is the only way you can get the true effect? What can you do if he implores and de-mands that you let him read to you for an hour or two, if he telephones again and again, offering to clarify certain passages which, he admits, cannot be appreciated without sustained attention under his supervision? Your blood pressure rises from call to call, in the end you bang down the receiver—and feel remorseful, angrier with yourself than with your tormentor. Does he not, after all, feel as frustrated as a true artist?

The occasionally humble, who bow quietly to my No and withdraw with dignity, are almost as bad. A throb of sympathy passes through me; this is obviously a fine human being. I want to mitigate in some measure the effect of my rejection. But one incautious word and I shall be committed.

For these time-wasting, energy-consuming, nerve-wear-ing episodes I blame Sholem Asch. If only he had been considerate enough not to achieve a *succès fou!* If only I had had the foresight to leave my name out as translator! But on the other hand I wanted it there for business reasons.

However, this complaint is partly balanced by a debt of gratitude. If the Jews have a higher proportion of scribbling maniacs than any other people, they also have a higher proportion of true literary talent. Some of this I have discovered for myself, some has been brought to my attention as the too well-known translator of Sholem Asch. How pleasant it is to come upon a good piece of work by an unknown! And what a sinking feeling follows: "We have to do something about this." More than one publisher, my own included, and more than one Jewish foundation, will testify to the persistence with which I have urged the merits of Jewish writers, and to the labor I have put, so often in vain, into getting an English-reading public for them.

Because Asch's portraits of Jesus, Paul, and Mary were warmly sympathetic, he was widely and stupidly accused of seeking to convert Jews to Christianity, from which it followed that he was himself a secret convert, a sort of undercover agent for the Church. This malicious invention still comes up during question periods of my lectures. As it happened, Asch was Jewish through and through; apostasy was as remote from him, with his make-up and attachments, as from an orthodox Jew.

Those who charged Asch with apostasy usually added that in his New Testament novels he had also sinned for money; he had deliberately descended from his natural level. Talk of this kind is silly on general grounds. A man with ingrained standards—and Asch had them—cannot get rid of them. He may try his hand at a potboiler, but here and there the craftsman creeps in, and pride being stronger than prudence, he lets the phrases stand, hoping the reader won't notice that he is confronted with literature. The result is neither the one thing nor the other. Even writers who declare, with what they hope will pass for disarming frankness, that they know they are writing trash, having no genuine talent, are lying. Only a saint is capable of such humility, and saints who think they can't write don't.

To one who knew Asch personally, the charge is silly on particular grounds. He had a massive conception of himself as an artist, and developed a deep grievance as year after year went by without bringing him the Nobel Prize. To him his New Testament novels were more than literary masterpieces; they were a Messianic attempt to reconcile Jewry and Christendom. He was dumbfounded when I refused to translate *Mary*. I would not tell him outright that I thought the book an artistic mess, but that was what my individual objections amounted to. The sympathy he had brought to his portrayals of Jesus and Paul became cloying sentimentality when he turned to Mary. Here he could indeed be unjustly suspected of secret Christological sentiments, and even of what many Christians have objected to, namely, Mariolatry. The rage of his slanderers had, however, spent itself on *The Nazarene* and *The Apostle*, where it had not a shadow of justification.

Protagonist, propagandist, teacher—all these descriptions fit me. My over-all message, addressed to Jews, is that a knowledge of Jewish history in the widest sense—the experiences and thoughts of the Jewish people from antiquity to the present—is indispensable to the Jew who wants to remain Jewish without becoming warped by anti-Semitism. I may also be described as a one-man Anti-Self-Defamation League, on the prowl for Jewish writers who transfer their Jewish self-hatred to their people; and I told an audience recently that I look upon myself as an employee of the Jewish people with a lifelong contract on which only one signature appears. I am a professional Jew, in a class with rabbis, fund-raisers, Hebrew teachers, executives of Jewish institutions, and the like, but while they are on regular salaries I peddle piecework. From the point of view of security this has its drawbacks, but the compensations outweigh them. I have no organization, no board of trustees, no executive committees to reckon with, no fellow-employees to adjust to. Nor can the accusation, so common in public life, of hanging on to a job, be leveled at me. Nobody is contractually committed to buying my books or listening to my lectures.

In the roles I have mentioned—to which may be added Unofficial Minister for Jewish Self-Improvement—I am a much misunderstood man. A questioner at a lecture once said: "Whatever happens anywhere in the world you ask right away: 'Is that good for the Jews?'" I answered: "The criterion has its merits. An improvement in the position of the Jews anywhere usually goes with an improvement in the condition of the host people. Oppression of the Jews indicates a deterioration." My questioner remained standing, dissatisfied. "Perhaps you mean," I said, "that I am narrow, parochial, Jewish-centered, to the exclusion of all other interests?" He nodded. I went on: "To be Jewish-centered is to be world-centered; we are a world-people." I quoted Zangwill's adaptation of Terence's line: *"Judaeus sum, humani nil a me alienum puto."*

But he had touched on old memories, on forgotten ambitions and discomforts. I had longed to be famous in the world at large, and yet I had let myself be absorbed in the Jewish problem, an unpromising area. Novels about Jews, yes; essays on general problems, yes; but essays

276

The recoil in American Jewry from an earlier melting-pot theory of assimilation is in part a response to the threat of depersonalization. It is mixed with other factors; the extermination of six million Jews and the birth of the State of Israel have left deep psychological effects; and the general American movement toward religious affiliation, often—and more or less correctly—characterized as a purely social phenomenon, has set up a kind of machinery for Jewish self-recovery. But it is quite wrong to stop at these factors. The young Jewish physicists, chemists, mathematicians, engineers (I have met hundreds of them) who find they have to provide some Jewish instruction for their children, and join a temple or a synagogue for that reason, are often puzzled at themselves. "Look," they expostulate, as if anxious to disassociate themselves at once from their superstitious grandfathers, "look, I'm beyond that sort of thing, but I want my son at least to know who he is." I mention the scientists because it is presumably the scientific outlook which is most intelligently (or should I just say articulately) at odds with the notion of Jewish affiliation; also because among them one might expect a certain amount of clear thinking on the subject. I probe and find confusion. I ask: "Can't your son be a Presbyterian and know who he is?" They answer: "I don't believe in any religion, but if my son has to get a certain amount of religion to know who he is, at least let it be Jewish." I continue: "But why on earth do you want him to know that he is a Jew?" Sometimes they answer: "Better for him to find it out from me than from an anti-Semite"; sometimes: "A man shouldn't be ashamed of his origins"; and sometimes: "Well, if he isn't a Jew, what is he?"

Now, this concern with the child's need for self-identification is genuine, and the answers have meaning for the speaker, on one level or another; what the parents often do not perceive is that they, finding themselves the begetters of a new generation, are urgently in search of their own self-identification. The unformulated anxiety runs: "We've got children! What shall we tell them about ourselves? And, for that matter, *who are we?*"

The spiritual confusion of the physicist, mathematician, etc., is not different from that of the doctor or lawyer in the same predicament, or, given a certain level of intelligence, of the plumber or pantsmaker. It begins with a misconception in the religious field. A member of an audience once said to me: "As a physicist I do not believe in the existence of God. I know that things take place in accordance with unchangeable laws. In years of experimentation I have never come across an instance of interference with those laws by an outside power." I commented: "You seem to be under the impression that only a physicist, or a scientist generally, is aware of the inexorability and inviolability of the natural laws of cause and effect. But a pantsmaker, too, has the right to say: 'As a pantsmaker I do not believe in the existence of God. I know that in the making of a pair of pants there are inexorable and inviolable laws of cause and effect, and in all the years of my pantsmaking I have not come across a single instance of interference with these laws by an outside power. Never, never, in the making of thousands of pairs of pants have I seen a single pair come out right if the cutting was wrong.' His scientific experience hasn't the range and subtlety of yours, but it is as decisive."

Belief in God does not by itself make a Jew, just as calling oneself an atheist does not make one an atheist (the intellectual discipline of atheism is extremely exacting). The Jew who thinks himself an atheist and, looking for self-identification, can find it only in the Jewish people, relies on the fact that Jewishness, unlike Christianity, regards *peoplehood* as an expression of religion. And people-

I was for a time a member of the American Zionist administration and for a year a member of the Actions Committee of the World Zionist Organization. I had to take sides, accept compromises, obey caucus decisions when it had so been agreed, and vote against my convictions or, against them, refrain from voting. I had to seek the votes of people I found noisome, and I stumbled over the gushing courtesies which are the lubricants of political co-operation, the pot calling the kettle white for the return compliment. I realized that there is no other way in political life, and "political life" extends into every variety of organized human activity—synagogue and church, yeshivah and university, and the most idealistic associations and brotherhoods. I realized that the man who is "above politics" is simply letting others do the disagreeable work which is indispensable to the conduct of human affairs.

Jewish leadership in America is almost entirely unprofessional; there are few important jobs and, if I may so put it, no pork barrels. Rewards therefore take honorific forms: presidencies, chairmanships, a place on a letterhead, newspaper publicity, oratorical encomiums by visiting bigwigs at local banquets. In most cases such rewards are well earned; much labor and devotion goes into the successful direction of a U.J.A. or Israel Bond drive, the creation of an institution, though the heavy spadework is of course done by professionals. All this I could let pass, but when the extorted reward is the privilege of delivering an address before an important audience, the result sometimes crosses the threshold of my endurance. The majority of amateur speakers have so little rapport with their listeners that they are insensitive to the most demonstrative inattention. They seem to be addressing themselves. A hum of conversation rises in the hall, a general dispersal sets in; they go on, undeterred. They remind me of my aunt Mallie, who never connected with anybody. I marvel that they should so hunger for an audience and, getting one, should have nothing to do with it.

My enthusiasm for the cause carried me along for a number of years, but, underneath, a double revolt was gathering. First, of the writer. I was miserably cramped for time; I could not periodically set aside a few weeks for leisurely production, tinkering with sentences and chapters. I could not set aside a daily interval. I could not as the representative of the Zionist Organization behave on lecture tours as I have done since. I was at the disposal of the Zionist community from arrival to departure. In New York I had my office duties. There was as little room here for "compulsions" as there had been in the army or at the Goodyear Rubber Company. The books I managed to turn out during that period were substandard even for me.

Second, of the free commentator. An organization man is bound by rules; if he agrees with them, he belongs by nature and conviction; otherwise, he must get out or go under. There is the sacred-cow rule: a certain man is useful to the movement. You think that his practical usefulness is more than offset by the demoralizing influence on Jewish life of his vulgarity and his unsavory business reputation. A certain rabbi plays a leading role in Zionism; it is your opinion that his arrogance and his pathological careerism are bad for the movement and worse for the rabbinate. You feel it your duty to make known your opinions in print; the organization does not consider this helpful. (I ought to add that I have known a saint in Jewish political life; that was Henrietta Szold, the founder of Hadassah, and it is inconceivable that even she did not now and again deviate from strictly saintly standards by silence or evasion.)

There is the rule that the organization is always right in its external relationships—the equivalent of "My country right or wrong" and "politics stops at the frontier." If you believe your organization to be in the wrong, you may, indeed, stay in it, and try to set it right; but you cannot be its employee.

I was at odds with the organization on some issues. Under the cruel pressure of a rising world anti-Semitism, it devoted little attention to the spiritual needs of the Jewish people, concentrating on the promotion of immigration into Palestine. I thought this understandable but wrong, a shortsighted self-defeating policy. The attention paid to the young generation was fitful and inadequate, and it seldom rose above the intellectual level of a Sunday school. The organization should have founded and maintained at a loss a periodical of high literary quality, a forum for established Jewish writers, an invitation to young writers of promise. I believed that a culturally and spiritually reawakened Jewry would ultimately yield larger practical results. But a cultural and spiritual renaissance is a vague thing, and the cry was for practical results now. Again, there crept into the movement a repellent Jewish jingoism which has increased with the founding of the Jewish state. Many leading Zionists disapproved; the organization could not make such disapproval its business.

For all these reasons I left the employ of the organization: but, chiefly, to be "free to write."

But how remote already was the literary *parole* of my Paris days: "Art for art's sake. If the writing is good it needs no other justification. The true artist takes in the literary field Cesare Borgia's motto in the political: *'Fais ce que voudras, advienne que pourra*—do what you want to do, come what may.' Express yourself. Don't teach, don't preach, don't play the world-improver, leave that to the deluded busybodies who anyhow do more harm than good."

That was gone—and yet twinges of it continued to haunt me, and do till this day. I want to write something just for the fun of it—to the extent that writing is fun. I once took off three months to write an intellectual thriller, *The Devil That Failed*, about a man who was kidnapped by a group of pygmies who managed, by the ingenious arrangement of his surroundings, to persuade him that they were of normal size and that he had suffered an attack of gigantism; his problem was to discover without help from outside his miniaturized surroundings, that he was normal and his captors abnormal. I still like the book, which was reprinted in England, though I am afraid that it is tainted by a moral. I once wrote a novel of husband-and-wife relations, *Beyond Woman*, and can read parts of it without distaste; I spoiled it by making the characters gentile while my models were Jewish. But for these, and my first two novels, whose names I won't mention, my books have had some sort of educational purpose chiefly for the benefit of Jews. However, with the reservation noted, there was occasional fun in the writing of these books. *The World of Sholom Aleichem*, which has been reprinted every two or three years since I wrote it twenty years ago (and lest the reader wonder why I need to lecture, let me mention that its sale has not yet reached the thirty-thousand mark), and *Prince of the Ghetto*, on Yal Peretz, were enjoyable tasks; the nearest to pure fun was *Certain People of the Book*, a reconstruction of a number of Biblical characters. *The Gentleman and the Jew* was hard going, and there was no fun at all in *The Professor and the Fossil*, a retort to Arnold Toynbee's *A Study of History*, with its nasty misprision of the Jews, or *Level Sunlight*, a critical examination of the State of Israel in

1953, with attention to negative features. Other books I have written I shall mention further on; and there are many more that I want to write.

I want to write a book to be called *The Charm of Yiddish,* and I would open with a detailed side by side comparison of Shtutchkoff's magnificent Thesaurus of the Yiddish language and Roget's Thesaurus of the English language, showing how the number of words and idioms gathered round particular objects and ideas in the respective languages mirrors the differences in the modes of thinking and of historical experience. Hints on this subject are scattered throughout my Jewish books, but they are not enough. The power and attractiveness of Yiddish owe much to its dual character. Its beginnings lay in simple economic necessity; Jewish traders in the Rhine Valley eight or nine hundred years ago, coming up from the south, had to learn the local dialects, and turned them into a jargon; into this jargon they ultimately infused the non-economic element of their lives, their Jewishness. The final result was a language far more strongly polarized than English or French or German into a spirit of practicality and a spirit of other-wordliness, of mercantilism and Messianism. I would have to do a great deal of reading for this book.

I want to make a study of Jewish apostates, of which there are many types: Heine, who "converted" for convenience and remained emotionally tied to his people and its traditions; in his class were Daniel Chwolsohn and Benjamin Disraeli—but it was the elder Disraeli who led his family into the Church; Karl Marx, too, grew up in a converted household, but he thought of the Jews with hatred; Boris Pasternak and Simone Weil were genuine converts, with widely different approaches; Jacob Frank and Sabbathai Tzvi were pathological cases. There are

283

non-religious Jewish "apostates" who demonstratively repudiate their people in the name of a secular cause, just as Pasternak did it in the name of his brand of Christianity. Such a man was David Bergelson, also a Russian Jew who, however, wrote in Yiddish; but whereas Pasternak's repudiation was compassionate and condescending, Bergelson's was filled with a Streicher-like loathing of Jewish things. Most of Bergelson's novels are merely indifferent to the subject, but his greatest book, *Bam Dnieper (By the Dnieper)*, a magnificent panorama of Russian and Jewish life at the turn of the century, is haunted by an obsessive disgust with Jewish life, and in passage after passage he descends to the level of *Der Völkische Beobachter*. Yiddish and Hebrew critics usually ignore *Bam Dnieper*, and thus his name is allowed to stand high on the roster of Yiddish literature. I suppose that in a way it should; but when Bergelson is included in the martyrology of Jewish writers who were liquidated by Stalin, I protest. At one time I wanted to see *Bam Dnieper* translated into English, for the record. I wanted this particular piece of Jewish history to be more widely known; I wanted the role of the *Yevsektzia* to be understood, and I wanted to point the moral of its miserable fate. But so many friends have disagreed with me, fearing the harm that would be done, that I have changed my mind. As to Ilya Ehrenburg, who writes in Russian, I am at a loss as to how to classify him. He has used and abused his self-identification as Jew with immense skill, to become the only prominent Jewish writer in Russia who has survived unpersecuted into a somewhat malodorous old age.

I would like to write a long essay on my relations to America, the country without which there would hardly be a Jewish people today and therefore no Jewish homeland; and a book on American Jewish writers, with special attention to the recent crop; and still another on the enthusiasms of intellectuals without wisdom and their unreliability as guides to enduring values.

But, above all, I want to write a book on the layman's relation to science or, rather, to scientific knowledge, recording, among other things, my sad belief—the result of some years of study—that scientific knowledge cannot be "popularized"; that without the equivalent of a sound high-school and first- and second-year university training in the subject, one can't begin to understand what the scientists are saying in their capacity as scientists; that most science popularizations and practically all TV scientific programs (excluding the tutorial ones) are, in that sense, frauds; and that the problem of the relation between the humanist and the scientist is a long, long way from solution. The problem has of late been haunting me with such persistence that I even tried to weave it substantially into this book as part of my life experience; but it got out of hand and I must return to it elsewhere.

It is generally held that as a writer ages he improves his style at the expense of his ideas. I will say nothing about my style, but I am bursting with ideas; they may not be good ones, but the urge to expound them is as compulsive as ever.

CHAPTER XVIII

The Maggid

❀

THE FIRST TIME a chairman, thanking me at the end of a lecture, made use of the kindly formula: "May he be spared many years to carry on the good work," I nearly laughed out aloud. I took it he was confusing me with another lecturer, as chairmen sometimes do. I glanced over the audience—not a smile anywhere. The absurdity of it! Why, only yesterday they had been using the other formula: "This brilliant young man . . ." Then it occurred to me that I had been addressing audiences for over half a century.

I see myself as one of the *Maggidim,* the wandering preachers of East European Jewry about whom I had first heard from Lamport, and my line of descent is through Shmarya Levin, himself a modernized version of the tradition. My lecture subjects are drawn mostly from books I have written on Jewish themes and books I intend to write, and, as I have indicated, I do not pretend to be merely a purveyor of information. I have an axe to grind. My general objective in lecturing, as in writing, is to help Jews acquire an interest in Jewish knowledge with the hope that they will transmit it to their children, though, with the recent improvement in Jewish youth education, the children sometimes know more than the parents, and then it is a question of encouraging the parents at least to keep up with their children. Where the interest already exists, I cater to it. My theory of Zionist propaganda is that the more a Jew knows of his people's cultural and spiritual heritage the more likely he is to be a Zionist.

It took me many years to create a market for my lecturers. I had to educate audiences to like the kind of education I offered. I was told that I was too highbrow, but the curious thing was that I never heard from the people I was too highbrow for. It was always: "As far as I'm concerned, you understand, it was wonderful. I enjoy an intellectual talk; but everybody isn't like you and me." Actually, as the attentive reader—if I still have one at this point—will have perceived, there is nothing of the highbrow about me as a writer; as a lecturer I am equally unambitious. I only asked my audiences to think along with me; it called for a very modest effort, and they were more than equal to it; but they had been conditioned into a prejudice that a lecture was not the proper place for that sort of thing. What with that and my interludes of unsociability, I got few invitations even at derisory fees. After about two and a half decades, I had as many engagements as I cared to accept, at better, though still moderate, fees —a confirmation of Sholom Aleichem's aphorism that every Jew would die a millionaire if he only lived long enough.

I find this crucial difference between writing and lecturing: in the first the feeling of accomplishment or failure is deferred; in the second it is immediate. It takes me a long time to decide—if ever I do—whether something I have written has done the job; lecturing, I know from minute to minute whether I am doing well or badly; and "doing well" does not simply mean holding the attention of the audience; it means holding the attention of the audience *while presenting and conveying the ideas I want to present and convey.*

But how do I know whether a substantial part of the audience is getting the ideas? It is not by the degree of attentiveness. It is something else, a special sense, a mutual interpenetration of the audience's mind and mine, a radar effect connected, perhaps, with otherwise not perceptible changes of expression and posture, and perhaps connected with as yet scientifically undefined modes of communication between persons face to face. When I feel that I am not getting the idea across, I change the line quickly, choose another approach, start with a new supporting anecdote, quotation, recent event, historical parallel, Biblical allusion. I must add that getting an idea across does not mean getting it accepted. The satisfaction lies in being understood, not in being agreed with.

There are lecturers who read from a manuscript and lecturers who have memorized their text. They belong to another species; their relationship to the personality of their audience is a mystery to me. Readers and reciters are not lecturers in my book, nor are political and religious orators; nor does the word apply to writers who take to the platform for a killing in the wake of a successful book, or to explorers just returned from a mountain peak or an ocean crevasse.

Next to the illusion of an inspired writing spell, I know of no higher pleasure than to stand before an audience and get into a streak when speech comes easily, the phrases are right, the quotations hit home, the thesis unfolds clearly and logically, and the audience follows; the highest point is reached when I suddenly perceive a novel way of presenting the material and exploit it successfully. Correspondingly, a botched lecture fills me with the acutest

288

misery. There are times when I fail to take hold of an audience; for all the echo reaching me, I might as well be talking into a barrel of sawdust. Or, taking hold of the audience, I fail to develop the thesis, I produce only an approximation and leave an impression tangential to my intentions. The audience may be attentive, it may be working with me, it may applaud heartily at the end, but I am filled with disgust at my ineptitude.

Sometimes I get off to a bad start, and the fault may not be wholly mine. The chairman has been prolix and foolish, the audience has lost its cohesion, and my stored-up initial momentum is dissipated. This handicap can be best overcome by rebuking the chairman; the audience is pulled together by the authoritative gesture and I have worked off my resentment. But this corrective can backfire in unexpected ways. I lectured once in Bloemfontein, South Africa, on Arab-Jewish relations. My chairman was a Rabbi Rohm, who introduced me for thirty-two minutes in a lecture of his own on the same subject. When I got the floor, I asked to be forgiven for saying that I had been burning while Rohm was fiddling. The audience didn't get over it, and every few minutes throughout the lecture a chuckle would break out and spread from row to row. Sometimes the audience cannot settle down; private conversations spring up; I let them go on for a minute or two, then point my finger at the culprits and ask them either to behave or leave the hall. A latecomer will enter at the back and start walking ostentatiously to the front; it is usually a lady wearing high heels, and the impudent tap-tap echoes from wall to wall, making heads turn automatically. I break off to say: "If you can't hear well, or are shortsighted, come early." Shmarya Levin's rule was: A lecturer must treat his audience with respect, and vice versa. I was at a meeting with him when a young woman in the front row began to chew gum audibly while she stared up at him. Levin leaned over and said icily: "Madam, swallow the damn thing or spit it out." I cannot remember which she did, if either, but she stopped chewing.

Getting and holding the attention of an audience is only the first step; the second, without which the first is pointless, is to make creative use of its attention. A lecturer must have, for each occasion, and at his fingertips, ten times as much material as he needs for his purpose. He must be able to pick and choose according to the response he is getting. Even so, addressing seventy or eighty audiences a year, he is in danger of growing stale to himself and therefore listless toward his audience. Repetition is inevitable, but the varieties of combinations and their improvisation help to keep him fresh. And there is always the windfall, the unexpected new vista of exposition which opens up right in the middle of the lecture. It has its dangers, of course; you adjust quickly to make room for it, perhaps to discover that it has led you astray. You remember an important point you were about to make when the visitation interrupted, but you must not go back; you must wait for an opportunity in the question and answer period. Shmarya Levin used to say: "Going back on a deal is poor business practice, going back to a lost point is poor lecture practice."

It may seem unnecessary to add that one must be absolutely honest with an audience, but many lecturers think they are honest enough if they do not quote unreliable statistics or repeat as fact what they have heard as rumor. Honesty demands that you never offer a plausible argument hoping that no one in the audience knows the effective counterargument. It is dishonest to shrink from the prospect of a hostile reaction, or to veil your convictions in deprecatory language, or to ingratiate yourself by turning folksy. These are the devices of the politician and the orator, not of the lecturer.

Like Gaul and Mr. Schiff, my average audience is composed of three parts; an informed and sophisticated core, an intelligent receptive mass, and a small nondescript periphery—harmless people with minds as difficult to locate as the whereabouts of an electron. For these last, attendance at a Jewish affair is an act of piety, a gesture toward the higher life. I can always identify them by their eagerness to thank me at the close of the evening. They are given to protracted handshakes with a pumphandling or rotatory motion or a complicated grip like a lodge signal. Their congratulations are warm and undiscriminating: "Mr. Samuels"—it is never Samuel—"you were absolutely marvelous. Last month we had a man who did card tricks. He was very good too." They expect to be remembered on the slenderest grounds. "Mr. Samuels, don't you recognize me? I was at your lecture in Knoxville twenty-five years ago." When I shake my head regretfully, they add: "It was a very rainy evening."

For most lecturers the question and answer period is a sort of afterbirth, to be disposed of quickly and hygienically; for me it is the climax of the evening, and I make it as long as possible. It is during this period that I check on my intuitions, and it is during this period, too, that I learn something of what is going on in the mind of American Jewry, or at least a certain sector of it. A thousand questions directed at me every year by audiences drawn from the most varied communities constitue a Gallup poll in reverse; and the changes in the type of question over a period of nearly fifty years build up a skeleton history of Jewish public opinion.

I prefer the spoken to the written question; I like to see

the questioner, it helps me to understand him, and I will take the risk that he will want to outline his autobiography. Sometimes the questioner flounders about; I have to guess at what is troubling him and find the words for it; it is pleasant to see his face light up when I succeed. I do not mind delivering five or six capsule lectures on top of the main lecture if the questions touch on important issues, the less so as they help me to bring up the good point I lost while chasing the new insight.

Some of the questions are merely silly, some simple and factual, and a few unfathomable. After a lecture on the character of Bloom in Joyce's *Ulysses* I was asked: "Mr. Samuel, are you in favor of human nature?" and after a lecture on Sholom Aleichem, whether I was in favor of vivisection. Late in the night after the Sholom Aleichem lecture I recalled having used some phrase like "dissection of human beings," but I never established a connection for the first question. There need not have been any; my questioner no doubt belonged to the small army of amiable cranks who haunt meetings in order to put in a word on vegetarianism, free love, Esperanto, faith healing, Bahaiism, moral rearmament, Yoga, spiritualism and kindness to animals; they form part of the periphery. The pest questioner is in a tiny class by himself; he attends every lecture and always has a question. He betrays himself the moment he opens his mouth by the pitch of his voice, which for some reason is half an octave or so higher than the average; the practiced lecturer can also identify him in advance by the dismay of the audience, which vents itself in a groan of resignation at the sight of him.

The loquaciously hostile questioner who wants to debate the issue with you from beginning to end must be disposed of decisively the moment he stops to catch his breath. An anti-Zionist rabbi named Foster rose after one of my addresses in Newark and began to deliver himself on the in-advisability, impossibility, and un-Americanism of creating a Jewish state in Palestine. At the first opportunity I slipped in the remark: "Sir, do not worry; the Jewish homeland will be built by the children of Israel, not the foster-children." After that the audience was deaf to him. In 1928, speaking on the Arab-Jewish problem, I found the same gentleman in my audience. I have referred, in telling of my last meeting with my old *Rebbe,* to the anti-Jewish riots which swept over Palestine in the fall of that year. The *Haganah,* or defense army, then clandestine, was in its primitive stage, and over a hundred and fifty men, women, and children were killed and thousands wounded before the British restored order. Even the anti-Zionist Jewish Communists of America, caught off guard, joined in the world-wide protests until they were ordered by Moscow to reverse their position, which they did with that bland and unembarrassed celerity which is, or used to be, such an engaging feature of dedicated Communism. Rabbi Foster put his question briefly this time: "Mr. Samuel, what would *you* do if you were an Arab?" I counter-questioned: "Rabbi Foster, what would you do if *you* were a Jew?"

Oddities remain imbedded in my memory, freak incidents, incongruities that are a joy forever, incredibilities that startle me afresh whenever I think of them—somewhat as if I had heard the train announcer at Grand Central say distinctly: "The Goddam five-twenty-five for Bridgeport is now ready on track nineteen." The first prize belongs to a 1933 meeting. At that time, world Jewry was divided on the issue of Jewish colonization in Russia. Most Zionists correctly saw in it nothing more than a device to divert Jewish funds to Russia; but some of them were taken in and one of them challenged me earnestly: "Mr. Samuel, don't you think it's better to give relief to Jews wherever they need it until we can build the homeland and all go and relieve ourselves there?" The atmosphere was so serious, the turn of phrase so unexpected, that the audience was paralyzed. In a similar stoniness an audience once heard me commit a ghastly spoonerism in a metaphor which intended to refer to a piston pushing. In spite of the sudden chill at my heart, I had the presence of mind to hurry on without correcting myself, thus creating a doubt in the minds of my listeners. I do not know whether it was incredulity or courtesy which prevented the audience from bursting into a shout of laughter when I was introduced at a meeting in the Bronx, where I was then living, in the following terms: "We have with us tonight Mr. Maurice Samuel, who is well known throughout America and in the Bronx as well. As the chairman of this evening, I will not bore you for long, since we have brought Mr. Samuel here for that purpose." This story has become something of a legend, and has been attached to various speakers, but unless my chairman of that evening reinvented the gem—he was too kindly and unsophisticated a man to have been quoting—I claim it as part of my saga.

An introduction is not, or should not be, an idle and hasty formality; its function, difficult and responsible, is to pull the audience together and dispose it to listen. It should be neither too long nor too short, neither fulsome nor dry, neither facetious nor pompous. It must contain mention of the subject and some polite remarks on the lecturer's qualifications for dealing with it. A nervous chairman infects the audience, and precious minutes are lost before it regains its composure. If the chairman has been chosen as a reward for various services but happens to know nothing about the subject or the lecture, he should confine himself to reading the introduction furnished by the lecture bureau. Had this rule always been followed, one flustered lady would not have introduced me as Mr. Furtlewanger because the late Lion Feuchtwanger had addressed the organization the previous month, and another as Sholom Aleichem because I had written a book about him.

The most difficult part of an evening comes when, being at leisure and glad to engage in conversation even after a two-hour stretch on the platform, I am buttonholed by the wrong people. Some have private grievances against the organization or the community leadership and want me to adjudicate in their favor; others want to tell me of a long and complicated personal experience which bears out or disapproves part of my thesis; and there are those who ask: "Mr. Samuel, do you *really* believe" something or other I said in the course of the lecture, as if they expected me to confess that I had only been fooling. But some are troubled by serious questions which they were too shy to ask in public, and these are among my best teachers.

The change in the character of my audiences, and in the matters which interest them, is, as I have hinted, a commentary on Jewish development in this country over the last half century. It is also an indicator of general changes. It goes without saying that the immigrant element has largely disappeared; those that come to hear me are eighty to ninety per cent American-born, more than half of them of American-born parents. One curious result has been the almost total disappearance of a perplexity that used to haunt my audiences thirty and forty and fifty years ago. It went under the name of "dual allegiance." Was it possible to be a "good American" with half one's heart attached to the idea of a Jewish homeland in Palestine? The question is still put here and there, but it emanates from a small, identifiable, extremist assimilationist minority.

The more American the Jews have become, the more natural does it seem to them to be, if not ideological Zionists, vigorous supporters of the State of Israel. It is not only that the timidity of the newcomers has dissolved in the tacit Americanism of their descendants; it is also that America herself has lost a good deal of her provincialism. The growing consciousness of the fateful world role which has devolved on her makes her sympathetic to the value of additional attachments. (I avoid the word "allegiance" because it is part of a loaded formula.) "Americanism" loses all contemporaneous meaning unless it is hyphenated with "One-Worldism," and One-Worldism finds encouragement in emotional and cultural bonds with other peoples; there cannot, in my opinion, be too many of them, for America's good and the world's. Certainly these double or multiple affections (I myself feel strong ties to England and France) will create problems occasionally, but how can the great transition which is now mankind's imperative be made without problems?

The transition is to something far more significant than a state of guaranteed peace. Beyond the danger of human self-annihilation lies the danger, less spectacularly horrifying but hardly less horrible to contemplate, of the annihilation of the human self, the gradual disappearance of those human group differentiations in which a self is rooted. In the introduction to Teilhard de Chardin's *The Phenomenon of Man,* Julian Huxley speaks of the tendency, emerging from technological progress, "which might destroy the effects of cultural diversification and lead to a drab uniformity instead of to a rich and potent pattern of variety in unity." Before us looms the spectre of a planet inhabited by six or ten or fifteen billion nobodies-in-particular (and why we should consider it an achievement to infect distant planets with such biological specimens is beyond me).

of a new generation, are urgently in search of their own self-identification. The unformulated anxiety runs: "We've got children! What shall we tell them about ourselves? And, for that matter, *who are we?*"

The spiritual confusion of the physicist, mathematician, etc., is not different from that of the doctor or lawyer in the same predicament, or, given a certain level of intelligence, of the plumber or pantsmaker. It begins with a misconception in the religious field. A member of an audience once said to me: "As a physicist I do not believe in the existence of God. I know that things take place in accordance with unchangeable laws. In years of experimentation I have never come across an instance of interference with those laws by an outside power." I commented: "You seem to be under the impression that only a physicist, or a scientist generally, is aware of the inexorability and inviolability of the natural laws of cause and effect. But a pantsmaker, too, has the right to say: 'As a pantsmaker I do not believe in the existence of God. I know that in the making of a pair of pants there are inexorable and inviolable laws of cause and effect, and in all the years of my pantsmaking I have not come across a single instance of interference with these laws by an outside power. Never, never, in the making of thousands of pairs of pants have I seen a single pair come out right if the cutting was wrong.' His scientific experience hasn't the range and subtlety of yours, but it is as decisive."

Belief in God does not by itself make a Jew, just as calling oneself an atheist does not make one an atheist (the intellectual discipline of atheism is extremely exacting). The Jew who thinks himself an atheist and, looking for self-identification, can find it only in the Jewish people, relies on the fact that Jewishness, unlike Christianity, regards *peoplehood* as an expression of religion. And people-

The recoil in American Jewry from an earlier melting-pot theory of assimilation is in part a response to the threat of depersonalization. It is mixed with other factors; the extermination of six million Jews and the birth of the State of Israel have left deep psychological effects; and the general American movement toward religious affiliation, often—and more or less correctly—characterized as a purely social phenomenon, has set up a kind of machinery for Jewish self-recovery. But it is quite wrong to stop at these factors. The young Jewish physicists, chemists, mathematicians, engineers (I have met hundreds of them) who find they have to provide some Jewish instruction for their children, and join a temple or a synagogue for that reason, are often puzzled at themselves. "Look," they expostulate, as if anxious to disassociate themselves at once from their superstitious grandfathers, "look, I'm beyond that sort of thing, but I want my son at least to know who he is." I mention the scientists because it is presumably the scientific outlook which is most intelligently (or should I just say articulately) at odds with the notion of Jewish affiliation; also because among them one might expect a certain amount of clear thinking on the subject. I probe and find confusion. I ask: "Can't your son be a Presbyterian and know who he is?" They answer: "I don't believe in any religion, but if my son has to get a certain amount of religion to know who he is, at least let it be Jewish." I continue: "But why on earth do you want him to know that he is a Jew?" Sometimes they answer: "Better for him to find it out from me than from an anti-Semite"; sometimes: "A man shouldn't be ashamed of his origins"; and sometimes: "Well, if he isn't a Jew, what is he?"

Now, this concern with the child's need for self-identification is genuine, and the answers have meaning for the speaker, on one level or another; what the parents often do not perceive is that they, finding themselves the begetters hood does not mean nationality or nationalism; it means a group-cultural personality within which the individual comes to birth, and this in turn means being rooted in the culture.

But by a certain age—say the late twenties or early thirties—much exertion is needed to send down new roots or to reactivate old ones that have withered. Usually something is still there, and not only because of reminders from the outside, a personal experience, an overheard jibe, exclusion from certain areas of employment; something beyond the fact that Jews habitually consort with Jews; something that nags quietly, or starts suddenly to life without apparent provocation, a regret, a sense of self-alienation and self-devaluation, an obscure perception of some kind of impiety. The something that is still there is also felt, often enough, as a confounded nuisance: "I didn't ask for it! I refuse to let myself be pestered by it. To hell with the past." Hence an ambivalence of attitude, a simultaneous hankering and resentment, respect and derision. "The Jews, Jewishness—you can't just wave it away; the Jews, Jewishness, just a lot of antiquated rubbish."

Thus, a popular Jewish woman novelist opens her autobiography with: "All my life I have been inordinately proud of being a Jew," and some fifty pages farther on explains: "It has always been my contention that the Jew, left in peace for two hundred years throughout the world, would lose his aggressiveness, his tenacity, his neurotic ambition, would be completely absorbed and vanish, as a type, from the face of the earth." Now, surely the lady cannot be "proud" of these Jewish characteristics, and surely she must look forward to the day when a world purified of hatreds will permit this somewhat repellent type to disappear. But no, what she is proud of in her Jewishness is the noble sentiment she quotes from the

Bible as the motto of her book: "Now, therefore, if ye will obey My voice, and keep My covenant, then ye shall be a peculiar treasure unto Me, above all peoples; for all the earth is Mine and ye shall be unto Me a kingdom of priests and a holy nation." On the other hand, it appears from her account that if the Jews have in some slight degree approximated to this lofty ideal, they owe less to God and the Prophets than to certain questionable historical characters: "For centuries we have been kept from complete absorption or utter oblivion by such fanatics and megalomaniacs as a Pharaoh, Ivan of Russia, or Philip of France, or Edward the First, of England . . . Adolf Hitler has done more to solidify and spiritualize the Jews of the world than any man since Moses."

Novels which depict Judaism or Jewishness as nothing more than a persistent historical trauma, and the Jewish people as the locale of a baffling non-filterable virus called anti-Semitism which has the curious faculty of keeping the host organism alive for centuries, are very popular with Jews engaged in the struggle for self-recovery; they find there relief for one side of their ambivalence. Whatever my subject at a lecture, I am sure to be asked for my opinion of such books while their brief and lucrative season is on; and since I consider it my duty to have an answer, I must, like the reader for the Catholic Index, regularly imperil my soul, or my sanity, for the benefit of my audiences.

I also imperil my soul occasionally by the intemperateness of my comments; but what other kind of comment can one make on the following piece of advice, which another Jewish novelist puts into the mouth of one of his sympathetic Jewish characters: "What you're afraid of, George [a fellow-Jew] is the world of the Gentiles. Somewhere, God alone knows the location, you've picked up and be-

lieve the same notions about Gentiles that *so many* Gentiles
have about Jews. That they're creatures of another planet,
with cloven hoofs and spiked tails and *a passion for drinking human blood.* [My italics]." The author does not know
where on earth some Jews have picked up these monstrous
beliefs about gentiles! It is for him no miracle that when
the concentration camps opened they did not let out on
the world a horde of lunatic survivors. It surprises him
that even among those who have only learned something
about the camps there should occur occasional delusions
(!) of persecution. One must assume that this is his attitude,
for a proper comment on the hideously coarse statement
I have quoted occurs nowhere in the novel. There isn't a
Jew or gentile in it with intelligence enough to make it.
And how ingeniously he turns the tables—"that so many
Gentiles have about the Jews. . ." Jewry and Christendom
are even-stephen. Gentiles misunderstand Jews, Jews misunderstand gentiles; there is an unfortunate mutuality of
self-perpetuating misunderstanding without a basic cause
on either side. The crowning touch is "the passion for
drinking human blood." The author might have spared
us this oblique reference to the ritual blood libel, so often
thrown by Christians at Jews but never by Jews at Christians. He might, in order to fill out the picture with the
honesty expected of a novelist, have had someone say:
"Yes, I know, George, certain terrible things have happened over the centuries, and recently, too; all the
same . . ." No, instead he has another perceptive Jew ad-
monish George: "Don't hide. Don't dig a hole for yourself . . . Do what your heart tells you, not your religion.
It's more important to be a man than a Jew." It appears
that, for the author, "Jew" and "man" are in some way
incompatible.

The recurrent impulse to get rid, somehow, of this

burden of Jewish identity, and the endless, banal discussion of it, are often characteristic of Jews who are fundamentally attached to Jewishness. Perhaps it is only a particular form of the longing that all human beings occasionally experience to be someone else for a change. So I am frequently asked: "Can't we assimilate?" and I answer: "Some of us certainly can, and do, but you must not make a programmatic thing of it; that would be like screaming at people: 'Relax!' "

Some years ago an "ex-Jew" wrote an article in *The Atlantic Monthly,* describing how, by the exercise of the proper tact, ingenuity, and determination, he had managed to "pass" completely. He wrote under a pseudonym, of course—otherwise he would have ruined his life's work—and offered himself as proof conclusive that "it can be done"; and Jews who complain that the gentile world won't let them assimilate are deceiving themselves; it is their own clannishness or self-assertiveness that stands in the way. No one, he reported, but no one except himself now knew him as an ex-Jew; and he advised Jews at large to follow his example.

I was surprised by the number of Jews who read the article and wanted to know what I thought of it; there must have been quite a run on that issue. I pointed out to my questioners that in addition to the particular qualifications which enabled the "ex-Jew" to carry out his farsighted plan, he had to thank that vast majority of Jews who lacked both his qualifications and his ambition. It is obvious that if all the Jews of America were to make a concerted attempt to "disappear," the country would be set by the ears, and the more widespread the attempt, the fewer, in the final account, would be the instances of success. Let us imagine the courts of New York, Philadelphia, Boston, Cleveland, Chicago, and Los Angeles suddenly

flooded with petitions for change of name—in most instances the first prerequisite; let us then imagine a miraculously rapid and uniform favorable disposal of all the
cases; then let us imagine the disappearance of the serried
columns of Cohens, Caplans, Levys, Horowitzes, Hurwitzes,
Samuels, and Slomowitzes from the telephone books. What
a hue and cry there would be, here and abroad! *"Where
are the Jews of America!"* The political commentators
would be in their element, propounding theories: at one
extreme that the Jews had gone underground in accordance
with the sinister plans outlined in *The Protocols of the
Elders of Zion;* at the other that they had been massacred
in a tremendous and marvelously organized St. Bartholo-
mew's night which had not left behind so much as a single
corpus delicti. (I ignore the various problems of relocation,
transportation, and economic reintegration: one need only
think of the chaos in the social security offices.)

What I really held against the "ex-Jew" was not his
imbecility but his ingratitude. He was like the millionaire
who earnestly counsels the poor to emulate him and repeat
his success, forgetting that a few people can be millionaires precisely because other people, much more numerous,
cannot. Those who have the necessary combination of
ability, craftiness, single-mindedness, imaginativeness,
avariciousness, and love of power (not to mention luck)
will become millionaires without his encouragement;
others are merely disturbed from time to time by the reflection: "He's right! I could have made it, too," when in
fact they haven't a dog's chance, not only because of social
handicaps, but because they just aren't built that way.

"Ex-Jew" was built in a certain way, and because of it
he was able to realize his ambition, though not quite as
completely as he imagined. There was one person, very
important to him, to wit, himself, who was in on the secret,

and how he took it is not clear from his statement. He may
have chuckled at the situation, thinking how he was did-
dling his neighbors, the Jewish people, and history. He
may have winced slightly when a good friend of his made
an anti-Semitic remark—say, something on the order of:
"A Jew can try to disguise himself as much as he likes,
but I can tell one a mile away" by some unpleasant characteristic or other—and then laughed up his sleeve: "Poor
devil! He doesn't suspect he's been having one in his home
for years." It is possible that he entered a mild demurrer,
just to test his feeling of security: "Oh, I don't know . . ."
I have sometimes wondered whether some of his best
friends were Jews; and I have wondered what became of
him. There is the horrid possibility that he was exposed
by a chance encounter, and perhaps even by himself—a
slip of the tongue at a Christmas Eve party where he had
taken a drop too much and was irresistibly impelled to
hint at the relationship between him and Jesus, or, God
knows, in a moment of unaccountable revulsion. But if he
carried on successfully to the end, his children would be
quite secure, assuming, as we must, that when they asked
him about his parents or other relatives he made up some
cock and bull story. Or he may have decided not to risk
marriage and fatherhood. The fact is that there is no such
thing as an assimilated Jew any more than there is a
digested potato. There are only assimilating Jews, and
they are never absolutely safe. One may be second-generation baptized, and a United States senator to boot, and a
granddaughter will take it into her head to join a *kibbutz*
in Israel.

Assimilationism as an organized movement, with national headquarters, organs, slogans, chapters, and chairmen, is an absurdity from the practical as well as from the
moral point of view. Pasternak, himself a convert to

Christianity, urges something like it in *Dr. Zhivago*. Referring to the sufferings of the Jewish people, he cries: "Of
what use is it to anyone, this voluntary martyrdom? Whom
does it profit? For what purpose are those innocent old men
and women and children, all these subtle, kind, humane
people, mocked and beaten up through the centuries? Why
didn't the intellectual leaders of the Jewish people ever go
beyond *Weltschmerz* and ironical wisdom? Why have they
not disbanded this army which keeps on fighting and being
massacred nobody knows for what? Why don't they say to
them: 'Come to your senses, stop. Don't hold on to your
identity. Be with all the rest. You are the first and best
Christians in the world. You are the very thing against
which you have been turned by the worst and weakest
among you.' "

These generous words about the Jewish people—I should
like to think they are deserved: "the best Christians in the
world!"; isn't it a bit overdone?—make nonsense of the
proposal. Why should David Gordon, the Christianized
Jew in the novel (he is one of the self-images of Pasternak),
want the dissolution of so exalted an example? If Jewishness produces "the best Christians," oughtn't the world to
turn Jewish? Which is perhaps what Jesus, the home-grown
Jew, intended, and Paul, the Hellenized Jew, could not
understand.

Assimilation takes place quietly, more or less simply,
and is a natural thing. Sometimes I will be invited by a
questioner to express disapproval of Jews who drift away,
intermarry, and initiate the slow process by which Jewish
identity dissolves. I am unable to comply. A Jew has the
same right to intermarry as an American or an Englishman
has to emigrate. All peoples regularly lose contingents of
their sons and daughters; to hold them by force when they
have the opportunity and the desire to leave is an abomi-

nable act of tyranny, an infringement of the basic right of the human being to seek his happiness where he thinks he can find it. Or else I am invited to express alarm at the volume of Jewish assimilation. Again I cannot oblige; for such distress as I feel is occasioned, not by the diminution of our numbers, but by the insufficiency of Jewish content and Jewish values in that mass which will persist with a Jewish designation into all the foreseeable future.

Jewish values! Again and again I am asked: "But what *are* those Jewish values you keep talking about?" and I must answer again and again that one doesn't explain them, one acquires them by a conscious effort; they are associated with a body of Jewish knowledge; and that body of Jewish knowledge is in turn associated with the Jewish view that without knowledge there is no Jewishness. This is the specific Jewish tradition of intellectuality, the dissipation of which is a loss to every country with a Jewish community. I think sometimes of the role that Jews ought to be playing in America as her intellectual pacesetters. We are still, I believe, in front, but only by the momentum of the past. Most of our young intellectuals are not with us; their children will be strangers to the tradition which carried their fathers. That is a pity, but the loss is not irreparable. The matrix is still here.

If the anti-Jewishness bias of some writers does not trouble me too much, the pro-Jewishness of others does. I am referring to the sentimental books, novels or memoirs, which are filled with exhibitionistic and smiling affection for our recent ancestry. "Nothing," says Professor Herbert Muller, "is more undignified than a past become quaint." Such books achieve the same popularity as their opposites and do more harm because they purport to tell us something about Jewishness. I had a boyhood friend in Manchester, Louis Golding, who grew up to be that sort of writer. When we were youngsters we were very fond of each other, and his father, a Hebrew teacher and a sternly orthodox Jew, used to thrash him for frequenting the company of a notorious apostate like me. In later years Louis and I developed a strong aversion toward each other's books, and we used to meet at intervals, in London and New York, to express it; if the intervals were too long, we wrote each other abusive letters about each other's latest productions. He died recently and I miss him, because I never really lost my fondness for him. Besides, my personal acquaintance with other writers of his type, where it exists at all (I don't move in literary circles), is too slender to provide me with this outlet. But the type will fade away as immigrant memories recede.

Though I am sure that my lectures do no harm, I cannot be sure that they do any good. The measure would lie in the number of people who have been prompted by them to take up Jewish studies. That number is steadily increasing, but who knows if I have had anything to do with it? Lectures about the value of Jewish culture can indeed be samples of Jewish culture, and that is what I try to make them; but if the listener is content to nod approval and leave it at that, he is like the man who goes to church or synagogue as an expression of his faith in the value of faith, which is a fair description of much of our contemporaneous religious revival—and nothing new, at that. Gissing said of the Victorian Englishman: "His religion, strictly defined, is *an ineradicable belief in his own religiousness*" [his italics]. I place in the same category the Jew who "believes" in Jewishness, his own Jewishness, and makes no effort to give it substance. From time to time I am asked wistfully why the Bible can't be made as attractive as Bible movies, and why an immortal work like the Talmud can't be reduced to twenty-five simple lessons.

I have to drive home the point that these inane longings, or rather velleities, are hostile to the very material, as it were, of Jewishness, its specifically moral-intellectual discipline and substance.

In that substance the spirit expresses itself, having no other means of expression for us. The One God of whom I get glimpses speaks to me, as a Jew, *in that substance,* making it the starting point and medium of my perception of the world, my mode of entrance into it and my identification with it. Exactly when that substance, in its earliest form, became the heritage of the group which evolved into the Jewish people, is to me a mystery. I cannot accept as literal the account of Genesis. I suggest that instead of God having spoken to Abraham (or Aram), He put into the heart and mind of the primitive group, no doubt through a prophetlike figure, the myth of His having spoken to Abraham. What He is thus purported to have said to Abraham concerning the destiny of the group, namely, that in it the families of the earth should be blessed (what a mad notion!), the group accepted as the *raison d'être* for its existence. When did this happen? That, I have said, is a mystery to me, and I cannot think it will ever be resolved. But the notion stuck. It was and is periodically repudiated and reasserted, disregarded and renewed in ascending perception. The records are superficially confused, the thematic consistency and continued clarification perfectly clear. The renewal of Jewishness can take place only in these terms, and if the re-creation of the State of Israel is conceived in other terms, that is (as certain ultra-Orthodox Jews assert, without, alas, being themselves an acceptable example) one of the periodic repudiations. Either Israel ultimately helps the Jewish people to be a world-serving community or it is, however successful in other respects, Jewishly speaking a failure.

These are the very high ideas I try to infuse into some of my lectures. They are seemingly so out of kilter with the ordinary tenor of our lives that one is tempted to laugh, to dismiss them as so much hot air. But either there is God and purpose, and then this ordinary tenor, with all its failures, absurdities, and shenanigans, indicates a meaningful direction, or else there is neither God nor purpose, and then, as I asked in my youthful years, what difference does it make if we inflate ourselves with empty delusions?

Epilogue of High Moments

❀

HIS IS where I intended to close the book. As a record it has many lacunae, even in the limited areas I have
chosen. To any reader who is dissatisfied on this score I
offer one of Zangwill's prefaces: "I must apologise to the
critics for this book not being some other book, but it
will not happen again, as my next book will be."

I must write this epilogue while there is still time, for
of late my memory has developed an interesting four-stage
trick no doubt familiar to others but new to me. In the
morning I suddenly will think of someone who was quite
close to me many years ago. The face, the posture, the
voice, the opinions, and other peculiarities will be as fresh
as if I had just left him; I know him as well as I know
myself, but for the moment I can't think of his name. But
precisely in that moment the image fades out and with it
the identity. I no longer know who the person was whose
name I was trying to recall. Then, after an interval of
some hours, I find myself saying, in the midst of quite
another train of thought: "What was it that I recalled
with such exasperating near-completeness this morning?
Was it a person? A book? A scene? A smell? A tune?"
This question, too, fades out. Then suddenly, at some

point in the evening, I am haunted by the recollection of a frustration. What was it that bothered me earlier in the day? Did I have an unpleasant encounter? Did I get a bad piece of news? Did I remember and forget again a neglected duty? A fragment of myself has slipped away from me. Is it gone forever or will it come back?

As a rule it comes back. That same night, or perhaps the next day, or the day after, and in rare cases a week or so later, a reverse process sets in, beginning with the last and unidentified frustration; and once it begins, it is very rapid, almost instantaneous. "Good heavens! It had to do with a memory! It did not occur to me there and then except as a memory. A person, a voice, a posture—all unmistakable—there they are! It is he!" The momentum carries me past the dead point and I triumphantly call out the name, to the surprise of anyone in whose company I happen to be.

Incidents, too, and whole chains of incidents out of my far-off past can thus play hide and seek with me. A place swims up in my mind; it is important because of what happened to me there. What place? I was looking at it a moment ago, and I cannot conjure it back by a direct effort. I must wait until something sets off the reverse process, and that something is invariably hidden from me. If it is an external object, like Proust's little cake dipped in tea, or the wobbly flagstone under his foot, I am unaware of it. It seems that, without prompting from me, the unreachable part of my mind has all the time been diligently at work, exploring the labyrinths, running up blind alleys, returning, scurrying this way and that, until it has found the episode in its niche, all of the episode, in all of its detail, beautifully immediate and alive.

This little inner drama of death and resurrection, silent and fragmented, will often use as its prologue a person

I have known only fleetingly, someone who has etched himself into my memory in connection with a large experience of which he has become one of the symbols. Such, I have indicated, are certain men and women I met in Vilna; such, also, was a young Englishman I happened to recall a few days ago, remembering only for the moment that he could have been one of the attractive characters in *The Forsyte Saga*. He was blond, tall, clean-looking; he spoke in the clipped, allusive, diffident way proper to such characters in Galsworthy. He was Tom Merry grown up and carrying his share of the White Man's Burden. Where had I seen him? Why was he lodged in my mind? To what important experience was he the clue?

He slipped from my consciousness via the familiar stages and was flashed back the next day in the familiar pattern of recapture. A morning in August 1937, *The Llangibby Castle* at anchor off St. Helena, the young Englishman standing at my side watching with me the boatloads of passengers being rowed ashore, a brief conversation—the only one I had with him during the seventeen-day voyage. He was a colonial administrator in Kenya, homeward bound on leave. I sat back to back with him at meals; I had heard him talk about his home, his people, tennis, hunting, always using odds and ends of sentences, a glancing kind of talk which might or might not conceal an articulate personality.

He addressed me suddenly: "Shall you be going ashore?"

"I don't think so," I answered. I did not care to see where Napoleon had died; I was working on a book; besides, the day was hot and close.

After a pause he murmured: "That man in Germany is going to be the Napoleon of the twentieth century."

I was startled. It sounded like an invitation to an exchange of views; and perhaps it was only a friendly admonishment not to miss a unique opportunity.

312

I said, cautiously: "You mean he's going to make a mess of it, like Napoleon?"

"I rather fancy he won't," he answered.

I read admiration and approval into his voice, and was depressed. I wished that he had at least said: "I'm afraid he won't." He added: "He won't make Napoleon's mistakes."

"Such as?"

"Fighting England, for one thing, I suppose."

"He'll make other mistakes," I suggested.

"Oh, I dare say."

"He's pretty hard on the Jews," I said.

"Yes, so one hears. But they do have to be put in their place, you know."

He was detached, thoughtful, unmalicious, even kindly. My depression became sickeningly acute. That is always my reaction when I run up against anti-Semitism in someone who in all other respects seems to be decent and considerate. It is there that the coarse anti-Semite, the obviously low, brutal, or deranged type—who disturbs me much less—finds his leverage. I dropped the conversation, and I may have betrayed my feelings, for he did not address me again during the remainder of the voyage.

I watched him descend the gangplank, and I changed my mind about visiting the island. The day was spoiled for me, I would do no work. I took one of the last boats, and there was an impulse in me to catch up with the young Englishman and reopen the discussion. But the moment I set foot on the shore I realized the absurdity of it.

St. Helena is—or was then—a pitiful and beggarly place. From a distance it looks desolate, without a touch of the imposing, and a closer view is even more dismal. The inhabitants are for the most part paupers; the colored and the black, descendants of slaves, seem to be little worse off than the whites. The houses, which are strung along the

313

narrow cleft of the rock and make up the one narrow street which is all of Jamestown, are primitive, brick, or stone, or yellowish clay. As we walked slowly inland, ragged children left their games of bobbers and kibs to beg for pennies. Adults peddled cheap lace handkerchiefs, Woolworth necklaces, and postal cards. On the right I saw a shingle: *Samuel, Saddler*. On the left there was a gully between the street and the mountainside; it was filled with half-cobbled courts surrounded by wretched huts, the kind I had seen in the Kaffir slums of Johannesburg.

On this island Napoleon passed the last six years of his life, the years of his prime; not in Jamestown, but farther up, at Longwood, the showplace of St. Helena. I let the group I had landed with drift away from me. Something was stirring in me, I wanted to think and make notes. Afterwards I took a carriage and arrived at "the house" when the others had left. It was less oppressive there than in Jamestown, but the heat still clung close, unrelieved by a breath from the dark, sullen, heaving Atlantic. Here, then, Napoleon ate his heart out while the climate ate at his liver; here he brooded, quarreled with the mean-spirited governor, played at being Emperor still, and brooded over his "mistakes." He paced the living room of the one-story building set aside for him, and took back his moves, like my friend Shmarya Levin at chess, but unlike Levin only in his mind, and too late. If he had not made such and such a move—that was the theme of his everlasting plaint—he would have won the game, he would not be here, on a volcanic pustule in the middle of the Atlantic. He should not have crossed the Memel so early; he should not have spared the Hohenzollern dynasty; at Waterloo he should have sent the Guard forward earlier; he should not have entrusted himself to the English; he should have gone to America. . . "What terrible mistakes I have made."

I had been reading a life of Napoleon on the voyage, and these were some of the notes I had made, thinking how strange it was that a man of this caliber should identify the forces of history with his hit or miss decisions on the field of battle. Less strange, great men being what they are, were his delusions of a world-revolutionizing moral mission. "My aim was the social regeneration of Europe . . . I was never the aggressor! Striving for dominion? I wanted to found a European system, a European code of laws, a European court of appeal; there would have been only one people throughout Europe . . . I was obliged to daunt Europe by force of arms . . . I am dying before my time, murdered by the English oligarchy."

Only now and again he permits himself a doubt. "In the present day, the way to convince Europe is reason." He does not follow up with the inevitable conclusion that his greatest mistake, the supreme and irreparable mistake, lay in his being a Napoleon.

These reflections floated on the surface of my mind. Under them, breaking through occasionally, was my young Englishman. What was it that attracted him to a figure like Hitler? How did evil men, demonic hungerers for power, establish their hold over "decent" people? Is it because "decent" people aren't really decent, because they too, the "simple, innocent ones" too, hunger for power and satisfy their hunger vicariously, by worship of the power-bearer and self- association with him?

On the way back from Longwood I left the carriage a half mile or so from the wharf and sat down on a stone opposite the house of Samuel, Saddler. I was in a tremendous state of excitement. The book I was working on had become unimportant; I wanted suddenly, overwhelmingly, to write about power and its relation to simple people, some kind of novel, in which the problem would unfold through personalities. But not a novel of contemporaneous life; a historical novel rather, a parable, illuminating our present perplexities while avoiding direct collision with the political passions and prejudices of our day.

I had not the faintest notion where to begin, what setting and what personality to fasten on, and all the way to Southampton I tried to shake myself free of the obsession. It was perfectly senseless. This was not my line of work; it called for qualities of the imagination in which I was lacking; and it would mean years of research.

Here again I must pause over the interplay between the purposive and the accidental in my life. The day after we docked I picked up in London, at Foyle's, Villari's four-volume life of Machiavelli, and I had not read ten pages before I realized that here was my perfect setting—Renaissance Italy; here was my perfect theoretician of Fascism, Machiavelli; and here was my perfect villain, Cesare Borgia, whom Machiavelli admired so extravagantly. They were made as if to order. And I ask myself: if the young Englishman on the boat hadn't addressed me, or, addressing me, hadn't said what he said, would I have gone ashore at St. Helena? Probably not. Would the obsession to write a novel on the power theme have taken hold of me anyhow? Perhaps. If I hadn't chanced on Villari's *Machiavelli* when I did, would I have chosen Cesare Borgia as my symbol of evil, and invented Giacomo Orso, child of the Romagna—Mussolini's birthplace and the scene of Cesare Borgia's first triumphs—as my symbol of the decent young man? Most probably not. Nor would I have devoted ten years to the study of the Italian Renaissance in order to write *Web of Lucifer,* of which one critic observed: "His knowledge of the times seems prodigious." Honesty compels me to say that my knowledge of the times was in fact considerable and I must add that the accumulation of the knowledge meant far more to me than the writing of the book.

I have done much traveling in connection with my profession, and I have noticed that practically all the information I have picked up in my travels I could have obtained from books. When I am introduced at a lecture as an authority on Israel because I have spent so much time in the country, I call to mind a conversation I once had in a place called Edgecomb, a suburb of Durban, on the Indian Ocean. I was taken to visit an invalid who because of some dangerous allergy had been confined to his room for twenty years. He was a dedicated Zionist. He had never seen Palestine and could never hope to see it. He contributed to the Zionist funds and subscribed to all the Palestinian dailies, weeklies, monthlies. He read, as fast as he could get them, all the books, in English, Hebrew, and Yiddish, that were in any way connected with Palestine; and he carried on a copious correspondence with a number of people in the country. I cannot tell whether he sent for me—as he did for every visiting Zionist lecturer—because he hoped to learn something from me or because he wanted to show off his knowledge, which was in fact "prodigious"—certainly far deeper than mine. He was at home in the geography of the country, and talked of its cities and villages as one who had moved among them all his life, had watched their development at first hand since their beginnings. He knew in detail the condition of every colony, whether commune, co-operative, or free enterprise, and followed passionately all the controversies that agitated the community. He was an expert on the politics and finances of Palestine. He asked me many questions, and corrected or supplemented whatever answers I gave him. One question in particular staggered me. "Can you tell me the inside story why Golden and Feitlovitch stopped

317

advertising in *Davar* though they continue to advertise in *Ha-Aretz*?" All I knew was the name of the firm of linen drapers, and its location on the Nachlat Benyamin Street in Tel Aviv.

Travel has meant for me, chiefly, stimulation and memory aid. What I read about a place I no doubt remember more easily for having been there, but if I were to spend on travelers' accounts the time and energy consumed by my traveling I would be better off. Macaulay tells us that Edmund Burke, preparing his case against Warren Hastings, read up so assiduously on India, which he had never visited, that he became the leading authority on it, far better informed than officials who had spent many years there. In our own day, Robert Graves produced his superb novels on Claudius without ever having set eyes on Rome; and Marchette Chute produced her classic account of Shakespeare and Shakespeare's London exclusively from materials in the New York Public Library.

The stimuli I have received from my travels have been those of a particular scene or episode during a particular moment of sensitivity; and the scene need not have been new to me. The account I give of the birth of my novel *The Second Crucifixion* in the opening chapter is in substance not fictional. I had often been in Rome, I had often lingered among the ruins of the Forum. But on the occasion I describe, something unpredictable and—for me—momentous did in fact happen. That something I have fictionalized as a woman's voice speaking to me across eighteen centuries. It was less, and more, than that. It was the onset of a compulsion to write a novel about Hadrianic Rome, about the Judaism and Christianity of that time, and about the manner in which anti-Semitism crystallized and fastened itself into the body of Christendom, to endure until our own time. I fought against the compulsion

318

just as, exactly ten years earlier, I had fought against the compulsion to write *Web of Lucifer,* and as on the previous occasion, I argued and fumed in vain. I had to write that book, and I wrote it as I had written *Web of Lucifer,* more or less mutinously. But I enjoyed thoroughly the ten years of research that went into it. I could have continued reading up on early Christian-Jewish relations for many years; so also with the Renaissance when I had finished *Web of Lucifer.* It was not a flagging interest that made me stop in both cases—I still leaf through the books with enjoyment—it was rather the fear that if I went on for much longer I would turn into a scholar, and then what would become of me? For the same reason I will go no further with my scientific studies, but content myself with keeping fresh in my mind the little I have acquired.

Thus far, not all my far-off experiences are subject to the recent caprices of my memory. I have a standby treasury, collected in the course of my travels, which is still immediately accessible, and on sleepless nights I choose at will what I want to relive.

I am flying southward along the Nile. There is a sliver of moon above the horizon as we leave Heliopolis, but it fails to illumine the ground, and the river is hidden from us as we move toward the Lybian desert. A hint of light is born in the east toward the Red Sea, it takes on color, it becomes an aureole shading softly into the vast, starry blue-blackness. It changes, it passes through pink and dull red into crimson and radiant rose. The depths pulsate, waves of counter-color come back from the zenith, subtle green and heliotrope and violet. The patches along the Nile become visible under us, rectangular little fields which might be the levels of an English countryside. The lamps of the villages glimmer here and there. The Nile curves away and we are above the empty desert. The light in the east gains, loses color. In the cool, lucid dawn the river comes back to us and we descend at Assyut. To one side of the field an Arab, kneeling on his mat, bows himself to the East three times. Someone nudges me and says: "Isn't that dumb?"

When we rise again, the fullness of day is upon us, and from a height of ten thousand feet I look down again upon the Nile. From that height it is a thin, rippleless, accidental, shallow spill drawn across the illimitable, arid waste, a green-bordered thread making an irregular diameter across an immense, circular vacancy. I feel, I understand, I am drawn into the immemorial struggle of life with the fierce wilderness. The strip of growth which persists along the banks never strays into the desert; the two never fraternize or intermingle; they hold each other at bay, neither of them giving or gaining an inch.

Seen thus, the Nile is a frail, provisional powerless thing. The desert on either side need only shrug its flank, send out a puff, unfold a lap, and the ribbon would shrivel and vanish. The persistence of the river has something awful about it; it is the persistence of life itself, an inexplicable obstinacy fed from an invisible and mysterious source. Now I understand why they had to worship the Nile, not simply because it was the fructifier and breadgiver, but because it was the affirmation of life in the midst of surrounding death, the cry of defiance in the face of the hot, engulfing desert.

Except for this incredible thing, the Nile, the desert under us seems omnipotent. Its intractable sands are reinforced by ridged, stony heights. When the sun is near the horizon, the desert is scarped, cracked, ravined, with every variety of design, every kind of hilltop, sides that slope, sides that are sudden and precipitous, sides that retreat into caverns. All is dappled with sharp light and shadow,

like the concave edge of the moon seen through a telescope. As the sun rises the shadows shrink, they become
flakes, they withdraw into the foot of the hills and disappear. Then the desert receives the full blast of the sun
and bakes, and bakes, and bakes, and the heart becomes
faint at the sight and thought of it.

They say that hereabouts rain never falls. Never! These
regions belong to a dead planet: below us, no birds, no
animals, no insects. There is not, I feel, even a microbe
in the air. There is only yellow, blistering sand turning
to bronze at the horizon; there is convulsive black rock,
and heat, relentless, intolerable heat. As long as we are
aloft I only see it, but as the downward glide begins, the
feel of it closes in on me, the capsule turns into an oven,
the arms of my seat are hot to the touch; and when I step
out of the plane I am caught in a double blast between
the burning earth and the fiery sun.

The heat is dry as far as Atbara in the Sudan; below
Khartoum it is a steaming, nauseous heat. In the north
the narrow runlet of the Nile asserts itself against the with-
ering hostility of the desert; in the south it is lost to view
in the *Soud,* which is neither land nor water but a primal
ooze. Here and there we see islands; they are mostly tangles
of vegetation, roots and scum without foundation, a replica
of the carboniferous era. Where the soil is firm, it is covered by an uncontrollable jungle, a richness of life in the
primitive which leaves no room for anything else; man is
almost choked out by the wanton generosity of nature. The
insects, birds, reptiles, like the insane vegetation, riot
unrestrained. In the north a little shifting of the desert
would dry out all the works of man; here an extra spurt
of biologic prodigality would engulf and dissolve them. I
think of ancient civilizations in the Sahara, in South
America, in Asia, which have been wiped out by too little

or too much, by nature's bitter parsimony or her ferocious, suffocating extravagance. The panorama of man's long contest with her unrolls before me, the supreme drama of our planet, the story of stories. Where and how did it begin? At what point in place and time did this animal get the start toward the mastery of the blindly indifferent environment which had given it birth? The shambling biped with opposable finger and thumb which is our image of the first hominid emerges far down the road of evolution. Remote ancestors of his had already learned the crucial trick of passing on to their progeny, by means of special sounds and gestures, something more than instincts developed through random mutations played on by natural selection; they had already overcome life's built-in handicap of the sequestered genes, circumventing the intransmissibility of acquired characteristics by transmitting acquired knowledge. Man had arrived, the halfway creature, doing what had never been done before—a species planning its future. Nature, groping undirected for a billion years, had begotten the directed; the accidental had monkeyed around until it had produced the purposive!

But was it so? Could intelligenceless atoms jigging about for a billion billion years have hit upon a self-conserving, self-developing intelligence? Here was the riddle of riddles, the ultimate riddle, by comparison with which all other themes are trivialities.

Below the Sudan the heat becomes dry and scarifying again. When I step out of the plane at M'beya, it is as if I had been shoved into Nebuchadnezzar's furnace. A scattered circle of all but naked Negroes, to whom the plane is still a novelty and a portent, is drawn about the field. I feel I am moving in a Wellsian fantasy. Everything is intensely unreal, surrealistic, and as I walk in a daze across the field it seems to me that I am hearing my name called in thin, selenite voices with a Yiddish accent. "Mr. Semuel!

Mr. Semuel!" I seem to see two figures running toward me.

I stop dead; this is pure hallucination.

The twinkling figures draw nearer; two smiling, eager faces, hands thrust out at me, voices in a mixture of English and Yiddish. "Mr. Semuel! Mr. Semuel! Welcome! God be thanked for your arrival."

It is not hallucination. The men are flesh and blood, their voices are human, and as I walk with them toward the airport hut, they continue to chant: "Excuse us! We recognized you from the picture. We couldn't wait. We can't tell you what this means to us."

In the hut I slowly get my bearings. The dazzle of the sun and the vertiginous panorama of the ages die away; I am in the here and now. A welcoming committee in this most improbable of places. But how? There isn't supposed to be a Jewish community within a thousand miles.

"You don't know us, Mr. Semuel, but we know you. I am Chaim Leffert and this is my brother Jacob Leffert. We read in the *Zionist Record* of South Africa that you are going to lecture down there and were coming by plane, and the plane goes from Cairo to Capetown every three days, so we reckoned, according to the date of your first lecture, that you'd be on the plane of three days ago or on this plane. So we were here three days ago, and no sign of you. But you are here today. And why were we here three days ago, and why are we here today? Because one perishes here for a Jewish word—and you come to us straight from the land of Israel."

The porter carries my bag to the rondavel assigned to me. The Leffert brothers accompany us, two lean, sunburned men of about my age, bearded, in shorts and open shirts and soiled topees. We sit over cold drinks and the story unfolds.

They come from Vilna, which they left in 1914 for

Central Africa, dreaming of gold and ivory and quick fortunes—and then Palestine, where they would buy themselves large orange groves. They found neither gold nor ivory, and in the meantime the war cut them off from their home. They went to South Africa and tried "smousing"—peddling—in the villages of the Rand. Others had reached wealth from such beginnings, but it took too long. The war ended and, poor and hopeful as ever, they went north again, lured by the rumor of quicker returns from sesame and coffee. The years went by and they still had not made enough for as much as ten dunams of orange land. Some of their relatives at home had died; others had migrated; no one was left to write to, and here they were, in the African wilds, and it was 1933, and what fools they had been! They should have gone to Palestine, barefoot and penniless, and pioneered there instead of squandering their youth in the wilderness, with never a Jewish word to delight the ear or freshen the heart.

All this came out in the midst of a hundred questions. Was the new Jewish homeland growing as marvelously as the papers said? Had I really seen Jerusalem and Tel Aviv and Haifa and the Jordan? they asked, and they laughed as they asked; it was only a manner of speech, they explained, for of course I had seen those fabulous places, I had just come from there. I wouldn't by chance have met so-and-so, a Vilna boy who went out to Palestine in 1913? Or so-and-so, from Grodno, a cousin of theirs? No? "Write down their names. You're going back to the *Yishuv*. You might come across them."

When they heard that I had been in Vilna they started from their seats and the tears came to their eyes. What? I had seen the Gaon's *klaus*, and the Ostrobramow, and the Bristol Hotel, and the Synagogue Yard? Did I know the Ramaille Street? Yes, I remembered that too. But they were *born* on the Ramaille Street, and I, a total stranger, had actually seen it!

It was as if, in their isolation, they had begun to suspect that their boyhood had been a dream which they had dreamed in common.

We talked through the afternoon, we told each other stores of *Chassidim* and *Misnagdim* and of famous Lithuanian Jews. I recited for them verses from Bialik and Abraham Reisin, and we sang together Peretz's *The Three Seamstresses* and Goldfaden's *In a Corner of the Temple*. When they left they embraced me as if I had been a brother. "You don't know," they said, "what a *mitzvah* you have performed."

That night I thought no more about the aeons and the marvels of evolution. I thought of the Leffert brothers (will chance bring this page to their living eyes?), and it seemed to me that if there is a Hand that writes, and keeps an accounting of our good and bad deeds, my most valuable entries on the credit side of the ledger will be the moments of comfort which my travels have enabled me to bring to lost and homesick Jews "hungering for a Jewish word."

I will tell of one more *mitzvah* of this kind, one that is forever associated in my memory with the onset of a "high moment." It goes back nearly forty years, to the time of my service with the Zionist Organization of America. A Yiddish letter in an old man's hand came one day to the head office in New York from Tucson, Arizona. He had read in the newspaper, the writer said, that a certain Mr. Samuel, having recently returned from a visit to Palestine, was being sent to address meetings in Los Angeles. There were then thirty thousand Jews in Los Angeles (they number nearly half a million today), in Tucson there was only a handful of Jews, most of them elderly people who had settled there for their health. "It is true," said the letter, "that we are fewer than the few who went down with Jacob our Father into Egypt, and we can do little toward the Redemption; therefore your speakers always pass us by, coming and going between Los Angeles and New York, and we are left like a lodge in a cucumber field. But our souls are Jewish, and surely," the letter went on, with many apt Biblical quotations, "surely for once your speaker can set out a day earlier or return a day later and bring to this Remnant of the Escape a living Jewish word from the land of our fathers." Thus it came to pass that as a summer night was drawing to its close I stepped off the train at Tucson, where a committee was waiting for me; and what with the dim moonlight, and the palm trees, and the exotic softness of the air, and my lightheadedness due to lack of sleep, I was suddenly double. One me carried on according to program, a propagandist of the Zionist Organization on an unprofitable but ungrudged assignment to a tiny out-of-the-way community; the other me was elsewhere in time and space. Twenty-six centuries closed up, and the globe of the earth had spun through a third of a circle. I saw myself as an emissary of the Prophets among exiles on the banks of the Khebar or the Nile. The Destruction had taken place only yesterday; a few years would pass and God would give the signal for the Return. "Patience, fellow-Jews! God is slow to anger, but quick to relent."

These visitations, these "high moments," stand outside the ordinary excitements I often find in my work. They are special seizures and intoxications and trances, unearned bonuses handed out to me irregularly and unexpectedly, reassurances that I can still get out of life more than I consciously put into it, reminders, too, of the generosity of a world I never made.

A Note on the Type

THIS BOOK was set on the Linotype in "Baskerville," a facsimile of the type designed by John Baskerville, Birmingham, England, in 1754. The original Baskerville type was one of the forerunners of the "modern" style of type faces. The Linotype copy was cut under the supervision of George W. Jones of London.

Composed, printed, and bound by
The Haddon Craftsmen, Inc., Scranton, Pa.
Typography based on originals by
W. A. DWIGGINS

A Note About the Author

MAURICE SAMUEL was born in Rumania in 1895
and was educated in England. In 1914 he migrated to the United States, and since 1921 he
has traveled extensively in this country and
abroad, partly as lecturer and partly to acquire
information. His major interest for nearly fifty
years has been the position of the Jewish people
in the Western world; of his twenty books,
fifteen are concerned with the exposition of
Jewish values or the relations between the
Jewish and Christian worlds.

August 1963